The
# Annexation of Bosnia

# The
# Annexation of Bosnia
## 1908–1909

BY

BERNADOTTE E. SCHMITT

NEW YORK

Howard Fertig

1970

First published in 1937

HOWARD FERTIG, INC. EDITION 1970
Reprinted by permission of the Cambridge University Press

Library of Congress Catalog Card Number: 71-80588

PRINTED IN THE UNITED STATES OF AMERICA
BY NOBLE OFFSET PRINTERS, INC.

# CONTENTS

# PREFACE

IN October 1908 the former Austro-Hungarian Monarchy proclaimed the annexation of the provinces of Bosnia and Herzegovina, and Bulgaria declared her independence of the Ottoman Empire. These actions involved no change in either the territorial or the political arrangements of the Balkan peninsula, for Austria-Hungary had "occupied and administered" the two provinces for thirty years, while the sultan of Turkey had never exercised the slightest control over the autonomous principality of Bulgaria set up in 1878. But the steps taken by the two governments did constitute violations of the Treaty of Berlin, which were all the more resented because the other signatories of the treaty were not consulted by the offending governments. A diplomatic crisis of six months' duration ensued which came near ushering in the Great War, and memories of what happened between October 1908 and April 1909 were not without bearing on the events of July 1914.

Not long after the crisis had ended, rival versions of their preliminary negotiations were published in an English magazine[1] by the Russian and Austro-Hungarian governments, while conflicting accounts of how the crisis had been resolved were circulated by the Russian and German governments. Repeated attempts have been made by publicists and historians to unravel these mysteries; without, however, much success, for some of the essential documents have not yet been published. Meanwhile, no systematic account of the long negotiations has ever been written. To-day, it is possible to tell the story in considerable detail, even though certain points still remain obscure, and to examine the charges of disloyalty and unscrupulousness which were so freely bandied about at the time.

The narrative here offered is based primarily on the great collections of diplomatic documents published after the war by the Austrian, German and British governments. Use has been made also of certain Russian and Serbian documents

---

[1] *Fortnightly Review*, September, November 1909.

published privately by individual Russian and Serbian diplomatists; but these collections are far from complete and their
accuracy cannot be checked. Many features of Russian and
Serbian policy will perforce remain vague until the diplomatic
correspondence is authoritatively published.[1]  The French
documents, though in course of publication, have unfortunately
not reached the year 1908; this is, however, of less consequence
than might be supposed, for France played a minor rôle in the
crisis. In addition, the memoirs of many of the personages
involved have contributed not a little, and there are a few
monographs on certain aspects of the crisis.

The first seven chapters were published some years ago in the
*Slavonic review*, but have since been considerably revised.

A uniform system for spelling Slavonic names has been
adopted, regardless of the forms used in the several collections
of documents. Likewise "Serbia" has been used throughout,
even in quotations from British documents in which the then
conventional spelling "Servia" was regularly employed.

---

[1] The Soviet government has begun to publish the documents of the
tsarist régime, but has not yet reached the years 1908–9. In October 1935
the present writer was allowed to see Izvolsky's report from Büchlaü of
September 1908, now in the Central Archives in Moscow, and was promised
a photostatic copy; later, permission to use the document was withdrawn and
the photostat withheld, and no explanation of this change of attitude was
offered. A publication of Serbian documents by the Yugoslav government
has more than once been rumoured, but so far nothing has appeared. The
same thing may also be said of Italian documents.

BERNADOTTE E. SCHMITT

UNIVERSITY OF CHICAGO
11 *November* 1936

# THE ANNEXATION OF BOSNIA
## 1908–1909

## CHAPTER I

## *The Preliminaries*

THE CRISIS in the Near East which was concluded by the Treaty of Berlin signed on 13 July 1878 was precipitated in July 1875 by revolts in Bosnia and Herzegovina, the two most north-westerly provinces of the Ottoman Empire. During the crisis two agreements were successively reached between Russia and Austria-Hungary by which the main part of the two provinces was freely conceded by the Russian government to the Dual Monarchy. When, however, this understanding was ignored by Russia in dictating the Treaty of San Stefano, Austria-Hungary joined Great Britain in objecting to the proposed settlement, and the Congress of Berlin met to revise the Treaty of San Stefano.[1] At the congress Lord Salisbury proposed, and Article 25 of the Treaty of Berlin accordingly provided, that Bosnia and Herzegovina should be "occupied and administered by Austria-Hungary". In effect, the Dual Monarchy received an international mandate to restore peace and order in the two provinces, and in the minds of both the British who proposed it and of the other governments which accepted it, there was no expectation that the occupation would be otherwise than permanent.[2] But the Ottoman plenipoten-

[1] R. W. Seton-Watson, *The rôle of Bosnia in international politics (1875–1914)*, The Raleigh Lecture on history, British Academy, 1931 (London, 1932), pp. 15–23; W. L. Langer, *European alliances and alignments, 1871–1890* (New York, 1931), pp. 92–3, 113–14, 138–50; A. F. Pribram, *The secret treaties of Austria-Hungary, 1879–1914*, English edition by A. C. Coolidge (2 vols. Cambridge, Mass., 1920–1), II, 188–203 (for the Austro-Russian agreements of 1876 and 1877).

[2] The Austro-Hungarian foreign minister and plenipotentiary, Count Julius Andrássy, accepted "occupation" instead of annexation partly to overcome Turkish opposition, partly because he foresaw resistance on the part of the Austrian and Hungarian parliaments to the formal incorporation of more than a million and a half Slavs in the Habsburg state.

tiaries at the congress refused to sign the treaty until the representatives of Austria-Hungary made a declaration stating that

the rights of sovereignty of His Imperial Majesty the Sultan over the
provinces of Bosnia and Herzegovina shall not be affected by the
fact of occupation...; that the occupation shall be considered provisional and that a previous agreement [*entente préalable*] on the details
of the occupation shall be made by the two governments immediately
after the closing of the congress.[1]

Actually, the Austro-Hungarian government proceeded immediately to occupy the provinces, and it was not until 21 April 1879
that a convention was signed at Constantinople.[2] The convention
referred in its preamble to the "fact of annexation" as "not
prejudicing the rights of sovereignty of His Imperial Majesty the
Sultan", and provided, *inter alia*, for the circulation of Turkish
money and the expenditure of the revenues of the provinces
within their confines. The Austro-Hungarian government also
promised to retain such Turkish officials as were qualified and to
choose new ones from the native population. In spite of these
attempts to maintain some semblance of Turkish sovereignty,
Turkish money was subsequently excluded, the provinces were
brought within the Austro-Hungarian customs union, passports
for the inhabitants were issued from the Austro-Hungarian embassy in Constantinople, the administration was assimilated to
that of the Monarchy, the capitulations were abolished (with the
consent of the Powers), and the Austro-Hungarian military
service was introduced. For practical purposes, the provinces
became an integral part of the Habsburg dominions, and the
declaration that "the occupation shall be considered provisional"
became illusory in fact, whatever validity it might retain in the
eyes of the Turkish government.

A somewhat different situation was created by the Treaty of
Berlin in the Sandjak of Novi Bazar, which "extends between
Serbia and Montenegro in a south-easterly direction beyond
Mitrovitsa". There Turkish administration was to continue.

[1] A. Fournier, *Wie wir zu Bosnien kamen* (Vienna, 1909), pp. 64–75;
Carathéodory Pacha, *Le rapport secret sur le Congrès de Berlin* (Paris, 1919),
pp. 164–92.
[2] *British and foreign state papers* (London, 1887), LXXI, 1132–4.

Nevertheless, Article 25 provided, "in order to insure the maintenance of the new political status as well as freedom and security of the ways of communication, Austria-Hungary reserves to herself the right to maintain a garrison there and to have military and commercial routes in the whole area of this part of the former vilayet of Bosnia". Count Andrássy, the Austro-Hungarian foreign minister, adopted this expedient partly to humour the susceptibilities of Turkey, partly because he did not wish to assume the responsibility of governing a particularly backward and restless region; he believed that the presence of an Austro-Hungarian garrison would offer a sufficient guarantee against the union of Serbia and Montenegro, which he was determined to prevent in all circumstances. He sought, however, to provide for possible future developments by securing from the Russian plenipotentiaries at the congress a declaration stating that

the Imperial Government of Russia engages not to raise any objection if, as a result of inconveniences which may result from the maintenance of the Ottoman administration in the Sandjak of Novi Bazar, Austria-Hungary should see herself forced to occupy this territory definitely like the rest of Bosnia and Herzegovina.[1]

From an early date Austria-Hungary desired and determined to convert the occupation of the two provinces into annexation. It insisted, therefore, as a condition of joining the Three Emperors' League of 1881 that "Austria-Hungary reserves the right to annex the provinces at whatever moment she shall deem opportune".[2] Russia, being then primarily interested in Bulgaria, raised no objection, and the agreement lasted until 1887. Ten years later, however, when a new Balkan agreement was made between Austria-Hungary and Russia, the latter was not so complacent. Count Goluchowski, the Austro-Hungarian foreign minister, formulated the position of the Dual Monarchy thus:

The territorial advantages, accorded to Austria-Hungary by the Treaty of Berlin, are and remain acquired by her. In consequence, the possession of Bosnia, of Herzegovina, and of the Sandjak of

---

[1] Fournier, *Wie wir zu Bosnien kamen*, p. 74.

[2] Article 1 of the supplementary protocol of the treaty of 18 June 1881; Pribram, I, 43. For a project of annexation in 1882, see R. W. Seton-Watson, "Russian commitments in the Bosnian question and an early project of annexation", *Slavonic review*, VIII (1930), 586–7.

Novi Bazar may not be made the object of any discussion whatsoever, the Government of His Imperial and Royal Apostolic Majesty reserving to itself the right of substituting, when the moment arrives, for the present status of occupation and the right of garrison that of annexation.

But the Russian foreign minister, Count Muravyev, objected:

In subscribing to this principle we deem it necessary to observe that the Treaty of Berlin assures to Austria-Hungary the right of military occupation of Bosnia and Herzegovina. The annexation of these two provinces would raise a more extensive question, which would require special scrutiny at the proper time and places. As to the Sandjak of Novi Bazar, there would also be the necessity to specify its boundaries, which, indeed, have never been sufficiently defined.[1]

In other words, Russia wished to keep the question open; in any case, she would demand a *quid pro quo*. Since Austria-Hungary, probably because of internal difficulties, did not take advantage of Russian preoccupation in the Far East, the question remained dormant for years.

Two circumstances operated ultimately to bring the problem to the fore. In general, Baron von Aehrenthal, who succeeded Goluchowski in 1906, resented the subordinate position in European politics to which the Monarchy had been reduced in consequence of domestic crises and the great assertiveness of Germany. He determined to inaugurate a vigorous policy which, he hoped, would dispel *malaise* at home, restore Austro-Hungarian prestige abroad, and make an end of the irritating dependence on Germany. For such an active policy—and Aehrenthal was supported by the heir apparent, the Archduke Francis Ferdinand, whose nominee he had been, and by the chief of the general staff, General Conrad von Hötzendorf—the Balkans offered the only tempting opportunity. Here alone could the Dual Monarchy hope to find a ready and constant market for its goods, and the progressive decline of the Turkish power in Macedonia heralded a reopening of the Eastern Question of which Austria-Hungary might hope to take advantage. Still another incentive was the knowledge that the new Russian

---

[1] Pribram, *Secret treaties of Austria-Hungary*, I, 185–95.

foreign minister, A. P. Izvolsky, who had taken office a few months before Aehrenthal while the latter was still ambassador in St Petersburg, was an ardent believer in Russia's mission in the Near East and was hatching a new policy. More specifically, it had gradually become clear that the situation in Bosnia and Herzegovina required drastic treatment. Peace and order had been restored in the two provinces, some material improvements had been made; outwardly there were many signs of progress. But the administration, kept in the hands of German and Magyar bureaucrats, was not sympathetically viewed by the peasant masses, for whom little had been done and who were showing themselves receptive to agitation conducted by propagandist societies from Serbia. A solution of the Bosnian question appeared, indeed, as a first necessary step towards the settlement of the larger Southern Slav question, and even Baron Burián, the minister responsible for the provinces, who was a Magyar and an uncompromising supporter of the existing Dualism, came to advocate a liberalizing of the political system by the introduction of some kind of representative government.[1] As this step would be much easier if the Emperor Francis Joseph could act in the capacity of sovereign, the obvious course was to annex the provinces to the Monarchy, and in December 1907 Aehrenthal informed Conrad that the aim of his Balkan policy was "the annexation of Bosnia-Herzegovina and the incorporation of the non-Bulgarian parts of Serbia" in the Habsburg dominions.[2]

The incorporation of Serbia in the Monarchy had not hitherto, so far as is known, been an objective of Austro-Hungarian policy, which had been content to control the little state by means of a political alliance (1881–95) and an astute commercial treaty. Even the Serbian revolution of 1903 which put an end to the Obrenovich rulers and restored the dynasty of Karageorgevich did not at first seriously disturb the relations of Vienna and Belgrade,[3] for King Peter I could not be more difficult to deal

[1] S. Graf Burián, *Drei Jahre* (Berlin, 1923), pp. 218–21.
[2] Feldmarschall Conrad, *Aus meiner Dienstzeit* (Vienna, 1921), I, 528.
[3] The Emperor Francis Joseph was the first sovereign to recognize Peter as king.

with than the unfortunate Alexander Obrenovich. But Peter, sensible to the fate of more than one predecessor, determined to rule as a constitutional monarch and left the government of the country to the Radical party, which was the strongest political force in the country and Russophile in foreign policy. Under the leadership of Nikola Pashich, the Radicals attempted to free Serbia from Austro-Hungarian economic control by concluding a commercial treaty with Germany, negotiating a customs union with Bulgaria, and proposing to purchase artillery for the Serbian army from the French firm of Schneider (instead of continuing to buy from the Skoda factories in Bohemia). Faced with this challenge, the Austro-Hungarian government in 1906 denounced the existing commercial treaty with Serbia and made a new treaty dependent upon a Serbian promise to modify the Serbo-Bulgarian customs union as the cabinet of Vienna might require; when this demand was refused, the Hungarian frontier was closed to the importation of Serbian live stock by the issuance of a veterinary order. A further demand was made that preference should be given to Austro-Hungarian industry in supplying the ordinary needs of the Serbian government.

This drastic policy completely miscarried. Serbia was able to negotiate agreements with Turkey which permitted the export of live stock through Salonica, she borrowed money abroad for the construction of modern slaughter-houses, she bought guns from France and ammunition from Germany, and she resisted the demands for a preference to Austro-Hungarian industry. So successful in short was the Serbian defiance that Aehrenthal was constrained to negotiate a new commercial treaty which was more favourable to Serbia than that which Goluchowski had denounced.[1] In fact, it was so favourable that it was rejected by the Austrian and Hungarian parliaments. Thus Aehrenthal's policy of restoring Austro-Hungarian influence in Serbia by economic concessions was made ridiculous and impossible, and it may well have been this state of affairs which led him to adopt

[1] According to J. M. Baernreither, *Fragmente eines politischen Tagebuches: die südslawische Frage und Österreich-Ungarn vor dem Weltkrieg* (Berlin, 1928), p. 74, Aehrenthal in October 1907 declared to the council of ministers: "Our policy of making Serbia economically and politically dependent has failed completely."

the alternative policy of crushing Serbia and adding it to the Dual Monarchy.[1]

In any case, the agreement of 1897 required a discussion with Russia of any change in the status of Bosnia. Aehrenthal was not indisposed to such a discussion. When he assumed control of Austro-Hungarian foreign policy, his immediate aim was to revive the Three Emperors' League, and he was willing to take up a problem of fundamental interest to Russia, namely, the solution of the question of the Straits. But he was greatly annoyed when the Russian government elected to make the agreement of August 1907 with Great Britain, which was likely to render Russia less dependent, and Austria-Hungary more dependent, on Germany. Accordingly, in January 1908, without previous consultation with Izvolsky, Aehrenthal announced a scheme for the construction of a railway from Uvats, a town on the Bosnian frontier, across the Sandjak to Mitrovitsa in Old Serbia. As he had secured the consent of the sultan by sabotaging the judicial reforms which Great Britain and Russia were then pressing on the Turkish government, his action aroused great indignation in Russia and was interpreted as signifying the end of the Austro-Russian *entente*.[2]

But Izvolsky could not combat Aehrenthal very vigorously. Appointed to the foreign office on the morrow of the disastrous war in the Far East, which he had opposed, he was as keen to score a triumph by securing the opening of the Straits as was Aehrenthal to accomplish the annexation of Bosnia. Since he had received assurances, during the negotiation of the Anglo-Russian agreement, that Great Britain would be willing to discuss the question of the Straits, Izvolsky let his imagination toy

---

[1] Recent discussion of this controversy will be found in C. Dumba, *Dreibund- und Entente-Politik in der alten und neuen Welt* (Vienna, 1931), pp. 213–35 [Dumba was the Austro-Hungarian minister in Belgrade from 1903 to 1905; this chapter is omitted from the English translation, *Memoirs of a diplomat*]; Dionys Jánossy, " Der handelspolitische Konflikt zwischen der österreichisch-ungarischen Monarchie und Serbien in den Jahren 1904–1910", *Jahrbuch des Wiener ungarischen historischen Instituts* (Budapest, 1932), II, 285–312; W. M. Markov, *Serbien zwischen Österreich und Russland, 1897–1908* (Stuttgart, 1934), pp. 45–74.
[2] G. P. Gooch, *Studies in diplomacy*, vol. I, *The grouping of the Powers* (London, 1936), pp. 320–4, 370–85.

with the idea of an Anglo-Russian military action against Turkey. When, however, he expounded his plans to the Russian council of ministers on 3 February 1908, shortly after Aehrenthal had announced his railway programme, the military chiefs pointed out that Russia was not ready for war; the minister of finance was equally discouraging; and the premier, P. A. Stolypin, declared frankly that an adventurous and aggressive policy might precipitate a new revolution and endanger the dynasty. "A policy other than pacific and exclusively defensive", said Stolypin, "would be, at this moment, the delirium of a government which has lost its reason."[1] Thus deprived of the possibility of using force and profoundly impressed by the power of Germany, Izvolsky contented himself by making a counter-proposal for a railway from Rumania across Serbia and Montenegro to the Adriatic—to which Aehrenthal professed to have no objection. More than that, the Russian foreign minister decided not only not to open the breach with Austria-Hungary, but to try to revive the accord of 1897 and reach his goal by diplomatic bargaining.

Accordingly, on 27 April 1908, he addressed to Aehrenthal an *aide-mémoire* in which he promised to "abstain loyally from all obstruction of the Austro-Hungarian [railway] project" and requested Aehrenthal to support at Constantinople the Russian request for the authorization of preliminary studies for the Danube-Adriatic railway.[2] In his reply Aehrenthal evaded the Russian request by seizing upon a remark of Izvolsky that "the question of railways possessed only an economic character", whereas the Austro-Russian collaboration in recent years had been essentially political. But he went on to say that if "the cabinet of St Petersburg wishes it to be understood that it remains faithful to the principles of disinterestedness set forth by Austria-Hungary and Russia by common agreement in 1897, the

[1] M. Pokrowski, *Drei Konferenzen* (Hamburg, 1920), pp. 17–30.

[2] *Aide-mémoire* of the Russian foreign office, 27 April 1908: *Oesterreich-Ungarns Aussenpolitik von der Bosnischen Krise 1908 bis zum Kriegsausbruch 1914*, edited by L. Bittner and H. Uebersberger (9 vols. Vienna, 1930), vol. I, No. 2. (This collection will henceforth be cited as "A", and the documents by number; the documents used in this study will be found in vols. I and II.)

cabinet of Vienna will be disposed to accept this formula with pleasure" [!], for it wished to maintain "political relations of friendship and confidence" with Russia, which "alone would correspond to the monarchical and conservative interest of the two countries".[1]

This declaration forced Izvolsky to show his hand, all the more so since the meeting of Nicholas II and Edward VII at Reval in June had aroused suspicions in both Germany and Austria-Hungary that, under the guise of demanding reforms in Macedonia, Great Britain and Russia were planning some decisive stroke against Turkey. In a memorandum of 2 July, Izvolsky therefore made definite proposals to Aehrenthal for an *entente*. (1) He repeated his previous offer on the railway question. (2) Stating that Russia "remains faithful to the principles of disinterestedness set forth in the agreement of 1897", he remarked that it "appeared desirable to define certain points of that *entente* in a more precise manner". He therefore suggested that the *status quo* consecrated by the agreement of 1897 should be interpreted to include the railway project and he outlined a territorial definition of the Sandjak of Novi Bazar. Turning next to the question of Bosnia, which he knew to be the most effective lever for any negotiation with Aehrenthal, he reaffirmed the position taken in 1897 and then remarked:

We continue particularly to be of the opinion that the question of modification of the state of things created by Article 25 of the Treaty of Berlin, that is to say, the annexation of Bosnia, Herzegovina and the Sandjak of Novi Bazar, possesses an eminently European character and is not of a nature to be adjusted by a separate understanding between Russia and Austria-Hungary. On the other hand, we are ready to recognize that the same reservation applies to the question of Constantinople, its adjacent territory and the Straits. Nevertheless in view of the extreme importance to the two countries to see the two questions mentioned above adjusted in conformity with their reciprocal interests, the Imperial government would be ready to enter upon a discussion in a spirit of friendly reciprocity.

In general, Russia was anxious "to preserve the most friendly and confidential relations" with Austria-Hungary. (3) Izvolsky

---

[1] *Aide-mémoire* for the Russian government, 1 May; A 3.

promised to communicate his programme of reforms for Macedonia as soon as he had reached an agreement with the British
government (which had been a main theme of the discussions at
Reval).[1]

The heart of this communication was, of course, the offer of
Russia to recognize the annexation of Bosnia, Herzegovina and
the Sandjak of Novi Bazar in return for Austrian support in the
matter of opening the Straits. It was apparently Izvolsky's idea
that if the two Powers could come to a preliminary agreement,
they might then approach the other signatories of the Treaty of
Berlin with reasonable expectation of securing their consent to
the proposed changes. There was nothing irregular in such a
procedure, but the fact that the Russian overture was made some
three weeks before the Young Turk revolution (24 July) shows
that Izvolsky was quite as ambitious and adventurous as
Aehrenthal.

Although the bargain seemed one-sided to Aehrenthal—he
was asked to support the Russian railway scheme, whereas
Russia merely promised not to oppose the Austrian plan, and the
annexation of the Sandjak was hardly the equivalent of a settlement of the Straits question[2]—he recognized the conciliatory
tone of the document[3] and determined to seize the proffered
hand, although he did not answer the Russian communication
immediately. He accordingly had prepared a long memorandum,
which is of the utmost importance. Since Russia had suggested
the annexation of the Sandjak, it was necessary, the document
pointed out, to determine the future policy of the Monarchy
towards that district. Its military occupation had been stipulated for in 1878 in order to prevent the union of Serbia and
Montenegro and to assist the maintenance of the Ottoman
Empire; the expectation was that when Turkey collapsed,
Austria-Hungary would seize the territory. Aehrenthal was
convinced that the latter policy was impracticable:

[1] *Aide-mémoire* of the Russian foreign office, 19 June/2 July; A 9.
[2] The Austrian view was that Russia had conceded the annexation of
Bosnia in principle by the agreements of 1876, 1877 and 1881; consequently
the only new point in the Russian offer was the annexation of the Sandjak.
[3] Aehrenthal to Berchtold, ambassador in St Petersburg, telegram, 14
July; A 15.

The occupation and annexation of the Sandjak would compel us to maintain a body of troops of the strength of an army corps in this defile for a long period of years; this army corps would have to strike out in three directions under the most unfavourable conditions—it would be attacked on the right flank by Montenegro, on the left by Serbia, and in front by the Albanians who, in the event of an Austro-Hungarian invasion, would doubtless make common cause with the Serbs and Montenegrins.

Furthermore, a military occupation no longer seemed necessary: "in view of the conflict between Serbian and Montenegrin aspirations which has again recently come to light,[1] a Serbo-Montenegrin union, even after a partition of the Sandjak, would hardly fall within the realm of possibilities". And a definitive occupation would impose "ruinous" financial burdens on the Monarchy. But even if the union of Serbia and Montenegro could thus be indefinitely prevented, "we should not thereby accomplish the main purpose of any far-seeing policy in the East, that is, the attainment of secure frontiers to the south in the event that Turkey in Europe should rottenly break to pieces".

Such secure frontiers could be obtained, the memorandum continued, only if the Monarchy were determined "to strike at the root of the evil and put an end to the Great Serbian dreams of the future":

The antagonism between Bulgaria and Serbia is already to-day a factor that can be reckoned with; in Bulgaria the conviction prevails that the road to Macedonia must lead over the body of the Serbian state, and it is certain that the most violent strife will break out between Serbia and Bulgaria for the possession of Uskub. If we take Bulgaria's

[1] Probably a reference to the plot to assassinate Prince Nicholas of Montenegro, which is supposed to have been hatched in Serbia by an Austrian *agent-provocateur*, George Nashtich, who then revealed it to Nicholas (1907). Well paid for these activities, Nashtich published in July 1908 a pamphlet called *Finale*, in which he denounced by name a number of Austro-Hungarian Serbs as traitors and declared that they were members of a Serbian revolutionary organization, the *Slovenski Yug* ["Slav South"], the object of which was to bring about the union of the Southern Slav provinces of the Dual Monarchy with Serbia. In August the accused persons were arrested by the governor of Croatia and kept in prison without trial until March 1909. The trial, when finally held at Zagreb (Agram), was a scandalous affair which had wide European repercussions and profoundly affected the development of the Southern Slav question.

side in this conflict and favour the creation of a Great Bulgaria at the expense of Serbia, the necessary preparation will have been made, and in the moment of a favourable European constellation, we can lay our hands on the rest of Serbia. Then we should have the secure frontiers of which I have spoken above: an Albania become independent under our aegis, a Montenegro with which we maintain friendly relations, and a Great Bulgaria which is indebted to us.

In this passage Aehrenthal disclosed the real aim of his policy: to make the annexation of Bosnia a first step towards the incorporation of Serbia (or what was left of Serbia after Bulgaria had been satisfied) in the Habsburg dominions. Taking these several considerations together, the Austro-Hungarian foreign minister proposed that the Monarchy should withdraw its garrison from the Sandjak and enter upon negotiations with Russia for the annexation of Bosnia and Herzegovina in return for a discussion of the problem of the Straits.[1]

Aehrenthal submitted the problem to a ministerial council held on 19 August. In reply to a question of the Austrian premier as to how the annexation was to be carried through diplomatically, he stated that "Italy could not raise any claims for compensation on the basis of the treaty of the Triple Alliance";[2] that "no opposition was to be expected from England"; and that while resistance from Turkey had to be reckoned with,[3] "yet she would be forced to hold back, for she was facing difficult times". The chief of staff, Conrad von Hötzendorf, stated that "at present Russia was not in a position to wage war and the military situa-

[1] Memorandum of 9 August (drafted by Musulin); A 32. Several days later the Russian government requested an early reply to its previous communication, in order that the two governments "might proceed to discuss the ultimate developments upon which they would have to agree", and be prepared for "proposals of collective intervention" from other Powers whose interests might be affected by recent events in Turkey, that is, the revolution of 24 July (aide-mémoire of 1/14 August; A 35).

[2] Aehrenthal had assured the Italian ambassador in Vienna that "the cabinet of Vienna was disposed to observe a waiting attitude" towards the developments in Turkey, and said that "a policy of non-intervention offered the best guarantee that the unity of the Powers would be preserved"; the Italian government readily agreed with this view (Aehrenthal to Somssich, telegram, 4 August; Somssich to Aehrenthal, telegram, 5 August; A 23, 26).

[3] The ambassador in Constantinople had advised Aehrenthal not to raise the Bosnian question (Pallavicini to Aehrenthal, telegram, 10 August, and private letter, 12 August; A 33, 34).

tion of Turkey was not such that an attack from her had to be feared". The Hungarian premier supported Aehrenthal's proposals because the withdrawal from the Sandjak "would make clear to Italy and the Balkan states that the Monarchy cherished no far-reaching aspirations for Turkish territory" and because "the subversive movements in the Southern Slav provinces would not cease until the annexation had been carried out". Although the Austrian and Hungarian premiers reserved their formal consent until certain details had been settled, the policy of Aehrenthal was accepted in principle.[1] It is worth noting that the decision was concealed from the Archduke Francis Ferdinand, who was opposed to the plan.[2] As the archduke was to visit the German Emperor shortly, he would be sure to speak to William II about the annexation,[3] and thus the great advantage of secrecy would be lost.[4]

A week after the ministerial council Aehrenthal replied to the Russian overtures. On the railway question he could not, he said, promise to support the Russian project while the cabinet of St Petersburg merely refrained from opposing the Austro-Hungarian enterprise, but if Russia did not insist on that support, he would observe "a sympathetic attitude"; in other words, reciprocity was in order. Since the Russian memorandum showed that "a complete identity of views prevailed in respect of the 1897 agreement, he would accept the Russian definition of the

[1] Protocol of the ministerial council, 19 August; A 40. For the doubts of the Austrian premier, Baron Beck, see Rudolf Sieghart, *Die letzten Jahrzehnte einer Grossmacht* (Berlin, 1932), pp. 132-7.
[2] Francis Ferdinand to Aehrenthal, 6 August 1908; L. von Chumlecky, *Franz Ferdinands Wirken und Wollen* (Berlin, 1929), p. 98. The archduke thought that the Bosnian question could be solved by the removal of Burián and the appointment of General Vareshanin with full powers.
[3] Aehrenthal to Francis Joseph, 23 August; A 43.
[4] Early in August, the Vienna correspondent of the London *Times*, Wickham Steed, was consulted by an influential official of the Austrian government as to the advisability of annexing Bosnia. Steed replied that immediate and direct annexation might bring on a serious European crisis and advised the grant of autonomy to the two provinces; if the inhabitants abused their privilege by electing deputies to the new Turkish parliament, no objection could then be raised to annexation (H. W. Steed, *Through thirty years* [New York, 1924], I, 278-80). In the ministerial council, Burián emphasized the necessity of introducing constitutional government in the provinces, but agreed that this must be preceded by annexation.

Sandjak, provided it permitted the maintenance of the Austro-Hungarian garrison. But he hinted that "in a certain eventuality" the Monarchy might be disposed to withdraw its troops, and in case the Ottoman Empire were to collapse, to "observe in respect of the Sandjak the same principle of disinterestedness as towards the rest of Turkey". Bosnia and Herzegovina, he went on to say, were "territories which we have possessed for thirty years, which we have entered upon by virtue of an international mandate, and which we have conquered by force of arms". He was willing that the two cabinets "should engage to abstain from all intervention in the Near East without a previous agreement between them". But "if nevertheless imperative circumstances should compel Austria-Hungary to annex Bosnia and Herzegovina", he expected that Russia would observe "a benevolent and friendly attitude", while at the same time the Monarchy would agree to withdraw from the Sandjak "and definitely give up the occupation of this territory". In return, Austria-Hungary was "quite disposed to have a confidential and friendly exchange of views" with Russia on the subject of the Straits.[1] By offering to evacuate the Sandjak, Aehrenthal secured the advantage of asking for less than Izvolsky had signified his willingness to concede, and was thus able to avoid a definite commitment concerning the Straits.

While the Russian foreign minister, who was taking the cure at Karlsbad, was considering this communication, Aehrenthal undertook soundings of Austria-Hungary's allies. At Salzburg, on 4 September, he met Tommaso Tittoni, the Italian foreign minister. Tittoni, so Aehrenthal recorded, assumed "a conciliatory tone" and "repeatedly expressed the wish to proceed in closest agreement with us and Germany"; he asked only to be kept informed of the decisions of Vienna, "in order that he might be in a position to prepare the public opinion of his country". Aehrenthal, for his part, promised not to "surprise him with any kind of decision". The Austro-Hungarian minister then remarked that "our presence in the occupied provinces was permanent and it only depended on circumstances that we should adjust permanently the form of our possession". Tittoni agreed,

[1] *Aide-mémoire* of 27 August; A 48.

nor did he object to the further remark that, in such an event, Austria-Hungary "had no obligation to offer compensation". Aehrenthal promised to give notice of any increase of the garrison in the Sandjak and said, finally, that if Serbia did not change her course towards the Monarchy, "we should be compelled to humiliate the disturber of the peace, who was developing into a real danger to peace in the Balkans".[1] He did not give the slightest indication of the steps really contemplated.

Aehrenthal was not much franker with Wilhelm von Schoen, the secretary of the German foreign office, whom he saw at Berchtesgaden on the following day. Stating that he was exchanging ideas with Izvolsky and that both Izvolsky and Tittoni had agreed to a policy of non-intervention and the maintenance of the *status quo*, Aehrenthal did not go beyond saying that "in time Austria-Hungary could not avoid proceeding to a definitive settlement of the relationship of Bosnia and Herzegovina and that this solution could and would have to be none other than *annexation*", and that "at the proper time" the Sandjak would be evacuated. He did not intimate at all that both steps were imminent. If, he added, the cabinet of St Petersburg agreed with these "plans for the future", he was ready to discuss with it the question of the Straits, though "only with the greatest prudence and reserve and in as dilatory a fashion as possible". The German diplomatist was more cautious than his Italian colleague, limiting himself to saying that "Austria-Hungary would always find us ready to take account of its needs, interests and wishes in the Near East in loyal and most friendly fashion". Although he thought the question of the Straits full of danger, yet he preferred to have Russia receive the concession from Austria-Hungary rather than from the Western Powers. But Aehrenthal did explain, "with a certain anxiety" and in strict secrecy, that the further aim of his Balkan policy was "the complete elimination of the Serbian revolutionary nest", by giving Serbia to Bulgaria (the real plan was to give *part* of Serbia to Bulgaria and add the remainder to the Monarchy), for Bulgaria was "a quiet, well-ordered state" which would provide an

[1] Memorandum of 5 September; A 67.

effective barrier to the Russian-Slavic flood.[1] Aehrenthal, then, did not reveal his intentions to Schoen, who, for his part, as he later assured the British ambassador in Berlin, derived the impression that "the annexation would not be carried out for some little time, perhaps for a year".[2] Evidently the Austro-Hungarian minister proposed to prove his independence of Germany by presenting her as well as the other Powers with a *fait accompli*.[3]

No soundings were made in Paris or London.[4] To his ambassador in Constantinople, who had warned him against "the most regrettable consequences" if the Bosnian question were raised,[5] Aehrenthal wrote that the Young Turks seemed to him "wise and reasonable politicians" who were interested not in conquests but in reforms. "Why, then," he asked, "should the mere change from a *de facto* to a *de jure* status drive them to extreme decisions, especially if simultaneously our troops leave the Sandjak and our renunciation of any further acquisition of Turkish territory is thus clearly manifested?" The ambassador was empowered to sound out some Turkish statesmen, such as Ferid Pasha, the former grand vizier.[6] Ferid, when approached,

---

[1] Schoen to Bülow, from Berchtesgaden, 5 September; *Die grosse Politik der europäischen Kabinette, 1871–1914*, edited by J. Lepsius, A. Mendelssohn Bartholdy and H. Thimme (40 vols. Berlin, 1922–7), vol. XXVI, No. 8927. (This collection will henceforth be cited as "G", and the documents by number; the documents used in this study will be found in vol. XXVI.)

[2] Goschen to Grey, 7 January 1909; *British documents on the origins of the war, 1898–1914*, edited by G. P. Gooch and H. Temperley (11 vols. London, 1927–37), vol. V, No. 507. (This collection will henceforth be cited as "B", and the documents by number; the documents used in this study will be found, unless otherwise indicated, in vol. V.)

[3] A few days before he assured the German chargé in Vienna, when requesting the German government to prevent a discussion of the Bosnian question in the German press, that "the [Austro-Hungarian] government did not now intend to take up a solution of the problem"—a deliberate untruth which needs to be remembered whenever there is a question of Aehrenthal's veracity (Brockdorff-Rantzau to Bülow, 1 September; G 8924).

[4] When Edward VII visited Francis Joseph at Ischl on 13 August, the latter did not mention to his guest that the annexation of Bosnia was under consideration. Two days later at Marienbad, King Edward was told by Wickham Steed that the annexation was being prepared, but refused to believe it, because "surely the Emperor would have said something to me" (Steed, *Through thirty years*, I, 283).

[5] Pallavicini to Aehrenthal, private, 12 August; A 34.

[6] Aehrenthal to Pallavicini, private, 27 August; A 47.

advised against any action: "You do not now have a government with which you can negotiate about such matters."[1] Pallavicini's own opinion was that they must await the return of normal conditions or act before the meeting of the Turkish parliament; but he feared that no Turkish statesman would negotiate before parliament met.[2] These admonitions, however, did not cause Aehrenthal to alter his plans; he merely instructed Pallavicini to refrain from more soundings.[3]

Of course, no inkling of the intended action was conveyed to Serbia. When the Serbian foreign minister, Milovan Milovanovich, in a conversation with Aehrenthal on 14 September, expressed the conviction that "Serbia could secure her future only by leaning on her powerful neighbour", the latter replied that he must be sceptical, for he had received the same assurances from Milovanovich's predecessor; "we can no longer rely on mere words, but must demands deeds". He added that "the fog which had for a short time stretched between here and St Petersburg had been dissipated, and a complete identity of views with respect to the Near East was again established between the two cabinets".[4]

[1] Pallavicini to Aehrenthal, telegram, 2 September; A 61.

[2] Pallavicini to Aehrenthal, telegram, 31 August, and private letter, 2 September; A 53, 62.

[3] Aehrenthal to Pallavicini, telegram, 6 September; A 68.

[4] Memorandum of 14 September; A 78. Shortly before this conversation, Milovanovich had told the British ambassador in Vienna, Sir Edward Goschen, that "it seemed to be the whole object of the directors of Austro-Hungarian policy to humiliate Serbia as much as possible and to make her feel that politically and economically she was entirely at the mercy of her powerful neighbour": he intended, he said, to discuss the question with Aehrenthal "with the utmost frankness". He also expressed the opinion that the idea of an impending annexation of Bosnia was "entirely erroneous": "he could not bring himself to believe that at a critical moment like the present Austria-Hungary would care to open such a dangerous and complicated question, one which was, moreover, an European rather than an Austro-Hungarian affair" (Goschen to Grey, 31 August; B 265). Milovanovich was soon disillusioned, for on 4 September he saw Izvolsky at Karlsbad and, to quote a subsequent statement of Milovanovich, "the Russian minister informed him that the annexation of Bosnia by Austria-Hungary was only a question of time and would take place in the near future". Izvolsky added that Russia "was not in a position to offer serious opposition to this step being taken", but suggested that "nevertheless it might be convenient if Serbia raised a howl over the business" (Cartwright [Goschen's successor at Vienna] to Hardinge, private, 10 June 1909; B, vol. IX, Part I, No. 14). According to another account, Izvolsky asked Milovanovich to

At a second ministerial council held on 10 September Aehrenthal reported that the diplomatic situation seemed in general favourable and succeeded in allaying the apprehensions of the Austrian premier, Baron Beck, who had shown some nervousness at the previous council. "From Russia", said Aehrenthal, "no difficulties were to be expected over the annexation"; from the side of Italy "nothing serious was to be feared"; and "the Turkish army was at this time so disorganized that scarcely more than a protest was to be feared from Turkey and perhaps the rupture of diplomatic relations". Inasmuch as the Serbian propagandist society *Slovenski Yug* was getting in touch with the Young Turks, Aehrenthal urged immediate action; for "they should be under no illusion that Serbia was setting every lever in motion to prepare difficulties for the Monarchy in Bosnia, Croatia and Dalmatia, and create a situation favourable to her own aspirations". Apparently—there is no formal decision recorded in the minutes—the foreign minister was authorized to proceed as he desired.[1]

suggest "compensations" for Serbia (Steed, *Through thirty years*, I, 291). This statement may not be correct in every detail, for on 4 September Izvolsky had not come to terms with Aehrenthal (though he had doubtless received the latter's *aide-mémoire* of 27 August) and could hardly have known that the annexation would "take place in the near future". But he doubtless did inform his visitor that something was in the wind and that Serbia should be prepared for the worst. In his conversation with Aehrenthal Milovanovich did not hint that he knew anything of the impending stroke.

[1] Protocol of the ministerial council in Budapest, 10 September; A 75. For a brief semi-official presentation of the Austrian point of view for the entire period of the crisis, see Roderich Gooss, *Das österreichisch-serbische Problem bis zur Kriegserklärung Österreich-Ungarns an Serbien, 28 Juli 1914* (Berlin, 1930).

# CHAPTER II

## *Buchlau*

WHILE AEHRENTHAL was thus busy perfecting his plans, Izvolsky had left St Petersburg for a stay at Karlsbad, which was to be followed by visits to Italy, Paris, London and Berlin.[1] The tsar told Sir Arthur Nicolson, the British ambassador, that he had instructed Izvolsky not to take the initiative in suggesting a meeting with the Austrian minister, but to await a proposal from the latter.[2] As Aehrenthal was unwilling to take this initiative, his ambassador in St Petersburg, Count Berchtold, who was also at Karlsbad, persuaded Izvolsky to meet Aehrenthal at his estate of Buchlau, in Moravia, and there, on 15 and 16 September, they engaged in a thoroughgoing discussion of the Near Eastern problem.

With just what authority Izvolsky conducted the negotiations is not clear. Later in the month, when rumours began to circulate that the two ministers had struck some kind of a bargain for the annexation of Bosnia, Stolypin, the premier, made inquiries at the foreign office. Charykov, the assistant foreign minister who was in charge during Izvolsky's absence, declared that he knew nothing about the matter, asserting that before Izvolsky left St Petersburg "no preparations on this subject had been made nor had there been any references or memoranda presented to the tsar".[3] The tsar himself denied that he had given any special permission to Izvolsky, "as the latter had not asked for any".[4] Writing in exile after the war, Charykov gave a very different account. Izvolsky, he stated, drew up a memorandum in seven points, including the annexation of Bosnia by Austria and the opening of the Straits for Russia, together with the meeting

---

[1] He saw King Edward VII at Marienbad and Clemenceau, the French premier, at Karlsbad. Apparently he did not inform them of his negotiations with Aehrenthal.     [2] Nicolson to Grey, 14 August; B 217.
[3] Count V. N. Kokovtzov, *Out of my past* (Stanford University, Calif., 1935), p. 214. Stolypin informed Kokovtzov of the conversation.
[4] *Ibid.*, p. 216.

of a European conference; the tsar approved the memorandum and authorized the minister to negotiate with the Powers. The other ministers were not, however, informed of this plan.[1] Probably this is the correct version, for the tsar considered that foreign policies were the exclusive domain of himself and his minister of foreign affairs and as far as possible kept the other ministers in ignorance.[2] It is, indeed, highly improbable that Izvolsky would have embarked on his adventuresome course without the express permission of his master, and the denial of Nicholas to Stolypin that he had given authority to Izvolsky was no doubt merely an attempt to throw the responsibility on the latter when his policy was being attacked. But Stolypin was in a strong position to challenge the action taken by Izvolsky, and, as will be seen, did so successfully, to the great undoing of the luckless foreign minister.

According to Aehrenthal's memorandum of their conversations, Izvolsky declared that "if we [Austria-Hungary] were forced to proceed to annexation [of Bosnia-Herzegovina], Russia would assume a friendly and benevolent attitude". In return, he asked Austria-Hungary to observe the same attitude "in case Russia should see herself compelled by her interests to take steps for securing the free passage through the Dardanelles of individual [isolés] Russian men-of-war", with the understanding that the independence and security of the Turkish capital should not be affected and that the same privilege should be accorded the other states bordering on the Black Sea. Aehrenthal accepted this formula, on the conditions that the Russian ships should pass the Straits singly and not in squadrons, and that the Turkish possession of Constantinople should not be involved. They agreed that "a proclamation of Bulgarian independence and the definitive union [Angliederung] of Crete to Greece" should be regarded as steps "of a purely formal character" which would not change the existing situation de facto, but that "new territorial acquisitions by individual Balkan states at the expense of Turkey"

---

[1] N. V. Tcharykow, "Reminiscences of Nicholas II," Contemporary review, CXXXIV (1928), 445 ff.; ibid., Glimpses of high politics through war and peace, 1855–1919 (New York, 1931), p. 269.

[2] Kokovtzov, pp. 215, 217.

were to be prevented. Aehrenthal declared, à propos of concessions to Serbia and Montenegro, that "it was quite out of the
question for the Monarchy to negotiate with any Balkan state
over the cession of even one kilometre"; but Izvolsky might
hint to Serbia that if she conducted herself correctly "Austria-
Hungary would not oppose a territorial aggrandizement of Serbia
towards the south if and when great changes took place in the
Balkan peninsula". The Austro-Hungarian minister also agreed
to consider certain rectifications of Article 29 of the Treaty of
Berlin affecting Montenegro which were suggested by Russia.
Izvolsky promised to put in writing his understanding of the
agreement reached and to send a copy to Aehrenthal.[1] But
because of subsequent developments, he never did so.

Unfortunately, the reports which Izvolsky sent to St Petersburg
have not been published, so that it is impossible to control the
accuracy of Aehrenthal's version on certain very important details. From the accounts which, in the course of the next few
weeks, the Russian foreign minister gave to German and British
statesmen of his conversations with Aehrenthal, there is no doubt
that Izvolsky did agree not to oppose the annexation of Bosnia in
return for a similar attitude on the part of Austria-Hungary in
the matter of the opening of the Straits. What is not clear is the
precise bargain reached with reference to (1) the method of
carrying out the changes contemplated in the Treaty of Berlin,
and (2) the time of the annexation. Aehrenthal, according to his
account, proposed negotiations between the cabinets—"negotiations in which there could naturally no longer be any discussion of Bosnia and Herzegovina—followed by a conference to
record the results, which conference might be that of the ambassadors at Constantinople". Izvolsky, in his subsequent statements, always insisted that he expected the understanding reached
between Aehrenthal and himself to be submitted to the other
Powers. Thus he explained to Schoen, whom he visited at
Berchtesgaden on 25–26 September, that he desired a discussion
with the German chancellor after he had sounded the French
and British governments.[2] He told the British ambassador in

---

[1] Memorandum of 16 September; A 79.
[2] Schoen to Bülow, 26 September; G 8935.

Paris that he had said to Aehrenthal that "we [Russia] would consider the annexation as a question interesting the Powers signatory of the Treaty of Berlin and as a breach of that treaty", and that "in case of a revision we should demand the modification of its stipulations concerning the Straits in a sense favourable to Russia and the other Powers bordering on the Black Sea"; that he had likewise pointed out the necessity of concessions to Bulgaria, Serbia and Montenegro; furthermore, that he had stated merely his "personal opinion" and would have to submit the matter to the tsar. In short, the assertion of the Austro-Hungarian ambassador in Paris that the "consent" of Russia to the annexation had been secured, was "at least exaggerated".[1] This version seems to be borne out by a statement of Izvolsky's assistant in the Russian foreign office. When asked by the British ambassador whether the Russian government "had expressed their concurrence" in the annexation, Charykov said:

The statement was somewhat exaggerated; a confidential and preliminary exchange of views had taken place, but the Russian government had not yet given a formal reply. He added that the Russian government did not consider that eventual annexation of the two provinces by Austria-Hungary constituted a *casus belli*, and they did not intend to oppose it; but that the Russian government were preparing a circular despatch to the Powers, proposing that they should meet in conference for the revision of the Berlin Treaty, with a view to changing those articles of that act which were onerous to other parties, to Turkey, to Russia, and to the Balkan states.[2]

[1] Memorandum of Izvolsky to Bertie, enclosed in Bertie to Grey, 4 October; B 292. Bertie thought, however, that Izvolsky "did not quite tell me the truth, the whole truth, and nothing but the truth". From Izvolsky's remark that he understood that the provinces "would be incorporated in the Austrian Empire, the Kingdom of Hungary being probably compensated for this arrangement by concessions in regard to Croatia", Bertie deduced that "the question of annexation was pretty fully discussed and decided between Baron d'Aehrenthal and Monsieur Izvolsky, and that it was not a project for further discussion and consideration between Austria and Russia" (Bertie to Grey, 4 October; B 293).

[2] Nicolson to Grey, telegram, 5 October; B 303. After the war Charykov stated that on receiving Izvolsky's reports from Buchlau, he "obtained the emperor's permission to prepare a circular *à la Gorchakov* (as Izvolsky said) to the Great Powers signatories of the Berlin Treaty, inviting them to a conference for the modification of that treaty on the basis of our agreement with Vienna" (N. V. Tcharykow, *loc. cit.* p. 447). Izvolsky consistently maintained this thesis in conversations with various diplomatists subsequent to

Izvolsky always insisted that he had not understood the annexation to be imminent. To the British ambassador in Paris he represented Aehrenthal as saying that "certain circumstances might cause Austria to annex Bosnia and Herzegovina"; "he [Aehrenthal] did not, however, state that such a decision was definite nor did he say that it would be acted on at an early date".[1] He seems to have told Tittoni that Aehrenthal "made no formal declaration to him about Bosnia and Herzegovina", but "he, Izvolsky, had received the impression that Aehrenthal was pursuing plans for annexation".[2] On the other hand, Aehrenthal, in his memorandum of their conversations, stated that he had informed Izvolsky that the annexation would depend on the reports from Sarajevo and Plevlye.

But it might very easily be possible [he continued] that the annexation would be announced in the first days of October, just before the meeting of the Delegations. When M. Izvolsky remarked that he would prefer it if this event were carried through only after his return to St Petersburg—in the middle of October—because he would then be in a position to undertake himself the direction of Russian public opinion, I did not object to declaring that I should also much prefer it if M. Izvolsky could have arranged to be in St Petersburg at the moment of annexation, but that we found ourselves forced to act [*dass wir aber vor einer Zwangslage stünden*], and that I could not promise that the annexation would not go forward before the Delegations; in any event he would receive from me a previous notice at the proper time.

This seems very explicit, so explicit that the admission of

the announcement of the annexation: in Paris with Lancken and Radolin (G 9010, 9050), in Berlin with Szögyény (A 371), and with Cartwright, the British ambassador in Vienna (B 870). Cf. also Nicolson's report of 6 February 1909 (B 270), and Izvolsky's letter to the *Journal des Débats* of 5 October 1918, reprinted in H. Welschinger, *L'alliance franco-russe* (Paris, 1919), pp. 264–7.    [1] Bertie to Grey, 4 October; B 293.
[2] Memorandum of Stemrich of a conversation with the Italian ambassador in Berlin, 5 October; G 8943. The Duke of Avarna, Italian ambassador in Vienna, told his German colleague that Tittoni had first heard of the projected annexation from Izvolsky, but that, according to the Russian minister, "the talk had not referred to any date" and he had put forward his counter-demand concerning the Straits only in a quite general way, "in case the annexation should take place" (Tschirschky to Bülow, 12 October; G 8945). These statements do not necessarily prove that Izvolsky told Tittoni the truth, but they were made on 29 September, that is, before any controversy had arisen with Aehrenthal as to what had been said.

Aehrenthal's defenders that he might have given the information as to the time of the annexation "deliberately casually, as it were, in an aside",[1] and his own boast that he had deceived Izvolsky[2] seems to be of no consequence. Nevertheless, the matter cannot be considered settled. Three points may be noted. (1) The text of Aehrenthal's memorandum which exists in the Vienna archives is not the original document, but only a copy, and is undated. It is therefore at least possible that Aehrenthal, after the issue had arisen, modified the text to suit his story. (2) The German military plenipotentiary at the Russian court was told at the Austro-Hungarian embassy in St Petersburg that "Aehrenthal had spoken to Izvolsky about the possibility that the annexation of the two provinces would prove necessary, but in an indefinite manner, and indicating the possibility as lying in the vague future"[3]—which was exactly Izvolsky's version! (3) When speaking with Schoen, Izvolsky stated that he had received the impression that Aehrenthal "wished to proceed at an early date to the solution" of the problem, and added: "Without having received definite indications from Baron von Aehrenthal on this point, he was inclined to assume that the Austro-Hungarian minister would like to lay the plan for the annexation before the approaching Delegations."[4] This suggests that Izvolsky expected Aehrenthal to announce his plans rather than to present Europe with a *fait accompli*, and confirmation is seemingly found in a later incident. When the Austro-Hungarian ambassador in St Petersburg remarked that, according to Aehrenthal's memorandum, the Russian minister had been given plainly to under-

---

[1] H. Friedjung, "Die Zusammenkunft Aehrenthals und Iswolskys, 1908", *Historische Aufsätze* (Vienna, 1919), p. 196. Cf. also B. Molden, *Graf Aehrenthal* (Stuttgart, 1917), p. 77.

[2] H. Kanner, *Kaiserliche Katastrophenpolitik* (Leipzig, 1922), pp. 82–3. According to Kanner, Aehrenthal said that he had not informed Izvolsky that the annexation was imminent and that Izvolsky had not asked about the date.

[3] Hintze to William II, 9 October; G 9005.

[4] Schoen to Bülow, 26 September; G 8935. Charykov appears to have remarked to the Italian chargé in St Petersburg that "he had learned that the Austro-Hungarian government intends to modify the juridical [*staatsrechtliche*] position of Bosnia-Herzegovina on the occasion of the next Delegations"—a statement the meaning of which is not very clear (Call to Aehrenthal, telegram, 2 October; A 111).

stand that "the annexation would follow in the first days of October",

M. Izvolsky did not deny this at all [Berchtold reported], but said, he had not expected an "*acte brutale*"; rather he had assumed that Your Excellency [Aehrenthal], in accordance with diplomatic usages, would follow the course of confidential exchanges with the cabinets.[1]

From this welter of conflicting evidence, one is inclined to conclude that Aehrenthal said something to Izvolsky about the necessity of acting before the meeting of the Delegations, but left the Russian minister under the impression that he would have time to arrange *his* business about the Straits before Aehrenthal had shown his hand.[2] Certainly it is difficult to believe that, if he had understood the proclamation of the annexation to be imminent, which, according to his own statements, would not only be a breach of the Treaty of Berlin, but was likely to arouse much excitement in the Balkans, Izvolsky would not have modified his plans for a leisurely tour through Europe, in the course of which he intended to consult the German, Italian, French and British governments about the opening of the Straits.[3] Whether Aehrenthal intentionally deceived Izvolsky, as the latter repeatedly asserted, or whether Izvolsky, realizing his delicate situation,[4] took early to misrepresentation, cannot be determined until the Russian documents are made available.

[1] Berchtold to Aehrenthal, 30 October; A 465.

[2] That Izvolsky did not consider the matter entirely settled, but had negotiated subject to the approval of his government, is shown by what he wrote later to Aehrenthal: "I have already sent to St Petersburg, for submission to His Majesty the Emperor, my draft of a reply to your last memorandum, which I have drawn up on the basis of our conversation at Buchlau. If this draft obtains the sanction of my august master, our memorandum of reply will be transmitted to you with the shortest possible delay" (Izvolsky to Aehrenthal, 23 September; A 86).

[3] "My French colleague [wrote the British ambassador in Vienna], who is intimate with Izvolsky and saw him almost immediately after the Buchlau interview, tells me that Izvolsky informed him that d'Aehrenthal spoke vaguely at Buchlau about the necessity of annexing the provinces some time or other, and had given him the impression, also vaguely, that he, d'Aehrenthal, wanted him during his tour to sound other Powers on the subject and obtain their views. This shows that Izvolsky went off quite easy in his mind, only to find a 'fait accompli' by the time he reached Paris" (Goschen to Grey, private, 14 October; B 381).

[4] He was negotiating with Austria-Hungary behind the backs of France and Great Britain, and the British ambassador in St Petersburg was not slow in pointing this out (Nicolson to Grey, 6 October; B 322).

For the subsequent course of events, however, what actually was said at Buchlau was of less importance than what each minister believed, or professed to believe, had been arranged. Aehrenthal asserted that Izvolsky had agreed to the annexation and had been notified of its imminence. Izvolsky denied that he had agreed to it, affirming that he had only said that "Russia would not oppose it" when the question was brought before a European conference, the necessity of which he claimed to have made clear. Each man contended that the other was not acting loyally; Aehrenthal's version was accepted by Germany, Izvolsky's by France and Great Britain. The personal factor was introduced to a dangerous degree and constantly envenomed the negotiations.

From Buchlau, Izvolsky proceeded for a short holiday to Tegernsee, near Munich, and then visited Schoen at Berchtesgaden, to whom he gave an account of his conversation with Aehrenthal. He asserted that he would not have the courage to "set all these great questions in motion"(!), but that "if this were to happen through the initiative of Austria-Hungary, Russian policy would strive for a thorough solution of all the Balkan problems which would come up, and would always be inspired only by a sincere desire to effect a compromise in a peaceful way". The German foreign minister exhibited considerable reserve and avoided committing himself.[1]

From Berchtesgaden, Izvolsky went on to Desio for a meeting with Tittoni on 29 September. The Italian foreign minister, according to Izvolsky, "knew nothing of Austrian projects and was much perturbed on their being made known to him by M. Izvolsky".[2] But he raised no objection to the general plan, stating that Italy "would content herself, as moral compensation, with the evacuation of the Sandjak of Novi Bazar, to which he attached great importance, and the abolition of the article of the Treaty of Berlin restricting the rights of Montenegro".[3] He was apparently given to understand that Izvolsky "intended to propose a congress immediately".[4]

[1] Schoen to Bülow, 26 September; G 8935.
[2] Actually, Tittoni had received a letter from Aehrenthal on 26 September informing him of the annexation; but he may not have told Izvolsky of this.
[3] Bertie to Grey, 4 October; B 293.    [4] Grey to Egerton, 5 October; B 307.

Izvolsky proceeded from Desio to Paris, and on his arrival found a private letter from Aehrenthal informing him that the annexation had been fixed for 7 October and expressing "the firm conviction" that he could count upon "a friendly and benevolent attitude on the part of Russia".[1]

Meanwhile, Aehrenthal had been making elaborate preparations for staging his *coup*. Pallavicini, realizing that his warnings had not been heeded, now urged the presentation of a blunt note to the Sublime Porte stating that "Bosnia and Herzegovina are annexed"; negotiations of any kind should be avoided at all costs.[2] Aehrenthal, however, preferred to avoid the word "annexation". In the note which the ambassador was instructed to present, the change in the status of the provinces was justified by the argument that "an autonomous and constitutional régime, ardently desired by the entire population", had to be introduced:

Consequently the cabinet of Vienna sees itself in the imperative necessity of freeing itself from the restrictions contained in the convention of Constantinople [of 1879] and of resuming its complete liberty of action in respect of Bosnia and Herzegovina; it likes to believe that the relations between the two countries, relieved of uncertainty about the situation in Bosnia-Herzegovina and the Sandjak, will only improve as a result of the well-defined and normal state of affairs which we wish to establish.

Not a word was said about negotiation or compensation; and the ambassador was instructed to point out to the Turks, from whom "a formal protest" was to be expected, that the withdrawal from the Sandjak provided "an impressive and striking proof that we repudiate any idea of a territorial acquisition at the expense of the present territory of Turkey".[3] The withdrawal, in short, was to be sufficient compensation.

Next, Aehrenthal wrote private letters to Tittoni, Sir Charles Hardinge, the permanent under-secretary of the British foreign office, who was an old acquaintance, and Prince Bülow, the German chancellor, informing them of his plans. To the Italian

---

[1] Aehrenthal to Izvolsky, 30 September; A 103.
[2] Pallavicini to Aehrenthal, private, 23 September; A 85.
[3] Aehrenthal to Pallavicini, 30 September; A 99. Anlage I gives the text of the note to the Porte.

minister he promised to ascertain whether the Vatican still maintained its veto on the visit of Catholic sovereigns to the court of Rome.[1] The British diplomatist was reminded that it was Lord Salisbury who, in 1878, had proposed the occupation of Bosnia-Herzegovina by the Monarchy, "d'y établir une administration stable et forte", and he was assured that in consequence of the annexation, "it will be easier for us than it has been up to the present to act in concert with the other cabinets in the East".[2]

In the letter to Bülow, Aehrenthal stated that he had reached "a preliminary understanding with Russia", the terms of which were indicated, and he explained that in yielding to the Russian wishes in respect of the Straits, he had been animated in part by the desire "to separate Russia somewhat from England"—which was hardly in keeping with his overture to Hardinge. "We count", he added, "with complete confidence on Germany's support because she has received proofs from us that in a serious hour we stand firmly by our friends"—on which the German Emperor noted "?".[3]

Officially, the action of the Austro-Hungarian government was to be announced to the Powers by autograph letters which the Emperor Francis Joseph addressed to the German Emperor, the King of England, the President of the French Republic, the King of Italy, and the Tsar of Russia,[4] and which were to be presented by the ambassadors to the several heads of state on 5 or 6 October. The ambassadors were also provided with two circular despatches which they were to communicate to the respective foreign offices on 7 October, the day of the annexation.[5] In the case of the Balkan states, the King of Rumania and the Prince of Montenegro were to be officially notified of the annexation on 7 October, the latter being assured that "a correct and sympathetic attitude" on his part would be rewarded by subsidies for the building of roads and by modifications of Article 29 of the Treaty of Berlin. On the other hand, the minister in Belgrade

[1] Aehrenthal to Tittoni, private, 25 September; A 88.
[2] Aehrenthal to Hardinge, private, 28 September; A 91, B 288.
[3] Aehrenthal to Bülow, private, 26 September; A 89, G 8934.
[4] The letters were dated 29 September; A 92, 93, 95, 96, 97.
[5] Dated 3 October and carried personally by the ambassadors when they returned to their posts; A 116, 117.

was informed that "we naturally have no occasion to make any kind of communication about the matter to the Serbian government", which speaks volumes for the ultimate purpose of the action.[1] There remains to be considered the problem of Bulgaria.

[1] Circular to representatives in the Balkan capitals, 3 October; A 112. M. Boghitschewitsch, *Die auswärtige Politik Serbiens, 1903–1914*, vol. III, *Serbien und der Weltkrieg* (Berlin, 1928), pp. 73–7, thinks that in the presentation of his case to the Powers, Aehrenthal should have emphasized the danger to the Monarchy from the propaganda and subversive activities of Serbia.

# CHAPTER III

## *Bulgaria*

B Y THE TREATY OF BERLIN Bulgaria had been created an autonomous principality under the suzerainty of the sultan, while to the south of the Balkan mountains Eastern Rumelia had been established as an autonomous province of Turkey. The revolution of 1885 had brought about a kind of union, the Prince of Bulgaria being appointed Governor-General of Eastern Rumelia, and representatives from the latter being admitted to the Bulgarian sobranje. But the suzerainty of the sultan remained, and it became one of the cardinal aims of Bulgarian policy to achieve complete independence. Unfortunately, the Powers frowned upon any dislocation of the *status quo*,[1] so that the matter remained in abeyance until the Turkish Revolution of 1908 obviously altered the whole political situation in Eastern Europe. Very foolishly the new Turkish government gave Bulgaria an opening by neglecting to invite the Bulgarian diplomatic agent in Constantinople to a dinner for the foreign missions on 12 September, a step which, though technically justified, was contrary to established usage. To this the Bulgarian government replied first by recalling its agent and then by seizing the railway line running through Eastern Rumelia. As the railway belonged to an Austro-Hungarian company, Baron Aehrenthal protested against the Bulgarian action and demanded the return of the railway, in which he was supported by Germany.[2] But he waited till he had seen Prince Ferdinand, then on a visit to Budapest.

Aehrenthal's record of their conversation is a very interesting document. After saying that he and Izvolsky were agreed to "maintain Turkey within its present actual territorial extent",

[1] In 1907 the Bulgarian government considered proclaiming independence, but the Powers intervened (Buchanan to Grey, 7 August 1907; B 261).

[2] Romberg to foreign office, telegram, 27 September; Stemrich to Romberg, telegram, 27 September; G 8956, 8957: Buchanan to Grey, telegram, 27 September; B 268. The Austro-Hungarian documents are silent on the matter.

he assured the prince that he "would place no obstacle in the way of realizing any other wishes of the Principality", and called attention to two aspects of the international situation:

On the one hand, the Principality should not pursue a policy of adventure which could not obtain the support of the Powers; on the other hand, regard should be had for the fact that Bulgaria should not neglect an opportunity which was perhaps favourable to realize her legitimate wishes and allow to pass unused the superiority which the Principality enjoyed in the Balkans by virtue of its army, so long as it could be maintained at its present strength.[1]

The word "independence" was not mentioned, but Aehrenthal's language can only be interpreted as an encouragement to take that step. A few days later he told the German ambassador in Vienna that "he had the impression that Bulgaria will now proceed to a declaration of independence",[2] and explained frankly that he "needed the Bulgarians".[3] In other words, a step on the part of Bulgaria which would also be a violation of the Treaty of Berlin would provide a welcome diversion in the excitement which the annexation of Bosnia was bound to produce. The Bulgarians, on their side, did not take Aehrenthal's protest very seriously, for as a confidant of the Bulgarian premier explained, "Bulgaria was now pursuing Austrian policy".[4] It is impossible not to believe that Aehrenthal, to say the least, connived at the Bulgarian plans.[5]

Rumours that the Bulgarian government was considering the proclamation of independence began to reach the British foreign office,[6] and although the foreign minister gave assurances that "independence was not contemplated at present",[7] the British and French diplomatic agents in Sofia received information that

[1] Memorandum of conversations of 23 and 24 September, undated; A 87.
[2] Tschirschky to foreign office, telegram, 28 September; G 8953, note*.
[3] Tschirschky to foreign office, telegram, 29 September; G 8959.
[4] Romberg to foreign office, telegram, 30 September; G 8962.
[5] Aehrenthal subsequently admitted to the German Emperor that "Prince Ferdinand had been given to understand in Budapest that Austria-Hungary would do nothing against a proclamation of independence by Bulgaria", and from a remark of Aehrenthal, William II deduced that "the question of the royal proclamation had also been discussed between him and Prince Ferdinand" (Jenisch to Bülow, 7 November 1908; G 9088).
[6] Buchanan to Grey, telegram, 27 September; B 268.
[7] Buchanan to Grey, telegram, 29 September; B 272.

action was about to be taken.[1]  Great Britain thereupon proposed that "the Bulgarian government should be seriously warned of the gravity of such action of which it is impossible to foresee the consequences",[2] and appealed particularly to the Austro-Hungarian government "to use all their influence with the Prince of Bulgaria to discountenance the idea".[3]  The Russian government also used "the strongest language" in Sofia, warning the Bulgarians that "if they declared independence, they must bear all the consequences and Russia would not move a finger to help them if Turkish troops occupied their territory".[4]  But it was all in vain, for Bulgaria proclaimed her independence on 6 October 1908.[5]

[1] Buchanan to Grey, telegram, 1 October; B 275: Romberg to foreign office, telegram, 2 October; G 8966.

[2] Grey to Bertie, Goschen and Nicolson, telegrams, 2 October; B 278. Without waiting to hear from the Powers, Grey addressed his own warning to Sofia (Grey to Buchanan, telegram, 2 October; B 280).

[3] Grey to Goschen, telegram, 2 October; B 279. Aehrenthal, when approached by Goschen, "professed disbelief of rumours of imminent declaration of independence", for "he had only recently seriously warned Prince Ferdinand against any adventuresome policy and his advice had been well received" (Goschen to Grey, telegram, 4 October; B 289). "The rumours had not been confirmed by the Austro-Hungarian representative at Sofia", and he refused to take the step proposed by Grey (Goschen to Grey, 4 October; B 291). Grey did not believe Aehrenthal's assurances (Grey to Goschen, telegram, private, 5 October; B 299). Nor did Goschen (Goschen to Grey, 5 October and 14 October; B 305, 381). Belief in Aehrenthal's veracity was, in fact, impossible, for his ambassador in Paris had stated that the annexation of Bosnia would be preceded by one day by the proclamation of Bulgarian independence (Bertie to Grey, 4 October; B 294: Marschall to foreign office, telegram, 5 October; G 8987).

[4] Nicolson to Grey, telegram, 3 October; B 283. According to the Russian agent in Sofia, "Russia wished to show that Austria was not the mistress in the Balkans", but he gave it as his private opinion that "were independence proclaimed, Russia would be the first to recognise it" (Buchanan to Grey, telegram, 2 October; B 277). Izvolsky's statement to Bertie that "the question [of Bulgarian independence] had not been discussed between him and the Austrian foreign secretary" (Bertie to Grey, 4 October; B 293) is not consistent with Aehrenthal's record quoted in A 79 (on p. 20 above).

[5] The account here given is based on the contemporary documents. Much later Sir Fairfax Cartwright, who became British ambassador in Vienna in December 1908, received from J. D. Bourchier, the correspondent of the London Times in the Balkans, information which led him to doubt whether Aehrenthal had known of Prince Ferdinand's intentions. According to Bourchier, Ferdinand, who proceeded from Vienna to Rustchuk for a conference with his ministers, was as late as Sunday evening, 4 October, "fully determined to put off the declaration of independence until a further date", according to his arrangement with Aehrenthal. Cartwright also heard "on

Thus did two ambitious and unscrupulous men plan to take advantage of the Turkish Revolution to execute far-reaching plans. Probably Aehrenthal and Izvolsky were not honest towards each other; certainly they were not altogether so with their respective allies. Both were to be greatly surprised by the course of events.

very good authority" that copies of the proclamation of annexation had been printed with a date later than 20 October and that the corrected copies had to be printed "in a terrible hurry" to get them out on 7 October. "It all looks as if the annexation had not been contemplated for so early a date, and only intended to be carried out after the replies had been received to the Imperial letters addressed to the European courts." Count Zichy, who headed the Hungarian Delegation, had told him that on the evening of 6 October he was asked to make some allusion to Bosnia and Herzegovina in his speech, in order to give the government an opening to announce the annexation. "All this would tend to show", said Cartwright, "that the annexation was precipitated by the unexpected declaration of independence of Bulgaria, and that Aehrenthal had been as much deceived by Prince Ferdinand as the rest of the world" (Cartwright to Hardinge, private, 9 July 1909; B, vol. ix, Part I, No. 20). Cartwright thought it "incredible" that Aehrenthal, "who is no fool", should have lied to Goschen. "What could he gain by doing so, except to obtain for himself the damaging reputation of being a barefaced liar or of being an idiot?" Steed, who conveyed Bourchier's story to Cartwright, states that on 1 October, Count Henry Lützow, then Austro-Hungarian ambassador to Italy, informed him that "the proclamation of Bulgarian independence might be considered certain"; Lützow later added that he had been informed of this by Aehrenthal himself (statement of Wickham Steed, *ibid.* p. 778). Cartwright's argument from the alleged hasty reprinting of the proclamation of annexation is disproved by the fact that on 30 September Aehrenthal informed Izvolsky by private letter that the annexation had been fixed for 7 October (see above, p. 27). The ambassador, who had become an admirer of Aehrenthal, also endeavoured to discount the statement of the Austrian ambassador in Paris that the proclamation of Bulgarian independence would precede the annexation by one day (see p. 32). "Khevenhüller", said Cartwright, "is a man who is greatly given to inconsiderate talk and he may merely have meant that the annexation of Bosnia and the declaration of independence of Bulgaria were events which would follow each other in rapid succession without having the intention of fixing the precise dates when these should occur." On the basis of a private letter from M. de C. Findlay, British chargé in Sofia, to Hardinge, 27 July 1909, who received the information from an Austrian friend, the editors of the *British documents* state: "Apparently the Bulgarian code cypher was known to the Austro-Hungarian foreign office, so that all telegrams between Prince Ferdinand [while in Vienna] and his ministers were read in Vienna. This would make it possible for Prince Ferdinand's intentions to be known in Vienna, as Count Khevenhüller's statement that the Bulgarian declaration of independence would precede the Austro-Hungarian annexation of Bosnia-Herzegovina implies that they were, while at the same time Count von Aehrenthal could state definitely that there had been no understanding between Austria-Hungary and Bulgaria and that the subject had not been discussed" (*ibid.* p. 51).

# CHAPTER IV

## The Annexation

WHEN COUNT KHEVENHÜLLER, the Austro-Hungarian ambassador to France, returned to Paris on the morning of 3 October 1908, and asked for an audience of President Fallières on the 5th or 6th, in order to present the autograph letter of Francis Joseph, he was told that he could be received that afternoon or not until 7 October. Supposing that Izvolsky had already explained to the French government what was in the air, he decided for the earlier audience; not only that, but he informed the French foreign minister, Stephen Pichon, of the impending annexation, for which, he said, Austria-Hungary had "the concurrence of the Cabinets of St Petersburg, Berlin, and Rome".[1] When he saw Fallières he stated—according to French accounts—that the annexation would be preceded by the proclamation of Bulgarian independence.[2] Both Pichon and Fallières promised to keep the news secret until 6 October, but Clemenceau, the French premier, gave out a statement to the *Temps* the same afternoon,[3] which made a great sensation.[4] The British ambassador, Sir Francis Bertie, was also informed by the Quai d'Orsay.[5]

As a matter of fact, Izvolsky had apparently not told the French government of his bargain with Aehrenthal, and when he arrived in Paris the next morning (4 October), Khevenhüller's statement that Austria-Hungary was acting with the consent of Russia was thrown in his face. He at once denied to Pichon and

[1] Bertie to Grey, telegram, 3 October; B 281.
[2] This was stated to Grey and Marschall, the German ambassador to Turkey, by the French ambassadors in London and Constantinople (Grey to Bertie, 5 October; B 306: Marschall to foreign office, telegram, 5 October; G 8987). Khevenhüller subsequently denied that he had made any such statement, claiming, indeed, to have said that "there was no relation between the two events" (Khevenhüller to Aehrenthal, 17 October; A 314).
[3] Khevenhüller to Aehrenthal, 17 October; A 311, Beilage I.
[4] Lancken to foreign office, telegram, 4 October; G 8983.
[5] Bertie to Grey, telegrams, 3 October; B 281, 285.

Bertie that Russia had consented to the annexation, asserting that he had merely discussed with Aehrenthal certain questions which would have to be brought before a European conference.[1] He also called on Khevenhüller and took the same line, although he declared that Russia would not refuse her consent if Aehrenthal adhered to the conditions laid down at Buchlau.[2] And he telegraphed to St Petersburg:

I have applied myself above all to destroying the false impression created here by the ambassador of Austria-Hungary as though his government proceeded to the annexation with the approval of Russia and Italy. I replied immediately that on the contrary I had stated positively to Baron Aehrenthal that we considered the annexation as a violation of the Treaty of Berlin and a subject for the deliberation of the Powers.[3]

Aehrenthal promptly denied this: "M. Izvolsky never expressed himself to me in this fashion; we agreed in Buchlau that we would respond to the friendly attitude of Russia in the question of the annexation by a similar position in the question of the Dardanelles."[4] Thus almost before the Powers had had time to adjust themselves to the problem, the situation was badly complicated by the circumstance that Izvolsky and Aehrenthal were each challenging the good faith of the other.

Which of the two ministers was right cannot, as we have seen,[5] now be determined with certainty. But if recent revelations are to be trusted, Izvolsky's hand was forced by unforeseen circumstances and unexpected developments. When his reports from Buchlau were received in St Petersburg, his assistant Charykov consulted Stolypin, the premier, and Kokovtzov, the minister of finance. To his great surprise, Stolypin opposed the policy upon which Izvolsky had embarked, with the consent of the tsar. "He said, with great force and eloquence, that Russia should not give

[1] Khevenhüller to Aehrenthal, telegram, 5 October; A 142: Bertie to Grey, 4 October; B 292.
[2] Khevenhüller to Aehrenthal, telegram, 6 October, and report, 17 October; A 154, 311, Beilage II.
[3] Communicated by Charykov to Berchtold and by him forwarded to Vienna (Berchtold to Aehrenthal, telegram, 8 October; A 196).
[4] Aehrenthal to Berchtold, telegram, 9 October; A 218.
[5] See above, pp. 20–25.

her consent to the annexation of a Slavonic land by a German state, whatever political advantages this might bring to Russia, and added that if Izvolsky's plan were persevered in, he, Stolypin, would resign." Rather than force the resignation of the premier, "whose presence at the head of the government was our last and only hope of avoiding for Russia the cataclysm of a revolution", Charykov agreed to abandon the plan, and at his suggestion, "the necessary telegrams were sent to reach Izvolsky in Paris".[1] But nothing was known of this at the time. As Izvolsky could not publish the fact of his disavowal, he had to fall back on diplomatic argument.

Clemenceau described the Austro-Hungarian action as "a gross breach of a treaty engagement and an offence to public morality which if allowed to pass would form a very bad precedent". He thought that France and Britain should be "very stiff in their language", and suggested a conference,[2] which should preferably be proposed by Russia, France and Britain acting together, as this "would have a great moral effect in Europe".[3] On learning, however, that Britain objected to a conference "until there has been some preliminary understanding as to what questions are to be raised and how they are to be settled",[4] the French government promised to "do their best to persuade the Russian government to postpone the proposal".[5] For the moment, therefore, it contented itself with advising Serbia, where intense excitement reigned, to keep quiet.[6]

---

[1] N. V. Tcharykow, "Some reminiscences of Nicholas II", *Contemporary review*, CXXXIV (1928), 448–9; *ibid.*, *Glimpses of high politics*, pp. 269–70. When Stolypin discussed the matter with the tsar, Nicholas professed great indignation that Izvolsky had promised Russian support for the annexation of Bosnia. If the view advanced above (p. 20) that the tsar had approved Izvolsky's programme is correct, then the incident illustrates the well-known tendency of Nicholas II to agree with his last interlocutor. Stolypin thought that "the only step worthy of us would be to dismiss Izvolsky and announce publicly that he had acted without the permission of his government and that the entire matter would have to be considered as before" (Kokovtzov, *Out of my past*, p. 217).    [2] Bertie to Grey, 4 October; B 294.

[3] Bertie to Grey, telegram, 6 October; B 311.

[4] Grey to Bertie, telegram, 6 October; B 413.

[5] Grey to Bertie, 7 October; B 335.

[6] Bertie to Grey, telegram, 9 October; B 341: Khevenhüller to Aehrenthal, telegram, 8 October; A 193: Lancken to foreign office, telegram, 8 October: G 9009.

The French press, on the other hand, took a friendly view of the Austrian action, thanks to the activity of Khevenhüller.[1]

In London, the Austro-Hungarian ambassador, Count Mensdorff, had called at the foreign office on 3 October to present the private letter of Aehrenthal to Sir Charles Hardinge. The permanent under-secretary expressed the personal opinion that "it is not so much the proclamation of annexation which we should fear, but its consequences"; it "would be likely to encourage the Bulgarians" to demand compensation at the expense of Turkey.[2] But he seemed reassured by the statement that Russia and Italy would be favourable to the Austro-Hungarian action.[3] The ambassador then proceeded to Balmoral to present the autograph letter of his sovereign to King Edward VII. The king received the letter "with great coolness" and dismissed Mensdorff "with a few formal and unconciliatory words";[4] nor was he appeased by the circular despatch which was designed to place the Austrian action in the most favourable light.[5]

The Austrian action was indeed most unwelcome to the British government. British opinion had been distinctly hostile to Turkey because of the tyranny of Abdul Hamid, and the government had professed itself "perfectly helpless" to do anything for the tottering regime.[6] But the Young Turk revolution of July had completely changed the picture. Great Britain, as the home of constitutional government, became as popular in Turkey as she had hitherto been suspect, and her new ambassador, Sir Gerald Lowther, who arrived a few days after the revolution, was lionized in the streets of Constantinople. At the same time, German influence, which had been predominant in the counsels of the Sublime Porte for a decade, seemed to collapse overnight. These "marvellous" developments, as Grey characterized them,[7] were welcomed in London, and the British government, in public speeches and in messages to the Young Turk leaders, gave every

[1] Khevenhüller to Aehrenthal, telegrams, 4 and 5 October; A 119, 141.
[2] Memorandum of Hardinge, 3 October; B 287.
[3] Mensdorff to Aehrenthal, telegram, 3 October; A 114.
[4] Lee, *King Edward VII*, II, 633; Steed, *Through thirty years*, I, 283.
[5] Mensdorff to Aehrenthal, telegrams, 5 and 8 October; A 140, 192. The telegrams do not speak of the king's irritation.
[6] Grey to Barclay, private, 26 May 1908; B 197.
[7] Grey to Lowther, private, 11 August; B 207.

possible encouragement to the new course. There is no reason to doubt the sincerity of this attitude, even though certain material advantages were anticipated from an Anglophile Turkish government, such as an easing of the British difficulties in Egypt or greater opportunities for British trade and British capital.[1] British opinion, in short, desired that the new system should be given a fair chance.

The foreign office, however, was well aware of pitfalls and dangers. "It may well be", observed Grey, "that the habit of vicious and corrupt government will be too strong for reform", or that "there may be evolved a strong and efficient military despotism"; if the Young Turks went too fast, "they may either create confusion or provoke reaction", and they could accomplish little without sound finance.[2] Whatever might happen, the British course was clear: to encourage Turkey along the path of liberalism and reform and, if possible, to "keep the ring" while the experiment proceeded. At the same time, Grey remarked: "We must be careful not to give Russia the impression that we are reverting to the old policy of supporting Turkey as a barrier against her and should continue to show willingness to work with Russia when possible".[3] Since the Austrian action dealt a severe blow to the Young Turk regime, the new British policy was correspondingly damaged; while the fact that Russia was in some fashion involved in the business and had not yet explained her plans in respect of the Straits only added to the difficulties of the situation. Simultaneously to humour Russia and to protect Turkey from both Russia and Austria would require all the resources of a skilful diplomacy.[4]

Sir Edward Grey therefore lost no time in telling the Turkish ambassador that

we cannot admit the rights of any Power to alter an international treaty without the consent of the other parties to it; that we shall therefore refuse to recognize what has been done till the views of the

---

[1] Grey to Lowther, private, 31 July and 24 August; Lowther to Grey, private, 11 August; B 204, 207, 206.

[2] Grey to Lowther, private, 11 August, 23 August; B 207, 208.

[3] Grey to Lowther, private, 11 August; B 207.

[4] Cf. Jugo Burisch, *Englands Haltung in der Bosnischen Annexionskrise* (Halle, 1935), pp. 11–19.

other Powers are known, especially of Turkey, who is more concerned than any one else.[1]

He transmitted a formal protest to the Austro-Hungarian government urging "the necessity of reconsidering their decision to annex the two occupied provinces",[2] and to Bulgaria, who was advised "to minimize the consequences of her action by making it clear that she intended now to maintain a peaceful and unaggressive attitude".[3] To the German ambassador he complained of the "manner" in which Austria-Hungary and Bulgaria had acted: "It was no good having any treaties at all if they were to be altered in this way."[4] And to Mensdorff he said: "What Austria had done had given a great blow to public confidence, and it was in the interests of public morality that we should not recognize her action", which seemed to him "most inopportune and unfortunate".[5] Feeling very strongly that what the offending Powers had done "would be injurious to the new regime in Turkey, and might turn it from a peaceful movement into a military one",[6] he readily agreed to a French suggestion for "a simultaneous and immediate declaration to the Turkish government that the Treaty of Berlin cannot be modified without an agreement between the signatory Powers",[7] and he instructed the British ambassador in Constantinople to co-operate with his French and Russian colleagues in this sense.[8] But suggestions for a conference he put off on the ground that

[1] Grey to Lowther, telegram, 5 October; B 296. An official *communiqué* was issued to this effect, which was reported to Vienna (Széchényi to Aehrenthal, telegram, 6 October; A 153).

[2] Grey to Goschen, telegram, 5 October; B 302.

[3] Grey to Buchanan, telegrams, 6 October; B 319, 320.

[4] Grey to Lascelles, 9 October; B 350. Cf. Metternich to foreign office, telegram, 9 October; G 9003.

[5] Grey to Goschen, 9 October; B 351. Cf. Mensdorff to Aehrenthal, telegram, 9 October; A 213.

[6] Grey to Bertie, 5 October; B 306.

[7] Grey to Bertie, telegram, 9 October; B 343.

[8] Grey to Lowther, telegram, 9 October; B 347. He suggested similar declarations in Vienna and Sofia, but yielded to the French objection that a declaration at Sofia "may cause Prince Ferdinand to precipitate matters and do more harm than good", while one at Vienna was "likely to cause great irritation without producing any effect" (Bertie to Grey, telegram, 10 October; Grey to Nicolson, telegram, 12 October; B 352, 359).

there should be a preliminary agreement amongst the Powers who are to take part in it as to what subjects should be discussed, how they should be dealt with, and in what form Turkey can receive any advantages to compensate her for those gained by other Powers at her expense.[1]

He wished, as he explained to the German ambassador, Count Metternich, to await the arrival of Izvolsky in London.[2] Throughout, his cue was to pose as the disinterested friend of Turkey. At the same time he made clear to St Petersburg that he hoped to act in concert with Russia.[3]

Germany was equally determined to stand by Austria-Hungary, but this position was not reached quite automatically.[4] When the German chancellor, Prince Bülow, received Aehrenthal's private letter of 26 September,[5] which contained the first clear announcement of the impending action, he sent a long communication to the foreign office with directions for a letter to be prepared for the emperor, the essence of which was that Germany must support Austria-Hungary unconditionally.[6] He evidently expected his master to make no difficulties; for on

[1] Grey to Bertie, 6 October; B 321. He was already hinting to the Porte that Turkey might receive "some pecuniary compensation" (Grey to Lowther, telegram, 6 October; B 317).

[2] Metternich to foreign office, telegram, 9 October; G 9003.

[3] Grey to Nicolson, telegram, 5 October; B 301.

[4] For the question of Austro-German relations during the crisis, see O. H. Wedel, *Austro-German diplomatic relations, 1908–1914* (Stanford University, Calif., 1932), pp. 47–104, and Annie M. Popper, "Austro-German relations, 1890–1909", an unpublished dissertation of the University of Chicago (Chicago, 1930), pp. 155–222. The present writer does not always agree with the views expressed by these authors, but both studies are thoroughly objective.

[5] See above, p. 28.

[6] Bülow to Stemrich, acting foreign minister, 30 September, from Norderney; G 8937. Yet Stemrich, on 4 October, told the French and British ambassadors in Berlin that he knew nothing more about the annexation than what he had read in the newspapers (memorandum of Stemrich, 4 October; G 8981), and the latter believed him (Lascelles to Grey, telegram, 4 October; B 290). Later Stemrich admitted that Aehrenthal had mentioned the matter to Schoen, "but had conveyed the impression that these were remote contingencies and certainly had not intimated that they were in any way imminent" (Lascelles to Grey, telegram, 7 October; B 323). Stemrich's cue for the diplomatic corps was to express both his personal and his official " regret" that " Germany would have to espouse the cause of her ally Austria" (Stephen Gwynn, *Letters and friendships of Sir Cecil Spring Rice* [London, 1929], II, 127).

receipt of a telegraphic protest from Baron Marschall, the ambassador in Constantinople, complaining that Aehrenthal's action meant opening up "the whole Eastern Question" to the disadvantage of Germany and urging that Germany should pursue her own interests regardless of Austria-Hungary,[1] he replied that it would be going too far "to sacrifice or even in the slightest degree risk our alliance with Austria-Hungary for the friendly relationship with Turkey", and Marschall should assure the Turks that "Germany had known nothing of the annexation plan".[2] In addition, the cabinet of Vienna was informed that "it is for us an act of self-evident loyalty to hold fast to the alliance with Austria-Hungary", and no complaint was made that the Dual Monarchy had taken the initiative without consulting its ally.[3] In spite of repeated protests from Marschall,[4] the chancellor refused to take the crisis too seriously and thought that the Turks could be humoured by compensations, to which end Marschall was to exert himself to the utmost.[5] His only contribution towards a solution of the crisis was the advice to Aehrenthal to come to terms promptly with Turkey.[6]

The chancellor's letter to the emperor,[7] a copy of Aehrenthal's letter, Schoen's report of his conversation with Izvolsky,[8] and a telegram from Vienna,[9] were delivered to the emperor at Rominten on 6 October.

William II was greatly excited by the news thus brought to him. Complaining that he had not been informed by telegraph ten days before, he wrote a stinging comment:

That we shall do nothing against the annexation is evident. But I am personally most deeply wounded in my feelings as an ally that I was not previously taken in the least into the confidence of His

[1] Marschall to foreign office, telegram, 4 October; G 8980.
[2] Bülow to foreign office, telegram from Norderney, 5 October; G 8984. In due course Marschall made the desired declaration in writing (Lowther to Grey, telegram, 9 October; B 346).
[3] Stemrich to Tschirschky, telegram, 6 October; G 8988.
[4] Marschall to foreign office, telegrams, 4, 5, 6 and 8 October; G 8982, 8987, 8990, 8996.
[5] Bülow to foreign office, telegram from Norderney, 8 October; G 8998.
[6] Bülow to foreign office, telegram from Norderney, 9 October; G 9000.
[7] Bülow to William II, 5 October; G 8939.
[8] See above, pp. 24, 26.
[9] Tschirschky to foreign office, 28 September; G 8936.

Majesty [Francis Joseph]....Thus I am the last of all in Europe to learn something. That is nice thanks for our help in the question of the Sandjak railway....The lying Ferdinand and the worthy old emperor appear together on the stage in Bengal lights as spoliators of Turkey....Considered from the Turkish standpoint, the situation presents itself that after I have pursued a friendly policy for 20 years, my best ally is the first to give the signal for the partition of European Turkey. An agreeable situation for us in Stambul....If the Sultan in his necessity declares war and unrolls in Stambul the green flag of a holy war, I would not much blame him and it would be a sound move against the Christians of the Balkans—treacherous criminals.[1]

The imperial indignation was reported to the chancellor, who was still at Norderney, and he replied in a long telegram pleading for the Austrians. He had not been able, he said, to induce them to base their Balkan policy on Turkey, and the circumstances of their action were "highly unwished for". But the "Hauptsache" must not be forgotten: "we must maintain the alliance with Austria-Hungary intact and not let the confidence of the Austrians in us be shattered"; besides, the Monarchy must be repaid for its loyal attitude on the question of the naval rivalry with England—a clever argument, in view of the emperor's attitude on this question.[2]

William, although he complained of "the fearful stupidity of Aehrenthal" and foresaw "a great triumph for Edward VII over us", evidently was brought round by the foreign office official attendant upon him. For, although he complained to the Austro-Hungarian ambassador, Count Szögyény, who brought the autograph letter of Francis Joseph, that he had learned of the annexation "first from the newspapers" and that Fallières had been informed before himself, he accepted the ambassador's statement that Aehrenthal had informed Schoen at Berchtesgaden on 5 September (which was not true).

He assured the ambassador that he "fully recognized the necessity" of the Austrian action. Likewise he was persuaded to reject "the English insinuations" that the proclamation of Bulgarian independence had been arranged at Budapest between Aehrenthal and Ferdinand. Finally, he promised that if a con-

[1] Comment on Bülow's letter; G 8939.
[2] Bülow to Jenisch, telegram, 7 October; G 8992.

ference were proposed, he would accept only on condition that "it was laid down à priori that the annexation of Bosnia and Herzegovina, an accomplished fact, should in no wise be brought up for discussion", and that the opportunity should be utilized "to solve the question of the Dardanelles in accordance with Russian wishes".[1]

Szögyény was therefore able to inform Aehrenthal, after a conference with Schoen, that although Germany found herself in a difficult situation, since she, "as is well known, now as before has to take account of very important material interests in Turkey", nevertheless, "this would not prevent the German government, having regard for the valued relationship of ally, from emphatically supporting the action of Austria-Hungary", and that Marschall would be instructed to speak in that sense at Constantinople.[2] And a few days later, William II, in his reply to the letter of Francis Joseph, said that the latter "can count on my unchangeable personal friendship and respect as well as on the close friendship of alliance which binds our two empires together".[3] Germany thus took a position from which it would be difficult to recede.

The attitude of Italy was less clear-cut. Tittoni, when informed by Aehrenthal and Izvolsky of what was impending, asked the Austro-Hungarian minister "de suspendre l'action",[4] and requested German representations in Vienna to the effect that "no change in the *status quo* should be made by Austria without a previous understanding with Germany, Italy, and Russia".[5] But as Aehrenthal refused to suspend his action, Tittoni sought to save his position by promising not to oppose the annexation, provided the Austro-Italian declaration of disinterestedness concerning Albania[6] were extended to Montenegro, and the privi-

---

[1] Szögyény to Aehrenthal, telegrams, 8 October; A 182, 183: Jenisch to foreign office, telegram from Rominten, 7 October; G 8994.

[2] Szögyény to Aehrenthal, telegram, 9 October; A 205. Marschall was alarmed by the prospect that Russia would raise the question of the Straits (Marschall to foreign office, telegrams, 9 and 10 October; G 8999, 9001, 9002).

[3] William II to Francis Joseph, 14 October; G 9006, A 273.

[4] Tschirschky to foreign office, telegram, 2 October; G 8941.

[5] Memorandum of Stemrich, 5 October; G 8943.

[6] 29 December 1900, 9 February 1901; Pribram, *Secret treaties of Austria-Hungary*, I, 196–8.

leges accorded to Austria-Hungary by Article 29 of the Treaty of
Berlin in respect of Montenegro were renounced.[1] Aehrenthal
agreed at once and adopted with alacrity Tittoni's plan for an
Austro-Russian-Italian *entente*,[2] so that harmony seemed restored
between Rome and Vienna.

Unfortunately, Italian public opinion was greatly excited by
the announcement of the annexation, and the foreign minister
found his political position shaken. If he admitted that he had
known in advance of the annexation,[3] he would be held privy to
the plot; if he had not known of it, then he could be charged
with incompetence![4] To escape from his dilemma, he eagerly
espoused the suggestion of a conference, declaring it to be "the
only solution",[5] and refused publicly to sanction the action of
Austria-Hungary.[6] But his subsequent conduct leaves little
doubt that he was nonplussed by the situation and had no positive
policy.

In Russia the news of the annexation aroused great indigna-
tion, for nothing was known of Izvolsky's negotiations with
Aehrenthal, and the former's political head was demanded.[7]
But Aehrenthal was thought to be bluffing.[8]

Curiously enough, although the Russian government attempted
to open up the question of the Straits with the Porte,[9] the press
generally took the view that Russia should ask for no compensation for herself and be content with supporting and safeguarding

[1] Tittoni to Aehrenthal, private, 4 October; A 132.
[2] Aehrenthal to Lützow and Berchtold, telegrams, 6 October; A 157, 159:
Tschirschky to foreign office, telegram, 6 October; G 8944.
[3] He twice denied to Grey that he had consented in advance to the
annexation (Grey to Egerton, 5, 7 October; B 307, 331). This was true
enough.
[4] Lützow to Aehrenthal, telegram, 10 October; A 230.
[5] Egerton to Grey, telegram, 8 October; B 336.
[6] He admitted privately to Count Lützow, the Austrian ambassador, that
he was "almost content" with the annexation and that he was not sympathetic
to a conference (Lützow to Aehrenthal, telegram, 7 October; A 179). Tittoni's
statements were so contradictory throughout the crisis that it is frequently
difficult to determine what were his real views. Often he was obviously trying
to carry water on both shoulders.
[7] Miquel to Bülow, 10 October; G 9004.
[8] Hintze to William II, 9 October; G 9005.
[9] Marschall to foreign office, telegrams, 8, 9 October; G 8999, 9001:
Lowther to Grey, telegram, 8 October; B 338.

Slavonic interests.[1] On the official side, Charykov was hard put to explain Izvolsky's conduct to Sir Arthur Nicolson, the British ambassador; perhaps it was only the latter's anxiety to preserve the Anglo-Russian *entente* which caused him to be satisfied with the Russian promise "in all circumstances...to work hand in hand with His Majesty's government".[2] In any case, Izvolsky's task was made more difficult by the attitude of Russian public opinion.

The Turkish government received the Austro-Hungarian note with lively protests, the grand vizier, Kiamil Pasha, declaring that it could not recognize the annexation,[3] and the foreign minister, Tewfik Pasha, reminding the Austro-Hungarian ambassador, Marquis Pallavicini, that according to the Austrian declaration of 1878 the occupation was to be considered provisional.[4] But the latter, who throughout the crisis repeatedly watered down the strong language of the grand vizier, let it be understood that the formal protest handed in at Vienna[5] was made out of regard for public opinion and that "in reality the Porte would not follow up the matter".[6] So Pallavicini cheerfully reported that "the incident of the annexation of Bosnia...can be regarded as settled so far as Turkey is concerned".[7] He was due for a rude awakening!

The Porte did not communicate its protest against the annexation to the other Powers. But it promptly despatched a note protesting against the proclamation of Bulgarian independence as

[1] Nicolson to Grey, telegram, 13 October; B 366. In a later despatch Nicolson wrote: "M. Izvolsky...had assumed that, and had perhaps some historical justification for assuming, that if he could procure untrammelled egress for her ships of war through the Straits he would have accomplished an act that would have been universally applauded. But he had not foreseen, and, indeed, it is difficult that he should have foreseen, that the Russian public viewed the Dardanelles with comparative indifference" (Nicolson to Grey, 8 February 1909; B 270).

[2] Nicolson to Grey, telegram, 5 October, and despatch, 6 October; B 303, 322.

[3] Pallavicini to Aehrenthal, telegram, 6 October; A 149. Pallavicini got the impression that "the annexation would have caused no difficulties if it had not come in connection with the Bulgarian declaration of independence" —which is a commentary on Aehrenthal's foresight.

[4] Pallavicini to Aehrenthal, 9 October; A 211: Lowther to Grey, telegram, 8 October; B 339.

[5] A 208, Beilage.

[6] Pallavicini to Aehrenthal, telegram, 9 October; A 209.

[7] Pallavicini to Aehrenthal, telegram, 9 October; A 210.

an "illegal and arbitrary act", and proposing that a conference should meet "to discuss the conditions necessary for the re-establishment of the legal order in Bulgaria and Eastern Rumelia and the safeguarding of the various interests assured to Turkey by international treaties".[1] Thus the Turkish position was not unlike the Russian, although its programme for a conference was much more limited than that envisaged by Izvolsky. On the other hand, the Porte was immediately suspicious of the Russian plan to make the conference depend on the condition that "the riverain states of the Black Sea should have exclusive freedom of passage of the Dardanelles",[2] and let it be known that it relied upon Britain to oppose the plan.[3]

As it was known that Britain thought Turkey entitled to compensations for the alterations of the Treaty of Berlin, Turkey's interest in playing up to England was so obvious that the German ambassador suspected secret Anglo-Turkish negotiations for a treaty which he feared would seriously affect the Bagdad railway.[4] There is no evidence of any such negotiations, but this Anglo-Turkish solidarity was to prove an all-important factor in the development of the crisis.

The greatest excitement in any country was produced in Serbia. Huge crowds paraded the streets of Belgrade crying "Down with Austria!" and the more irresponsible spirits clamoured for war. The government, with a view to preventing possible excesses, ordered the mobilization of the first reserve—120,000 men[5]—a step which called forth an immediate warning from Austria-Hungary,[6] and summoned the skupshtina, where

---

[1] A 173; G 8973. Cf. Grey to Nicolson, telegram, 7 October; B 329.

[2] Lowther to Grey, telegram, 8 October; B 338.

[3] Marschall to foreign office, telegram, 8 October; G 8999.

[4] Marschall to foreign office, telegram, 10 October; G 9017.

[5] Franz to Aehrenthal, telegram, 6 October; A 147: Whitehead to Grey, telegram, 6 October; B 315. The foreign minister told the Italian chargé that "the government were in a most serious dilemma, as they found themselves between war or revolution".

[6] Aehrenthal to Franz, telegram, 7 October; A 164. The Powers were asked to advise Serbia in her own interests to show moderation and maintain a correct attitude (circular telegram of 7 October; A 167). The Serbian government replied that the step signified no aggressive intentions and was dictated by the necessity of preserving order (Franz to Aehrenthal, telegram, 8 October; A 181). The Powers were informed that only 20,000 reservists

patriotic orators might let off their steam. But since it could hardly remain passive in face of public opinion, it despatched a protest to the Powers in which, "invoking on the one hand the incontestable rights of the Serbian people...and on the other the clear and precise terms of Article 25 of the Treaty of Berlin", it demanded either "the full restoration of the situation created in Bosnia and Herzegovina by the Treaty of Berlin" or "a corresponding compensation".[1] And by way of emphasizing its position, it secured a war credit of 16,000,000 dinars from the skupshtina, which also passed unanimously a resolution of protest against the annexation. In the light of subsequent history, however, the most important incident of these days was the establishment of the society called *Narodna Odbrana* ["National Defence"], "which should protect and promote our interests in the annexed provinces"; for it was to the alleged activities of this organization that the Austro-Hungarian government ascribed the revolutionary ferment in Bosnia-Herzegovina which was made the basis for the ultimatum of 23 July 1914.[2]

The Austro-Hungarian government refused to receive the note of protest, for Serbia was not a signatory of the Treaty of Berlin,[3] and the German foreign minister declared that he could not see "what special interests and rights of Serbia had been injured by the annexation".[4]

Sir Edward Grey was willing to "take note of [the Serbian] point of view" about the annexation,[5] but advised moderation;[6]

had been called up and that the strength of the army would be only from 35,000 to 40,000 men (communication to British foreign office, 10 October; B 353).

[1] Circular of 7 October; G 9091. The Serbian chargé in London intimated as desirable compensation the concession of a railway to the Adriatic and a rectification of the Serbian frontier on the side of Bosnia (Grey to Whitehead, 10 October; B 356: Gruyich to Milovanovich, telegrams, 10, 12 October; M. Boghitschewitsch, *Die auswärtige Politik Serbiens, 1903–1914* [Berlin, 1928], vol. I, Nos. 9, 12. This collection will be hereafter cited as "S," and the documents by number).

[2] B. E. Schmitt, *The coming of the war, 1914* (New York, 1930), I, 179 ff.

[3] Müller to Aehrenthal, telegram, 8 October; A 180: Tschirschky to foreign office, telegram, 10 October; G 9096.

[4] Memorandum of Schoen, 8 October; G 9091.

[5] Grey to Whitehead, 5 October; B 308.

[6] Grey to Whitehead, telegram, 8 October; B 337. France gave similar advice (Bertie to Grey, telegram, 9 October; B 341). The French ambassador in Vienna informed the Ballplatz of this, 10 October (A 220).

and he pointed out the difficulty of securing territorial compensation from Austria-Hungary.[1]

But of all the Powers, Russia gave the least encouragement. Izvolsky told the Serbian minister in Paris, Vesnich, that Russia could not go to war on account of Bosnia and argued that the evacuation of the Sandjak signified a positive gain for Serbia, "for it opens up the prospect of a common frontier between Serbia and Montenegro";[2] while to the chargé in London he said that he could not understand why the Serbian statesmen allowed themselves to be carried away by the excitement of the masses: "it should have been quite clear to us that Bosnia and Herzegovina were lost to us long ago" and war would be "suicide" for Serbia.[3] Although he did promise in a vague, general way to try to secure territorial compensation, he declared that Serbia would fare best if she stopped her military preparations and restrained the warlike feelings of the people. For practical purposes, Serbia seemed left to face Austria-Hungary alone.

[1] Grey to Whitehead, 10 October; B 356.
[2] Vesnich to Milovanovich, 5 October; S 6.
[3] Gruyich to Milovanovich, 13 October; S 13.

# CHAPTER V

## *The Proposal for a European Conference*

IZVOLSKY, the chief proponent of a conference, arrived in London on 9 October, and saw Sir Edward Grey on the following day. It had undoubtedly been his original plan that at the conference Russia should be granted the opening of the Straits as compensation for the Austrian annexation of Bosnia,[1] and he was entitled to expect favourable consideration from the British government. His principal motive for making concessions in Asia during the negotiation of the Anglo-Russian agreement had been to secure British goodwill in the question of the Straits, and although the matter was not mentioned in the convention of 31 August 1907 the Russian government had let its wishes be known; and the British government had given assurances not only that "the question was one which we [Great Britain] were prepared to discuss", but that

if the negotiations now in progress between the two governments with regard to Asiatic questions had a satisfactory result, the effect upon British public opinion would be such as to facilitate a discussion of the Straits question if it came up later on.

It is true that the informal discussions had revealed differences of opinion between the two governments, the British being suspicious of the Russian desire to obtain a special or privileged posi-

---

[1] In the autumn of 1918 Izvolsky stated to Auguste Gauvain, the foreign editor of the *Journal des Débats*: "Ce que je voulais proposer à la conférence, c'était la revision complète des stipulations surannées touchant aux Détroits qui dataient de la Convention de 1841, et qui avaient été successivement confirmées à Paris en 1856, à Londres en 1871 et à Berlin en 1878. Dans ma pensée, ces stipulations devaient être remplacées par une convention speciale...dans laquelle le droit de passage par les Détroits des navires de commerce de toutes les nations serait defini d'une manière beaucoup nette et placée sous la sauvegarde collective des puissances. D'autre part, la Russie et les autres pays riverains devaient recevoir le droit de faire passer leur navires de guerre de la mer Noire dans la Mediterranée et vice-versa" (Hélène Iswolsky, "Les papiers d'Alexandre Iswolsky: correspondance inédite (1906)", *Revue de France*, XIV [1934], 431).

tion in the Black Sea; but inasmuch as Grey had expressly said that he "did not wish to discuss the particular conditions under which the existing arrangements with regard to the Straits might be altered", Izvolsky declared himself satisfied that an "identity of views" had been established "dans les grandes lignes" and stated that he would expect "a favourable reception" when he presented "a definite proposal".[1]

There the matter had rested. The Russian minister did not inform the British government of his negotiations with Austria-Hungary, either before or after the meeting with Aehrenthal at Buchlau, and it was only when he reached Paris that Izvolsky revealed to Sir Francis Bertie, the British ambassador, that Russia would raise the question of the Straits.[2] He seems to have anticipated little or no opposition at least to a discussion of the question, for, in an interview given to a Paris newspaper, he remarked, *à propos* of the general situation, that he was going to England and "he did not doubt that, seeing the cordial relations now existing between the two countries, he would be able to arrive at an agreement as to the view to be taken of the situation".[3]

The British government was indeed committed to discuss the question of the Straits, but it thought the moment "very inopportune":

> Turkey was hurt and sore at the slight put upon her by Austria and Bulgaria. It was hard enough that she should suffer this at the outset of what we hoped was a new and better era at Constantinople. We could not agree to add to her hardships by forcing upon her at once the embarrassing question of the Straits. If, later on, the consent of Turkey was obtained, this must be by satisfactory voluntary agreement and not by pressure or squeeze.[4]

Consequently, at the first hint that the question might be raised, a warning was issued that "the question of the passage of the

[1] Memorandum of Grey on conversation with Benckendorff, Russian ambassador in London, 15 March 1907; memoranda of Izvolsky, 14 April and 10 July 1907; Grey to Nicolson, 19 March 1907; memorandum of Grey, given to Benckendorff, 27 April 1907; B, vol. IV, Nos. 257, 265, 275, 258, 268.

[2] Bertie to Grey, 4 October 1908; B 292, 293.

[3] Bertie to Grey, 7 October; B 332.

[4] Viscount Grey of Fallodon, *Twenty-five years, 1892–1916* (London and New York, 1925), I, 172.

Straits is one which His Majesty's government must have time to consider very carefully and for which public opinion in England has hardly had time yet to prepare" and that it was not yet known "what objections Turkey may raise to it".[1] The Turkish objections were, however, soon made known. According to the Turkish foreign minister, "Russia was prepared to go to a conference on condition that the riverain Black Sea states should have exclusive freedom of passage of Dardanelles", in return for which Russia would abandon her war indemnity (under the Treaty of Berlin) and her post offices in Turkey. The minister was reported "suspicious of these suggestions and anxious that the conference should be limited to the two questions now raised by Austria and Bulgaria".[2] In the foreign office it was thought "not likely that Russia would agree to such a limitation".

On the other hand if the scope of the conference is widened and the question of the Straits is there discussed and modifications introduced in favour of Russia there will almost certainly be an outcry in this country unless something really substantial is done for Turkey which will at the same time strengthen the position of the Young Turk party and give a material proof that England, France and Russia intend to stand by and support that party.[3]

The visit of the Russian foreign minister cannot have been looked forward to with much enthusiasm.

How far Izvolsky was made aware of the British attitude cannot, in the absence of Russian documents, be determined. But since both the prime minister and the foreign secretary had given public assurance that "the interests and status of Turkey will receive full consideration and be adequately safeguarded",[4] the Russian minister knew what to expect. So when he saw Grey on 10 October, Izvolsky stated, apparently without any preliminary observations, that "Russia would not raise the question of the Straits at the conference". All that he asked for, he said, was an assurance that "if Russia could satisfy Turkey that an arrangement about the Straits was safe for Turkish interests,

---

[1] Grey to Bertie, telegram, 6 October; B 314.
[2] Lowther to Grey, telegram, 8 October; B 338.
[3] Minute of Hardinge on B 338.
[4] Speeches of Asquith at Leven and Grey at Wooler on 7 October.

England should not oppose it". His proposal to Turkey would be that ships of war of the riverain Powers on the Black Sea should have a right of way through the Straits.

They would not be allowed to remain in the Straits. There might be regulations that not more than three vessels should go through at a time, and that no other vessels should go through for 24 hours after the first. Such regulations would, of course, only apply in times when Turkey was at peace. In time of war, Turkey would be able to do as she pleased. In other words, the closing of the Straits would be maintained, subject to a limited servitude of this kind in favour of Russia and the riverain states.

Izvolsky declared that "the Russian desire now was to be friendly with Turkey" and argued that "if Russia did not make the proposal now, it might be blocked by Germany or Austria at some future time". Grey replied that the proposal was not the same as that put forward when the Anglo-Russian negotiations of the previous year were in progress, and he would not do more than promise to consult his colleagues. For the rest, Izvolsky offered an explanation of what had passed between himself and Aehrenthal, denying that "he had given his consent in advance to what Austria had done about Bosnia". The breaches of treaty must be dealt with by a conference, "but it would not be enough simply to ratify what had already been done", for "that would not secure enough compensation either for Turkey or the other Balkan states". Izvolsky did not, however, reply to Grey's suggestion that "some immediate proof of confidence in the new régime in Turkey and good will to it should be shown by offering a guaranteed loan if Turkey desired it".[1]

After consulting the cabinet, the British foreign secretary informed the Russian minister that the programme for the conference—Izvolsky submitted nine points[2]—would be acceptable if Germany agreed to it, but that the Russian proposals on the

[1] Grey to Nicolson, 14 October; B 379. Grey wrote of their conversation: "Directly I began to speak to him his eyes became very dull and defensive" (Grey to Nicolson, private, 26 October; B 409, b). Izvolsky informed Metternich and Mensdorff of his interview. He asked for German mediation in Vienna, and, though full of recriminations for Aehrenthal, said that he desired an agreement (Metternich to foreign office, telegram, 10 October; G 9023: Mensdorff to Aehrenthal, telegrams, 10, 12 October; A 227, 257).

[2] Memorandum of Izvolsky, 12 October; B 363.

Straits were "one-sided" and that there would be "great difficulties in any arrangement which was not reciprocal".[1]

Subsequently a memorandum was given to Izvolsky stating that "His Majesty's government agree that the opening of the Straits is fair and reasonable, and in principle they will not oppose it", provided "the Straits should be open on terms of perfect equality to all" and the consent of Turkey were obtained.[2] Izvolsky agreed to accept this, "although it did not give all that he had hoped for",[3] and Grey tried to make it more palatable by an assurance that his motive "has not been a desire to keep the Straits closed":

On the contrary, I positively desire to see an arrangement made which will open the Straits on terms which would be acceptable to Russia and the riverain states of the Black Sea, while not placing Turkey or outside Powers at an unfair disadvantage. Some such arrangement seems to me essential to the permanent establishment of goodwill between Russia and ourselves....And I believe that feeling both at Constantinople and in England will be so favourably affected by a disinterested co-operation between Russia and England to pull Turkey through the present crisis, that this will do more than anything else to prepare the way for dealing with the question of the Straits later on, a state of feeling which I shall welcome.[4]

[1] Grey to Nicolson, 12 October; B 364. Izvolsky was so dissatisfied by this statement that he saw Grey again on the same day and proposed a compromise by which in time of war, when Turkey was neutral, equal facilities should be given all belligerents for passage through the Straits. Grey promised to submit this to the cabinet, but declared the moment "exceedingly inopportune" and emphasized "the advantage of settling the present crisis in the Near East satisfactorily without seeking advantages for Russia or England" (Grey to Nicolson, 13 October; B 371). Grey supported this proposal in the cabinet (Hardinge to Nicolson, private, 13 October; B 372), but only four members—Asquith, Grey, Morley and McKenna—were for acceptance. On the other hand, King Edward was more disposed to humour Izvolsky. He was, he wrote to the prime minister on 13 October, "afraid that unless some hope is given to Russia that England and the Powers might grant the national aspirations of Russia on this question, Monsieur Izvolsky will return to his country a discredited man, and will have to resign...after the Russian convention with England of a year ago, we are bound, if we wish to retain her friendship, to give way on this important point" (Lee, *King Edward VII*, II, 639–40).

[2] Memorandum by Grey, 14 October; B 377.

[3] Grey to Nicolson, 19 October; B 394.

[4] Grey to Izvolsky, private, 15 October; B 387. Nicolson was instructed to point out at St Petersburg that "in order that Russia should gain Turkey's confidence", she should "co-operate in getting Turkey out of present

From this time on nothing more was heard of the question of the Straits.[1] Grey certainly played his cards with skill. He both evaded a Russian proposal which, in the form presented, was unsatisfactory, and strengthened his own position with Turkey; at the same time he convinced Izvolsky of his goodwill and kept the Anglo-Russian *entente* in being. As a matter of fact, the British minister had the Russian at his mercy, for the price of Izvolsky's plan for the Straits was the acceptance of the annexation of Bosnia, which he was compelled to oppose because of the orders from St Petersburg.[2] The bitter pill was sugared by an ample dose of attention and flattery from the British official world and press, and the Russian minister seems to have made *bonne mine à mauvais jeu*. With the troublesome question of the Straits out of the way, he and his British colleague could devote their whole attention to the question of Bosnia.

Before leaving London Izvolsky agreed with Grey on a programme of nine points which might be considered by the conference:

(1) Bulgaria; (2) Bosnia and Herzegovina; (3) Sandjak of Novi-Bazar; (4) Article 23 of the Treaty of Berlin; (5) Article 61, relating to Armenia; (6) Article 29, which limited the sovereign rights of Montenegro; (7) "Avantages à procurer à la Serbie et au Monténégro"; (8) the Balkan states and the Danube; (9) the capitulations and foreign post offices in Turkey.[3]

The Russian minister also assured the German and Austrian ambassadors in London of his desire for a satisfactory settlement.[4]

difficulties before pressing her about the Straits", and that "it would surely be desirable for Russian government to consult with [Izvolsky] at leisure before deciding to take any steps" (Grey to Nicolson, telegram, 16 October; B 389).

[1] The French government declined to express any opinion on the matter, but did not suppose that "His Majesty's government would adopt, or Turkey accept, the proposals as they stood" (Bertie to Grey, telegram, 13 October; B 368).

[2] See above, p. 36. It may be assumed that Izvolsky did not inform Grey on this point!

[3] B 390. The question of Crete, which had declared for union with Greece, was to be considered by the four Protecting Powers—Great Britain, France, Italy and Russia—in direct negotiations with Turkey and then be referred by them to the conference.

[4] Metternich to foreign office, telegram, 12 October; G 9031: Mensdorff to Aehrenthal, telegram, 15 October; A 288.

But the two ministers had not reckoned sufficiently with the resolution and resourcefulness of Aehrenthal. For, encouraged by William II's hint that the conference must exclude any discussion of Bosnia,[1] he informed Izvolsky that while he did not oppose a conference in principle, yet the condition on which Austria-Hungary would participate was that Turkey should previously recognize the annexation and that the conference should merely take account of this agreement without debate,[2] and when renewed assurances had been received that Germany was opposed to any discussion of the annexation,[3] Aehrenthal reaffirmed his position, this time to both Grey and Izvolsky.[4] But their failure to communicate the programme officially to Austria-Hungary,[5] although Aehrenthal had stated that his acceptance of a conference depended upon "a programme carefully formulated in advance",[6] enabled him to put off a formal

[1] Aehrenthal to Szögyény, telegram, 11 October; A 222.
[2] Aehrenthal to Mensdorff, telegram, 11 October; A 242.
[3] Szögyény to Aehrenthal, telegram, 13 October; A 266. Cf. Bülow to Tschirschky, 23 October; G 9033. The German Emperor was originally not indisposed to a conference (note on G 9007), and even suggested that it meet in Berlin (Jenisch to foreign office, telegram from Rominten, 7 October; G 9012). But Bülow objected to Berlin and was opposed to any other capital; moreover, he feared that decisions might be reached at the expense of Turkey and the Bagdad Railway (Bülow to foreign office, telegrams, 7, 9 October; G 9011, 9016). Inquiries of the French and Italian ambassadors were put off with evasive answers (Schoen to Bülow, 10 October; G 9022) until Bülow returned from Nordeney and made a formal statement to Szögyény. Metternich pleaded in vain with his government to act as mediator between Austria and Russia (Metternich to foreign office, telegrams, 11 October; G 9024, 9027: Mensdorff to Aehrenthal, telegram, 11 October; A 243).
[4] Aehrenthal to Mensdorff, telegram, 14 October; A 276.
[5] A copy was given to Mensdorff for his personal information. Hardinge explained that, since the programme placed Bosnia on the agenda and Aehrenthal had declared his opposition to a conference if Bosnia were to be discussed, Grey had thought it would be an "impertinence" to communicate the programme (Mensdorff to Aehrenthal, telegram, 19 October; A 336). Izvolsky asserted that he had understood that the French government would transmit the programme in the name of the Triple Entente (Szögyény to Aehrenthal, telegram, 23 October; A 371). But Pichon subsequently denied that there had been any such understanding (Khevenhüller to Aehrenthal, 31 October; A 470). Since the German, Italian and Turkish ambassadors in London were promptly given copies of the programme (Metternich to foreign office, telegram, 15 October; G 9045), it looks as if an attempt was being made to isolate Austria-Hungary. In fact, Paul Cambon, the French ambassador in London, hinted as much (Mensdorff to Aehrenthal, telegram, 13 October; A 269). [6] Aehrenthal to Khevenhüller, telegram, 9 October; A 214.

answer until he had had time, as he hoped, to secure Turkish recognition of the annexation. And he promptly seized upon point 7 of the programme as a line of attack. Its wording, "Avantages à procurer à la Serbie et au Monténégro", was undoubtedly vague.[1] But since Izvolsky had emphasized in London the necessity of territorial compensation to Serbia and Montenegro, and Grey had said that such compensation at the expense[2] of Turkey was out of the question,[3] Aehrenthal declared point 7 unacceptable "because it permits the interpretation of territorial compensations at our expense" and by encouraging the aspirations of Serbia and Montenegro would "sharpen the situation".[4] He was willing to consider compensations other than territorial, such as recognition of Serbia's position as a Danube state[5] and a connection through Bosnia to the Adriatic (i.e. a railway line),[6] but as Izvolsky continued to hold out for a territorial compensation,[7] a deadlock was produced which left both the conference and its programme in the air.

Meanwhile the German government had been manœuvring with a view to extracting profit for itself from the situation. Fearing that the British championship of Turkish interests would still further weaken Germany's already compromised

[1] Izvolsky's first version read: "Rectifications de frontière en faveur de la Serbie et du Monténégro sur la partie du territoire Bosno-Herzegovinien qui avoisine le Sandjak de Novi-Bazar" (B 363). Pichon protested and secured Grey's approval of the vaguer wording (Khevenhüller to Aehrenthal, telegram, 15 October; A 292); Grey himself insisted on the omission of "territoriaux" before "avantages" (B 390, note 2). Ultimately "consentir" was substituted for "procurer" (Khevenhüller to Aehrenthal, 17 October; A 312). The original version was published in the *Temps* of 16 October, supposedly with the connivance of Izvolsky, though he denied the accusation (Radolin to foreign office, telegram, 17 October; G 9050).
[2] Mensdorff to Aehrenthal, telegram, 15 October; A 290.
[3] Flotow (Berlin) to Aehrenthal, 16 October, received 18 October; A 295. For Grey's statement to Metternich, see Grey to Lascelles, 13 October; B 373, and Metternich to foreign office, telegram, 15 October; G 9045.
[4] Aehrenthal to London, Paris, Rome, and St Petersburg, telegrams, 19 October; A 335. Grey replied that it was the action of Austria and Bulgaria which had excited the aspirations (Mensdorff to Aehrenthal, telegram, 20 October; A 344). Izvolsky urged "a small territorial indemnification" as a "move of spontaneous generosity" (Khevenhüller to Aehrenthal, telegram, 20 October; memorandum of 20 October; A 345, 346).
[5] Aehrenthal to Szögyény and Berchtold, telegrams, 21 October; A 350.
[6] Aehrenthal to Berchtold, 24 October; A 385.
[7] Berchtold to Aehrenthal, telegram, 30 October; A 462.

position at Constantinople, it hinted to London that British proposals to secure compensation and a financial indemnity for Turkey would receive its approval and support[1] and that Germany was at one with England "in the wish to maintain the Turkish Empire intact".[2] Grey replied, logically, that Austria-Hungary must compensate Turkey; only then could he advise the Porte to admit that discussion of the annexation might be excluded from the conference.[3] But since Bülow insisted that "it was impossible for Germany to abandon her ally, and if Austria-Hungary declined to take part in conference, Germany would decline also",[4] an Anglo-German understanding was evidently out of the question.

In the course of a long harangue addressed to Count Hoyos, a member of the Austro-Hungarian embassy in Berlin, the German Emperor accused England of aiming to make the conference "a second Algeciras", and declared himself personally opposed to the plan in the strongest terms.[5] He promised that no satisfaction would be granted to Izvolsky, who was hoping by means of the conference to "save his honour" from a great diplomatic defeat.

Before proceeding to Berlin from London, Izvolsky returned to Paris, where he appealed to the German ambassador for assistance. Serbia, he argued, was entitled to compensation; Austria-Hungary had secured Bosnia-Herzegovina, Turkey Novi-Bazar, Bulgaria her independence, and Montenegro the

[1] Schoen to Metternich, telegram, 9 October; G 9013.
[2] Bülow to Metternich, telegram, 13 October; G 9028. The ambassador was asked whether he thought the moment favourable "to ask a concession from England on the Bagdad Railway, something as a *quid pro quo* [*Gegenleistung*] for support on our part of the conference idea". In view of the German promises to Austria, Bülow's suggestion was disloyal to either Aehrenthal or Grey. Metternich promptly discouraged any such overture (Metternich to foreign office, telegram, 13 October; G 9037). It is significant that Bülow instructed Marschall to insinuate to the Turks that "if England does not give up Cyprus, retains Egypt, further extends her position in the Persian Gulf, and does not at once energetically oppose the plans of Russia at the Dardanelles, it ought to be hard for Turkey to believe in the real friendship of England" (Bülow to Marschall, telegram, "ganz geheim", 13 October; G 9029).
[3] Metternich to foreign office, telegram, 14 October; G 9039: Grey to Lascelles, 14 October; B 380.
[4] Lascelles to Grey, telegram, 14 October; B 376.
[5] Memorandum of Hoyos, 16 October; A 294.

lifting of Article 29. "There would be incalculable consequences", he warned Prince Radolin, "if Germany, out of love for Austria, abstained from the conference." "What interest", he asked, "did Germany have in humiliating Russia?"[1] He was greatly depressed, feeling that he could not return to Russia "with empty hands";[2] but he seems to have expected to accomplish something by his interviews with the German statesmen.

These overtures were all in vain. Aehrenthal had provided Bülow with his version of the conversations at Buchlau, adding that he could not run the risk of a Turkish protest at the conference.[3] In Berlin elaborate preparations were made for the conversations with Izvolsky. Two memoranda were drafted, one setting forth the general lines of German policy, the other stating the reaction to the nine points of the Grey-Izvolsky programme. There was, it was stated, no objection in principle to a conference, provided complete agreement were reached beforehand on all questions; "firm and honourable support of Austria-Hungary, our valued ally, is for us a command of loyalty as well as of wisdom"; consequently Bosnia and the Sandjak must be excluded from the discussions; point 7 was rejected; no necessity was recognized to support Turkey, "since England has now taken Turkey under her special protection and is more Turkish than the Turks"; lastly, Germany had "no primary interest in the Straits". The emperor, to whom the memoranda were communicated, was asked not to talk politics with Izvolsky.[4] In short, Bülow, who viewed the Anglo-Russian *entente* with increasing dislike, was delighted to show Izvolsky what price Russia had to pay for abandoning the traditional close relationship with Germany, and he determined to be merciless.

The Russian foreign minister spent three days in Berlin (24–26 October), during which he was entertained at luncheon by the emperor, talked with Schoen and Bülow, and made a last desperate appeal to Aehrenthal through Szögyény, the Austro-

---

[1] Radolin to foreign office, telegram, 17 October; G 9050.
[2] Radolin to foreign office, telegram, 18 October; G 9058.
[3] Aehrenthal to Bülow, private, 15 October; A 281, G 9055. Aehrenthal transmitted copies of Izvolsky's memorandum of 2 July and his own reply of 27 August.
[4] Bülow to William II, 22 October; G 9061.

Hungarian ambassador.[1] Schoen listened to his complaints against Aehrenthal, but refused to be impressed by his warning that failure to satisfy Russian opinion would produce "a deep distrust between Austria-Hungary and Russia which might, in certain circumstances, lead to the most serious complication". Germany, said Schoen, could not undertake the rôle of mediator in Vienna and would only inform Aehrenthal of Izvolsky's wishes.[2] Bülow was equally firm,[3] and he informed Aehrenthal that the German attitude had been that of "complete refusal" of the Russian wishes,[4] even to the point of formulating an *aide-mémoire* of those points of the Grey-Izvolsky programme which the German government found acceptable.[5] The only satisfaction accorded to Izvolsky was the issue of a colourless *communiqué* which affirmed that the German government would consent "only to proposals which are acceptable to Austria-Hungary".[6] Szögyény was able to report to his government that "there was no question of a change in German policy" and Germany intended to "support our policy strongly in the future also".[7] All this was confirmed by Bülow himself, with the added promise that whatever decisions might be taken by Aehrenthal in respect of Serbia would be accepted "as those required by circumstances".[8]

[1] Szögyény to Aehrenthal, telegrams, 23, 24 October; A 371, 382. According to Szögyény, Izvolsky seemed to think that Aehrenthal was opposed in principle to a conference, which Szögyény denied. Aehrenthal authorized the ambassador to inform Izvolsky that this was not the case, but that he would not admit a discussion of Bosnia or recognize Serbia's claim to compensation (Aehrenthal to Szögyény, telegram, 25 October; A 390).

[2] Memorandum of Schoen, 24 October; G 9064.

[3] Memorandum of Bülow, 24 October; G 9065: Bernhard Fürst von Bülow, *Denkwürdigkeiten* (Berlin, 1930), II, 394–7.

[4] Bülow to Tschirschky, telegram, 25 October; G 9066. Cf. Szögyény to Aehrenthal, telegram, 25 October; A 391.

[5] Szögyény to Aehrenthal, telegram, 25 October; A 393.

[6] Bülow to Tschirschky, telegram, 26 October; G 9068: Szögyény to Aehrenthal, telegram, 26 October; A 403.

[7] Szögyény to Aehrenthal, 28 October; A 436.

[8] Bülow to Aehrenthal, private, 30 October; G 9079, A 451. The results of Izvolsky's negotiations were communicated to the British chargé in Berlin, whose report concluded with the statement that "the German government are anxious to avoid exercising any pressure on Austria-Hungary, but will make every effort toward a just and practical solution" (De Salis to Grey, telegram, 27 October; B 410). In the British foreign office this was considered "very satisfactory on the whole". Grey understood it to mean, as he

Izvolsky was under no illusion; of all the impressions carried away from his visits to the European capitals, so he told the British ambassador in St Petersburg, "the impression of the intention of Germany to support Austria-Hungary in all circumstances and in all quarters has been the deepest".[1] This was rubbed in by Count Pourtalès, the German ambassador, who, acting under instructions from Bülow,[2] read the Russian minister a long lecture on Russia's ingratitude towards Germany and her folly in concluding the *entente* with England, which had upset the European balance:

In face of this situation there was now nothing left for Germany but to adhere all the more closely to her allies and champion their interests even more than was required by the letter of the treaties of alliance.[3]

The Russian foreign minister was indeed a beaten man.[4]

How thoroughly Izvolsky appreciated the strength of the Austro-German combination can be gauged from his handling of a subordinate dispute with Aehrenthal. On the day of the annexation, the Austro-Hungarian foreign minister had informed

---

explained to Count Benckendorff, the Russian ambassador, who thought it "very cold and unsatisfactory", that while Germany agreed to a conference only as a ratifying body, "if, however, Turkey could be satisfied [by Austria-Hungary], then there would be no difficulty in getting Austria and Germany to include the question of annexation in the programme" (Grey to Nicolson, 27 October; B 411).

[1] Nicolson to Grey, 31 October; B 421.

[2] Memorandum of Bülow, 27 October; G 9074.

[3] Pourtalès to Bülow, 1 November; G 9085.

[4] The situation of his Italian colleague was not much better. Tittoni supported the proposal for a conference, in order to save his political position (Lützow to Aehrenthal, telegram, 15 October, A 293); his remaining in office was, he declared, essential for the harmony of Austro-Italian relations, and he discreetly raised the question of an Italian university at Trent (Lützow to Aehrenthal, telegram, 13 October; A 271). He even hinted that he would like the conference to be held in Italy (Lützow to Aehrenthal, telegram, 21 October; A 360). But he agreed with Aehrenthal about point 7, bluntly asking Grey how he proposed to secure compensation for Serbia and Montenegro (Grey to Egerton, 19 October; B 395). Aehrenthal tried to compromise Izvolsky by sending to Tittoni copies of Izvolsky's memorandum of 2 July and his own reply of 27 August (Aehrenthal to Tittoni, private, 19 October; A 337). Bülow urged that neither France nor England would or could help Italy in the Mediterranean and that Italy would risk everything if she abandoned the Triple Alliance (Bülow to Monts, telegram, 26 October; G 9067). Tittoni's professed fear of an Anglo-Austrian conflict (Monts to foreign office, telegram, 27 October; G 9072) was not taken seriously in Berlin (Bülow to Monts, telegram, 28 October; G 9073).

the Russian government that at the approaching session of the Delegations, he proposed to say that his conversations with Izvolsky at Buchlau entitled him to assume that Russia would observe "a friendly attitude", but that he did not intend to mention their agreement about the Straits.[1] Both Charykov and Izvolsky protested, on the ground that the consent of the Powers must be obtained,[2] to which Aehrenthal replied with a threat to publish the Austro-Russian protocol of 1878[3] and to state publicly that Izvolsky had himself proposed the annexation of the Sandjak of Novi-Bazar by Austria-Hungary.[4] When the Delegations met, Aehrenthal confined himself to stating to the Austrian Delegation that "an exchange of views had taken place between ourselves, Russia and Italy with reference to the possible eventualities in the Balkans arising out of the annexation of Bosnia and had led to a satisfactory result". He did not communicate this to the press. At the same time he hinted that he would have to justify himself openly if Izvolsky spoke in the duma,[5] and since both Charykov and Izvolsky at once exhibited nervousness,[6] Aehrenthal used more pointed language:

A direct denial of the fact that between ourselves and Russia negotiations took place which preceded the annexation, will compel me, entirely against my will, to repeat the declarations which I made in the confidential sessions of the Delegations, and to repeat them with the addition that I am in a position to offer documentary proof of the declarations made by me.[7]

[1] Aehrenthal to Berchtold, telegram, 6 October; A 158.
[2] Berchtold to Aehrenthal, telegrams, 8 October; A 196, 198: Izvolsky to Urussov, telegram from Paris, 8 October; A 219, Beilage.
[3] See above, p. 3.
[4] Aehrenthal to Berchtold, telegram, 10 October; A 232.
[5] Aehrenthal to Berchtold, telegram, 16 October; A 303. Izvolsky had spoken to Mensdorff of the possibility that he would have to "explain himself" to the duma (Mensdorff to Aehrenthal, telegram, 15 October; A 288).
[6] Berchtold to Aehrenthal, telegram, 17 October, and despatch, 18 October; A 318, 327: Izvolsky to Sverbeyev, telegram, quoted in Aehrenthal's telegram to Szögyény and Berchtold, 21 October; A 349.
[7] Aehrenthal to Berchtold, 24 October; A 386. The documents he had in mind were the protocol of July 1878, the Three Emperors' League of 1881, and the Russian memorandum of July 1908 (Tschirschky to Bülow, 30 October; G 9081). Aehrenthal drily pointed out that since Charykov insisted on substituting the words "Russia will create no difficulties" about the annexation for "Russia will observe a friendly attitude", Russia had forfeited the prospect

If Izvolsky persisted in his intention, he was to be warned of the consequences, which would prejudice "a further friendly exchange of views between the two cabinets".[1]

These repeated warnings were effective, for Charykov assured Count Berchtold, the Austrian ambassador, that Izvolsky would be discreet and probably not refer to the conversations at Buchlau.[2] But this did not satisfy Aehrenthal, who was quick to seize his advantage and demanded a friendly attitude on the part of Izvolsky:

A public statement by the minister or his assistant which is not in accord with what was agreed upon by both sides at Buchlau in respect of the questions interesting both Russia and Austria-Hungary (Bosnia and the Dardanelles) will unavoidably compel me to justify my policy and my language, to publish the secret protocol of 1878 and the memoranda exchanged during the summer.[3]

And Berchtold was instructed to explain to "other leading political personages, especially M. Stolypin and M. Kokovtzov", what had happened at Buchlau. Izvolsky was now at his wits' end. Since he had never transmitted to Aehrenthal his version of their conversations, he had no means of counteracting the effect which the publication of his memorandum of the summer would have on the Russian public; he would be convicted, as was already being charged against him, of indifference, if not treachery, to the Slavonic cause in the Balkans. He therefore protested against the publication of the memorandum and suggested instead that the Convention of Budapest of 15 January 1877,[4] the secret protocol of 1878, and the treaties of 1881 and 1884 might be published in an Austrian newspaper.[5] This would enable him

of a "friendly attitude" on the part of Austria in the question of the Straits (Aehrenthal to Berchtold, 24 October; A 387).

[1] Aehrenthal to Berchtold, telegram, 28 October; A 444. Bülow advised Aehrenthal to publish the documents only if forced "by further Russian insinuations" to do so (Bülow to Tschirschky, 2 November; G 9083).

[2] Berchtold to Aehrenthal, telegram, 29 October; A 448.

[3] Aehrenthal to Berchtold, telegram, 30 October; A 461.

[4] Pribram, Secret treaties of Austria-Hungary, II, 190–203.

[5] Berchtold to Aehrenthal, telegrams, 3 and 6 November; A 494, 520. Apparently Izvolsky had never heard of these agreements until he went to Buchlau, where they were adduced by Aehrenthal as a reason why Russia should consent to the annexation of Bosnia. On his return to St Petersburg,

to argue that Prince Gorchakov and Alexander III, whose Slavic sentiments could not be doubted, had, long before his own time, consented to the annexation of Bosnia. Aehrenthal was willing enough to build this bridge for the Russian minister,[1] provided the Convention of 1877 was edited.[2] But then Izvolsky, in characteristic fashion, began to waver. He asked himself, he said, whether "publication would not cause more harm than good",[3] apparently because an article in the *Fortnightly review*[4] had presented an "incomplete and distorted" version.[5] But while he was debating whether to publish a rectification, a second article, in the *Neues Pester Journal* on 24 November, written supposedly by Baron Dóczy, private secretary of the elder Count Andrássy, revealed the secret Austro-Russian convention of 1878. Aehrenthal professed to reget this indiscretion,[6] but it served his purpose quite as well as an official disclosure. Perhaps it suited Izvolsky equally well, for the revelation was accurate.[7] At the same time, it was a hint to the Russian minister to be careful, and he desisted for a time from the strong language which he had been using about Aehrenthal.

Meanwhile Izvolsky had resumed negotiations for a con-

he asked the legal adviser of the foreign office, Baron Taube, to look up the documents in the archives and prepare a memoir for the tsar (Baron M. de Taube, *La politique russe d'avant-guerre et la fin de l'empire des tsars (1904–1917)* [Paris, 1928], pp. 194–9). Perhaps no other incident illustrates so well the carelessness with which Izvolsky conducted his negotiations with Aehrenthal. Taube (pp. 104–14) gives a scorching, but amusing picture of Izvolsky's vanity and snobbery.

[1] Tschirschky to Bülow, 7 November; G 9089.
[2] Aehrenthal to Berchtold, telegram, 8 November; A 534. How completely Aehrenthal felt himself master of the situation is revealed by his statement: "I must naturally leave it to the judgment of M. Izvolsky whether he deems it more opportune to promise at least a neutral attitude on the part of Russia to the fact of the annexation by referring to the publication of previous secret agreements, or whether he is willing to set himself in opposition to the spirit of the Buchlau conversations and thereby compel me publicly to refer to an exchange of views of the most recent date" (Aehrenthal to Berchtold, 14 November; A 577).
[3] Berchtold to Aehrenthal, telegram, 10 November; A 546.
[4] "Diplomaticus", "The secret treaty of Reichstadt," *Fortnightly review*, xc (1908), 828–37. The version given is quite inaccurate.
[5] Berchtold to Aehrenthal, 22 November; A 630.
[6] Aehrenthal to Berchtold, telegram, 24 November; A 639.
[7] So he admitted to Nicolson (Nicolson to Grey, telegram, 27 November; B 467).

ference, but, as will be seen later, he conducted them without enthusiasm or conviction. Evidently he was fearful that Aehrenthal would be as good as his word and publish the memorandum of July. Yet a conference seemed, from the Russian point of view, more necessary than ever, for the relations between Austria and Serbia were becoming steadily worse and threatening to develop into a rupture.

# CHAPTER VI

# The Austro-Serbian Tension

THE hot indignation manifested in Serbia on the morrow of the annexation gradually burnt itself out, and after assurances had been given that Serbia could count on "help from several Great Powers in the approaching revision of the Treaty of Berlin", the skupshtina passed a unanimous vote of confidence in the government.[1] The policy of demanding "compensation", to which the Serbian government had already committed itself, was hardly a wise one, for Serbia had no case at law, and she would have pursued a more dignified course by merely protesting against the violation of the Berlin Treaty in the name of the principle of nationality and allowing her friends to conduct the diplomatic campaign against Aehrenthal without consideration for Serbia's material interests.[2] But the foreign minister, Milovanovich, evidently felt it necessary to provide some kind of sop for the feelings of his countrymen, more especially as Pashich and his Radicals were inclined to war. So, in spite of a categorical statement from Count Forgách, the Austro-Hungarian minister, that "Serbia could not receive any territorial compensation", Milovanovich begged for a "rectification of frontier, even if ever so small",[3] and this request was to be

---

[1] Franz to Aehrenthal, 13 October, 1908; A 265. The Austrian chargé in Belgrade continued to be alarmed over insults to Austrian and Hungarian subjects in the Serbian capital; he was instructed to demand protection for them, but to refrain from threats (Aehrenthal to Franz, 17 October; Franz to Aehrenthal, 18, 19 October; A 306, 320, 321, 330).

[2] Boghitschewitsch, *Serbien und der Weltkrieg*, pp. 77–8. For a hostile account of Serbian policy during the entire crisis, see Hans Uebersberger, "Zur Vorkriegsgeschichte Serbiens", *Berliner Monatshefte*, XI (1933), 31–9.

[3] Forgách to Aehrenthal, 23 October; A 369. Aehrenthal, who had already refused a similar request from Izvolsky, seems to have returned no answer. Milovanovich subsequently admitted to the British ambassador in Vienna that "the Serbian statesmen were perfectly well aware that no compensation of any practical value was obtainable for their country, but public opinion demanded that something should be done and all that could be done was that Serbian 'amour-propre' should be flattered and that the Serbian question should become one of international importance" (Cartwright to Grey, 17 August 1909; B, vol. IX, Part I, No. 39).

repeated *ad nauseam* in the ensuing weeks. But, well aware of the Austro-Hungarian opposition, he endeavoured to enlist Turkish assistance for a joint resistance to the policy of Vienna and despatched several diplomatic missions abroad to explain and secure support for his point of view.

The overture to Turkey was natural enough, for the Young Turks were determined not to recognize the annexation without compensation (as Aehrenthal was demanding) and had instituted a boycott of Austro-Hungarian goods.[1] At the end of October, Stoyan Novakovich, a former premier and one-time minister in Constantinople, was sent to the Turkish capital on a special mission, in order to bespeak Turkish support of the Serbian pretensions at the forthcoming conference. Serbia, he explained to Tewfik Pasha, the Turkish foreign minister, desired Austria-Hungary to "cede sufficient Bosnian or Herzegovinian territory that a connection would be established with Montenegro"; as a *pis aller*, the autonomy of the two provinces would be acceptable, but otherwise Serbia would resort to the sword.[2] Tewfik told the representatives of the Central Powers that he had replied that "Turkey had sufficient to do in the adjustment of her internal affairs and did not wish to involve herself in an adventuresome policy".[3] Actually, he proposed "a military convention or defensive alliance between Turkey, Serbia and Montenegro,[4] on condition that neither of latter states should be allowed to declare war without the consent of Turkey",[5] and submitted a draft convention in six articles.[6]

It must be doubted, however, if the Porte was sincere in this offer. For after the usual diplomatic routine had been inaugurated by Serbia's proposing certain amendments and Tur-

[1] The Austro-Turkish controversy is discussed in a subsequent chapter.

[2] Marschall to foreign office, telegram, 26 October; G 9104. The Serbian materials available contain no documents on this mission, so that we have to depend on Austrian, German and British evidence.

[3] Pallavicini to Aehrenthal, telegram, 31 October; A 467: Marschall to foreign office, telegram, 26 October; G 9104.

[4] A Montenegrin general, Yanko Vukotich, had arrived in Belgrade to discuss an alliance between Serbia and Montenegro. Cf. A 283, 389, 421, 450, 541, 599.

[5] Whitehead to Grey, telegram, 26 October; B 405.

[6] Whitehead to Grey, 10 November; B 440.

key's hinting that she would accept them,[1] the Turkish government proposed a new amendment to the effect that "in case of a victorious war against Bulgaria the conquered territory should be divided between Serbia and Turkey".[2] From the beginning of the crisis the Porte had been willing to bargain with Austria about Bosnia, whereas its attitude towards Bulgaria had been quite intransigeant. Serbia was a useful lever against Austria, but now that Aehrenthal had opened up indirect negotiations (through the Young Turk Committee at Salonica),[3] the obvious course was to break off the negotiations by proposing impossible conditions. At that moment an alliance against Bulgaria had no point for the Serbs, even if they had not been admonished by the British and Russian governments against it;[4] they were forced to make counter-proposals, which the Turks pretended to consider;[5] no agreement was reached,[6] and Novakovich had to justify his long sojourn in Constantinople by pretending to busy himself "chiefly with economic questions".[7] From the Serbian point of view, his mission was a complete failure.[8]

Meanwhile the Serbian foreign minister was making the round of the western European capitals. In Berlin, Herr von Schoen listened politely to Milovanovich's appeal, but said that Germany could not undertake the rôle of mediator and Serbia "should not

[1] Serbia desired that the obligation not to declare war without the consent of Turkey should be made reciprocal, and that neither Serbia nor Turkey "would accept any proposed solution of the question of Bosnia and Herzegovina without previous agreement with the other" (Whitehead to Grey, 10 November; B 440).

[2] Whitehead to Grey, telegram, 13 November; B 443.

[3] Aehrenthal to Rappoport, at Salonica, telegram, 28 October; A 443.

[4] Grey to Whitehead, telegram, 14 November; Whitehead to Grey, telegram, 20 November; B 447, 455.

[5] Whitehead to Grey, 25 November; B 462.

[6] The British government refused "official countenance to any convention specifically directed against any Power or Powers designated by name", and urged that "any agreement concluded by Serbia with Turkey and the other Balkan states should be of a purely defensive character" (Grey to Whitehead, telegram, 1 December; B 468). Russian pressure was also exerted in Belgrade in the same sense (Nicolson to Grey, 1 December; B 470).

[7] Pallavicini to Aehrenthal, 4 December; A 689.

[8] The Montenegrin general Vukotich proceeded from Belgrade to Constantinople with the hope of concluding a Turkish-Montenegrin alliance against Austria; but nothing came of it. The British government discouraged this scheme also (Grey to O'Reilly, telegram, 17 November; B 451).

pursue unrealizable desires".[1] Izvolsky, whom Milovanovich waited to see on his way back to St Petersburg, admitted that Germany would not influence her ally. But the Russian states-man gave his Serbian colleague "the categorical assurance that Russia would not recognize the annexation" in case Austria re-fused a conference, and declared that Bosnia was not lost, "even if the annexation were to be recognized", for he intended to liquidate questions outside of Europe in order to lead Russia back to her European aims, and "in this policy Serbia, as the centre of the Southern Slavs, was an important factor".[2] Izvolsky's policy had moved far since, three weeks before, he had urged the Serbian minister in Paris to accept the annexa-tion![3] It should be added that he advised Milovanovich to avoid a conflict with Austria then, but the reason given—"because the ground is prepared neither from a military point of view nor diplomatically"—revealed a policy which, while no doubt still inchoate, was bound to lead ultimately to disaster.

In London, Milovanovich saw Grey and Hardinge, the latter several times. The British foreign secretary did not have "much sympathy with the clamour of Serbia and Montenegro for terri-torial compensation", but he wrote to his ambassador in St Peters-burg, "I do not want to cold-shoulder Izvolsky on the Serbian question, if the Russians are keen about it, and I will do my best to support him"[4]—a kind of *amende honorable* for declining the Russian proposals in respect of the Straits. So Grey, while

---

[1] Memorandum of Schoen, 20 October; G 9100: Szögyény to Aehrenthal, telegram, 21 October; A 351. Milovanovich was not allowed to see Bülow or the emperor and no official luncheon or dinner was given for him. His plea to the Austrian ambassador was coldly rejected (Szögyény to Aehrenthal, telegram, 23 October; A 370: Boghitschewitsch, *Serbien und der Weltkrieg*, p. 81).

[2] Milovanovich to foreign office, 25 October; S 19. Milovanovich subse-quently stated, in June 1909, to a friend of the British ambassador in Vienna that Izvolsky "again declared that Russia was not in a position to give serious support to Serbian aspirations, but nevertheless he advised the Serbian government not to abandon them. He also advised them to clamour for compensation as loudly as possible, as the more stir they made over the Bosnian annexation, the more likely it would be that in the end Austria would give way a little on economic questions under the pressure of the European cabinets" (Cartwright to Hardinge, private, 10 June; B, vol. IX, Part I, No. 14).

[3] See above, p. 48.

[4] Grey to Nicolson, private, 27 October; B 412.

pointing out the difficulties of inducing Austria to make concessions, promised British diplomatic support to Russia in her attitude about the Serbian demands. But since Milovanovich went so far as to say that "we must prepare for war, which is unavoidable in the near future, if this compensation is refused us", Grey made clear that "it must not be expected that we should push matters to the point of provoking a conflict". He also declined to accept the Serbian argument that if compensation could not be secured, the question of annexation should be left open. It was pointed out to Milovanovich that in this case Austria, while retaining Bosnia and Herzegovina, might any day resume her liberty of action in the Sandjak and that the Powers might feel that to leave the question open indefinitely involved danger of war.[1]

The British government also expressed "the greatest sympathy with a *rapprochement* of the Balkan states".[2] In the final interview with Milovanovich, however, Hardinge, "in his own, Grey's and the king's name, advised, in the most pressing manner, to keep the peace and avoid any provocation of Austria-Hungary".[3] Just as William II and Bülow decided to support their Austrian ally in a course of which they privately disapproved, so Grey, for diplomatic reasons, lent his support to a policy for which he was not enthusiastic. The disadvantages of the system of alliances were manifesting themselves most unpleasantly.

In Paris, Milovanovich was told by Pichon, the French foreign minister, who had disapproved of the Serbian pretensions from

---

[1] Grey to Nicolson, telegram, 29 October; B 416: Milovanovich to foreign office, telegram, 29 October; S 21. According to Grey's version, Milovanovich "insists upon cession of a band of territory to connect Serbia and Montenegro; failing this he might be content with undertaking from Austria to maintain Bosnia and Herzegovina as a separate constitutional unit". In his report, Milovanovich did not mention the latter contingency. The Serbian minister also advocated railway communication to the Adriatic with the cession of Spizza to Montenegro and desired some small concessions on the Danube.

[2] Milovanovich to foreign office, telegram, 29 October; S 22

[3] Milovanovich to foreign office, telegram, 1 November; S 26. Cf. also Grey to Whitehead, telegram, 31 October; B 419. King Edward declined to receive Milovanovich, and also asked that the Crown Prince of Montenegro be discouraged from visiting England (Lee, *King Edward VII*, II, 643).

the beginning and was disposed to play up to Aehrenthal,[1] that there was "no chance" of territorial compensation and that "excessive demands" would not be supported by France.[2] But when he got to Rome, the Serbian foreign minister found a most congenial atmosphere. Tittoni and King Victor Emmanuel expressed not only their sympathy with Serbia, but their approval of her demands, and promised Italian diplomatic support as long as Russia desired it.[3] The former promised to suggest to Russia that she should ask Great Britain to send a fleet to the Adriatic and accepted the Serbian contention that the question of territorial compensation must not be eliminated from the conference; the latter expressed his confidence that Milovanovich would be able to bring the Serbian question before the conference, as Cavour had raised the Italian question at Paris in 1856. Although the premier, Giolitti, did not expect that Austria could be induced to grant territorial compensations and the Russian ambassador, who was drawn into the conferences between Tittoni and Milovanovich, insisted that Russia could not go to war, the Serbian visitor found everywhere "the best frame of mind".[4] At the beginning of the crisis, Tittoni had talked of an Austro-Russo-Italian *entente*; now he was secretly advocating Italo-Russo-Serbian collaboration. Just before the arrival of the Serbian minister, he had suggested to Aehrenthal the desirability of "declaring publicly in the most categorical manner that in no circumstances imaginable could there be any talk of territorial compensations",[5] and while Milovanovich was still in Rome, Tittoni sketched to the Austrian ambassador the speech he proposed to make in the Italian parliament, in which not a word was mentioned about territorial compensation.[6] A few days later he assured the Ger-

[1] Khevenhüller to Aehrenthal, telegram, 26 October; A 412.
[2] Khevenhüller to Aehrenthal, telegram, 4 November; A 501.
[3] Tittoni had hitherto opposed the idea of territorial concessions. See above, p. 60.
[4] Milovanovich to foreign office, telegrams, 10, 12, 16, 18 November; S 29, 32, 33, 34. The German ambassador, who did not refrain from criticizing the policy of his own government and of Austria, told Milovanovich that "only England could exert any influence on Austria-Hungary and force her to show more regard for Serbia" (Milovanovich to foreign office, telegram, 11 November; S 30).
[5] Lützow to Aehrenthal, telegram, 8 November; A 533.
[6] Lützow to Aehrenthal, 17 November; A 592.

man ambassador that he had induced Milovanovich to reduce the Serbian claim to "a small neutral strip to be reserved for the projected Danube-Adriatic railway".[1] Italian policy left little to be desired in the way of ambiguity and disingenuousness. Aehrenthal was being repaid with interest for his cavalier treatment of Tittoni.[2]

A third Serbian effort to obtain assistance was the visit made to St Petersburg by the Crown Prince George and Nikola K. Pashich, the Radical leader. They found much sympathy in the Russian capital for their cause, which Pashich stimulated by several interviews in the press.[3] The tsar received the visitors, and subsequently telegraphed to King Peter that it had been "a real pleasure" to see his son.[4] On the other hand, the crown prince, who was reported to have made anti-Austrian speeches in Belgrade, had it impressed upon him by the tsar that "Serbia should observe the greatest prudence and moderation".[5] Nor was Pashich able, at least at first, to get much comfort from Izvolsky, who was haunted by the fear of an impending Austrian attack on Serbia.[6] The Russian minister said bluntly:

Serbia must remain quiet and should do nothing which could provoke Austria and provide an opportunity for annihilating Serbia. Russia is not yet ready with her armaments and cannot now make war, and she is not willing to do so now on account of Bosnia and Herzegovina, come what may.... We Russians have not abandoned

[1] Monts to Bülow, 23 November; G 9122.
[2] Through the former Serbian minister in London, Miyatovich, Milovanovich sounded Mensdorff on the possibility of his visiting Aehrenthal on the way back to Belgrade (Mensdorff to Aehrenthal, telegrams, 8, 9 November; A 532, 537). Aehrenthal replied that if the request were made through the Serbian minister in Vienna he would receive Milovanovich, but on the express condition that the question of territorial compensation—which was to be the object of the visit—should not be raised (Aehrenthal to Mensdorff, telegram, 10 November; A 545). It subsequently appeared that the idea of visiting Aehrenthal was suggested to Milovanovich by the Rumanian minister in London, Catargi, who "hated the Serbs more than sin" and wished to "humiliate them" (Széchényi to Aehrenthal, 13 November; A 566).
[3] Berchtold to Aehrenthal, 12 November; A 560.
[4] Forgách to Aehrenthal, telegram, 11 November; A 547.
[5] Nicolson to Grey, 31 October; B 421.
[6] Nicolson to Grey, 2 November; B 424: Pourtalès to Bülow, 13 November; G 9112.

the demands for territorial compensation for Serbia, but according to all that I have heard, we cannot make them good.[1]

Izvolsky also assured the ambassadors at the Russian court that he had impressed on the Serbian visitors the necessity of modera-tion,[2] and Berchtold was satisfied with the "correct" attitude of the Russian government.[3]

This does not, however, tell the whole story. Subsequently, perhaps because of the news that Great Britain would give diplo-matic support to the Russo-Serbian position, the Russian government modified its attitude. Unless assurances were re-ceived, so Pashich was told, that Serbia and Montenegro would get territorial compensation and certain guarantees respecting the administration of Bosnia and Herzegovina, "Russia will not go to the conference and will not recognize the annexation". This was certainly an encouragement to Serbia, even if the warning was repeated that "Russia cannot and will not now go to war on account of Bosnia".[4] And when the tsar stated that "the Bosnian question will be decided only by war" and that the policy of Serbia for the present should be "understanding with Turkey, a quiet attitude, military preparation and waiting",[5] the Serbs had good reason to be content. Perhaps, in view of the excited state of public opinion, Izvolsky felt unable to abandon Serbia,[6] and there is no doubt that he sincerely desired at this time to prevent an Austro-Serbian war; hence to restrain the Serbs by holding out promises for the future was, for the moment, good politics. But such a course, if actually followed, could lead only to disaster, and it is significant that the Russian government did not reveal its ulterior policy to Great Britain.

In Serbia the continuation of the boycott against Austro-Hungarian goods evoked a protest from the Austro-Hungarian

[1] Memorandum of Pashich, 29 October; S 24.
[2] Nicolson to Grey, telegram, 2 November; B 422: Pourtalès to Bülow, 13 November; G 9112.
[3] Berchtold to Aehrenthal, 6 November; A 519.
[4] Pashich to foreign office, telegram, 2 November; S 27.
[5] Pashich to foreign office, telegram, 12 November; S 31.
[6] See his complaints in a letter to Nelidov, the ambassador in Paris, of 5 November; B. von Siebert, *Diplomatische Aktenstücke zur Geschichte der Ententepolitik der Vorkriegsjahre* (Berlin, 1921), p. 72 (cited hereafter as "Siebert").

minister.[1] Count Forgách believed that the government wished to keep the peace but was afraid of public opinion,[2] and in a difficult audience with the king, he offered assurances that

if Serbia gives up her illusions in respect of territorial compensations, we should be glad to help her secure other advantages, for example, the Danube-Adriatic railway, since we regarded tranquillity in Serbia and the strengthening of the dynasty as desirable in our neighbourly interest.[3]

Nevertheless, he advised Aehrenthal to make preparations for a rupture by collecting materials which would reveal "the fantastical insolence and the incredible machinations of Serbia", more particularly the official fitting out of bands of komitadjis and the command of them by a general on the active list.[4] For while the bands had been withdrawn from the frontier, the "unlimited correctness" of the government was simply a "pose", in order to gain time and to prejudice public opinion in Europe against the Monarchy.[5]

This suggestion was apparently not taken up by Aehrenthal, who had not yet found a basis of negotiation with Turkey. On the contrary, since, at the suggestion of Italy,[6] strong representations had been made in favour of moderation and prudence by the British, French, Russian, German and Italian representatives in Belgrade,[7] the Austro-Hungarian foreign minister addressed

[1] Forgách to Aehrenthal, telegram, 26 October; A 402.
[2] Forgách to Aehrenthal, 27 October; A 418. He was of the opinion, however, that "a reckoning with Serbia, our irreconcilable enemy, will have to come, but perhaps only after some years, eventually in connection with the solution of the Southern Slav question" (Forgách to Aehrenthal, 27 October; A 419).
[3] Forgách to Aehrenthal, telegram, 27 October; A 417. The king protested against the Austrian veto on the export of munitions to Serbia, but he could not answer Forgách's retort that the Monarchy could hardly allow munitions to go to a country "which was unanimously demanding war against us". Cf. also Ratibor to foreign office, telegram, 28 October; G 9105.
[4] Forgách to Aehrenthal, 3 November; A 487.
[5] Forgách to Aehrenthal, 6 November; A 512.
[6] Grey to Nicolson, telegram, 31 October; B 420: Forgách to Aehrenthal, telegram, 1 November; A 478.
[7] Grey to Whitehead, telegram, 31 October; Nicolson to Grey, 1 November; B 419, 424: Forgách to Aehrenthal, telegrams, 3 November; A 485, 486: Ratibor to foreign office, telegram, 3 November; G 9109. These representations caused the Serbian government to ask the Entente ministers and the Italian chargé for advice, which they declined to give, although they would

a circular to the Powers calling attention to the military activity of Serbia and Montenegro and asking them "to continue their efforts at Belgrade in the interests of peace".[1] This gave Izvolsky an opening, and he promptly proposed an identic *démarche* by the Powers,[2] who agreed to it.[3] The exact nature of the *démarche* was left to the representatives in Belgrade.[4] They decided that, in order not to arouse Serbian feeling too strongly, it would suffice to advise the withdrawal of troops from the Austro-Serbian frontier and to call attention to "the disastrous consequences which might result from the eventual formation on [Serbia's] territory of bands directed against Bosnia".[5] A note in this sense was presented to the Serbian government on 18 November by the representatives of the five Powers in immediate succession. The Serbian premier, Velimirovich—the foreign minister having not yet returned from his tour—replied that orders had already been given for withdrawing the troops and measures taken to prevent bands from forming or crossing the frontier; and he tried to turn the tables by presenting to the representatives of the Powers an *aide-mémoire* in which Austria-Hungary was charged with violating the frontier and with preparing for war and which

have liked to advise Serbia to withdraw her troops from their position on the rivers near the frontier (Whitehead to Grey, telegram, 6 November; B 431). This suggestion was communicated to Vienna by Grey, who asked whether "Austria would respond to it" (Grey to Whitehead, telegram, 7 November; B 434). Aehrenthal apparently did not "respond".

[1] Circular telegram of Aehrenthal, 6 November; A 513. Aehrenthal subsequently sought to deny that he had asked for an "intervention" at Belgrade or was responsible for the *démarche* undertaken by the Powers (Aehrenthal to Széchényi, London, telegram, 13 November; Aehrenthal to Forgách, telegram, 20 November; A 564, 614).

[2] Memorandum of Benckendorff, 9 November; B 438: Berchtold to Aehrenthal, 9 November, telegram; A 540: Kiderlen to Ratibor, telegram, 10 November; G 9110.

[3] Grey to Whitehead, telegram, 9 November; B 437: Kiderlen to Ratibor, telegram, 14 November; G 9111: Flotow to Aehrenthal, telegram, 9 November; Széchényi to Aehrenthal, telegram, 11 November; A 535, 549.

[4] Aehrenthal's complaints were to be made the *point de départ* (Izvolsky to Sergeyev, telegram, 12 November; B 445).

[5] Whitehead to Grey, telegram, 14 November; B 448: Ratibor to foreign office, telegram, 16 November; G 9115. The German and Austrian ministers desired some reference to the increased strength of the Serbian army and the orders for munitions, but the former declined to press these views (Ratibor to foreign office, telegram, 16 November; G 9116: Forgách to Aehrenthal, telegram, 16 November; A 582).

invited the Powers to offer "friendly counsels" in Vienna against such activity.[1]

Aehrenthal was irritated by the "impertinent" tone of the Serbian reply,[2] but since the Powers did not give effect to the Serbian request,[3] he could do nothing. Meanwhile, however, the military preparations of Austria-Hungary had begun to cause alarm,[4] and the Serbs evidently thought that they could make capital out of the situation. They accordingly requested the Powers early in December "to urge upon the Austrian government the cessation of these measures and the restoration of the normal military situation on the frontier as has already been effected on the part of Serbia".[5] The German government, as

---

[1] Ratibor to foreign office, telegram, 18 November; G 9118: Forgách to Aehrenthal, telegrams, 18 November; A 596, 597. Forgách, who, of course, took no part in the diplomatic action at Belgrade, was of the opinion that Serbia would undertake "no adventurous enterprise" for the next few weeks or months, in spite of the excitement caused by the return of Crown Prince George from St Petersburg, the activity of certain Italian journalists, and the "illusions" spread in Belgrade by Valentine Chirol, of the London *Times* (Forgách to Aehrenthal, 7, 12, 16, 26 November; A 523, 553, 554, 583, 649). Perhaps the most interesting episode of this period was the lecture given in Belgrade by the famous Serbian geographer, Professor Tsviyich (Cvijič), on the "Serbian problem", in which he remarked that "the solution of the 'Serbian question' could also be accomplished within the framework of the Monarchy by the association of Serbia and that this was being striven for by many Serbian politicians"; he spoke openly of the formation of "a great Southern Slav kingdom" which could be federated with the Monarchy (Forgách to Aehrenthal, 26 November; A 648).

[2] Tschirschky to foreign office, telegram, 21 November; G 9120.

[3] Since Mensdorff had assured the British foreign office that "his government would take no action against Serbia unless they were attacked" (Grey to Carnegie, 16 November; B 450), Grey appears to have instructed the British chargé in Vienna to sound the ambassadors there on the desirability of communicating the Serbian reply to the Austro-Hungarian government (Tschirschky to foreign office, telegram, 20 November; G 9119: B does not mention this incident). Germany and Italy declined the suggestion (Szögyény to Aehrenthal, telegram, 22 November; A 623), for which Aehrenthal was duly grateful (Aehrenthal to Szögyény, telegram, 26 November; A 650).

[4] Grey to Carnegie, 16 November; B 450: Berchtold to Aehrenthal, telegram, 18 November; A 603. Aehrenthal admitted that the 15 corps (in Bosnia) had been strengthened by several thousand men and that additional battalions had been sent to Dalmatia (circular telegram, 16 November; A 588). Preparations were also under way for a mobilization against Serbia; Conrad, chief of the general staff, expected war in the spring, and pressed for more elaborate military measures (Conrad, *Aus meiner Dienstzeit*, I, 120–8, 601–27).

[5] Grey to Bertie, telegram, 2 December; B 471.

might have been expected, rebuffed the demand, declaring it "only natural that Austria-Hungary should take measures of precaution, since for weeks the war trumpets had been blown in Serbia and arming carried on with the greatest zeal".[1] But Serbia's friends were also hesitant. Izvolsky thought it "a serious step, which could not be decided upon in a moment",[2] and Grey, after consulting the Powers, decided to reply that the British government "do not consider that there are sufficient grounds for making representations at Vienna".[3] Grey, in fact, accepted the explanations of Mensdorff that "the Austrians were only increasing their peace footing, as the men had been over-taxed by recent events, and that the Austrians were not doing anything which amounted to a mobilization",[4] and the Serbian chargé in London was told that the Austrian preparations were "intelligible".[5] So nothing came of the Serbian plan.

Austro-Serbian relations were thus left in a most delicate position. The little Slav state had not recognized the annexation, it maintained its claims,[6] and it declined to dismiss its reservists; although Milovanovich sought to convince Forgách that he desired "only a peaceful solution", the latter concluded otherwise from his secret information:

The minister does not conceal from a limited circle his conviction that Serbia cannot satisfy her demands in a peaceful manner; so war must be prepared for the spring in order to strike then, in case assistance or intervention can be hoped for.[7]

[1] Schoen to Tschirschky, telegram, 2 December; G 9125.

[2] Grey to Nicolson, 7 December; B 479.

[3] Grey to Bertie, telegram, 4 December; B 474.

[4] Grey to Carnegie, 7 December; B 480. Grey told Mensdorff, however, that it seemed to him, from what he had heard, that "the movements of Austrian troops went beyond what Count Mensdorff had indicated". On the same day, Grey had received from Benckendorff, the Russian ambassador, a statement according to which 60,000 men had been called up and measures taken for the mobilization of three corps (memorandum of Benckendorff; B 479, enclosure).

[5] Gruyich to foreign office, 17 December; S 38.

[6] "If the programme of the conference should exclude discussion of the annexation and the territorial compensation of Serbia, then the kingdom must try to secure that no conference took place, that the question remained open and its solution sought on another basis", said the Serbian foreign minister.

[7] Forgách to Aehrenthal, 1 December; A 682. It is not clear what basis there was for the information which reached London to the effect that "Serbia

If, for the moment, the country was quiet, the government was weak,[1] and the manifestations of sympathy between the Serbs and the Czechs were an unfavourable symptom.[2] Aehrenthal, for his part, though he informed Bülow that he did not desire a conflict with Serbia, stated that he was "not disposed to continue the policy of patience and forbearance *ad infinitum*", and that if in the next two months the attitude of Serbia gave occasion for serious complaint, "the time will then come when we must come to a more decisive resolution".[3] He likewise warned the British government that "Austria could not tolerate much longer Serbian provocation"—language which caused "uneasiness" in St Petersburg[4]—and "accused England of causing half the trouble through the action of her press".[5] If neither Austria nor Serbia dared

is disposed to content herself with guarantees for the construction of the Danube-Adriatic railway, in case complete freedom of import and export by this were assured by special stipulations and unlimited transit conceded by Austria" (Metternich to Bülow, 13 December; G 9128).

[1] Forgách to Aehrenthal, 12 December; A 727.

[2] Forgách to Aehrenthal, 12 December; A 728.

[3] Aehrenthal to Bülow, private, 8 December; A 703, G 9127.

[4] Nicolson to Grey, telegram, 15 December; B 486. Izvolsky said that "if Austria attacked Serbia there might be explosion of Russian public opinion, which might force the hands of the Government. He did not see what Serbia had recently been doing which could be called provocation, and he wished that some means could be found for encouraging the peace party in Austria or for mediating between Austria and Serbia".

[5] Cartwright to Grey, telegram and despatch, 11 December; B 483, 484. Cf. Aehrenthal to Mensdorff, private, 17 December; A 767. Aehrenthal's accusation against the British press led to a series of unedifying recriminations between the British and Austrian governments. Grey replied that "Baron d'Aehrenthal's views as to England's responsibility for the present situation are on a par with the statements in part of the Austrian press, which writes as if it were England and not Austria which had first disturbed the *status quo*" (Grey to Cartwright, telegram, 14 December; B 485), and that "as far as the press was concerned, I considered that we were the injured party" (Grey to Cartwright, private, 16 December; B 487). The impression, indeed, obtained in London that "the greatest part of the Vienna press receives its inspiration from the Ballplatz" (Mensdorff to Aehrenthal, private, 20 December; A 781). Aehrenthal then complained of the activity of Noel Buxton, a member of the Balkan Committee, in Serbia, asserting that "this gentleman disposed of considerable funds and that he employed a large number of agents in the nefarious work of propagating aspirations among the ignorant Serbian population which it would be impossible for the European Powers ever to satisfy without the shedding of a great deal of blood" (Cartwright to Grey, 23 December; B 489). Grey replied that "the accusation was absurd" (Grey to Cartwright, private, 6 January, 1909; B 505), and, after investigating, that Buxton "seems to have endeavoured to exercise a moderating

proceed to extremes, the situation remained full of danger and was kept in hand for the moment only because its adjustment depended upon the solution of other pressing questions.

influence" (Grey to Cartwright, telegram, 26 January; B 533). In January the *Neue Freie Presse* declared that "England's object is to humiliate us, by showing through a striking example that no nation can remain faithful to the German Empire without hurt to herself " (Cartwright to Grey, 6 January; B 503); the *Neues Wiener Tagblatt* published an article which aroused the irritation of King Edward and led Hardinge to speak sharply to Mensdorff (Mensdorff to Aehrenthal, telegrams, 9, 11 January; A 866, 874: Grey to Cartwright, 18 January; B 521); finally the *Mittagszeitung* openly attacked King Edward (Cartwright to Grey, telegram, 18 January; B 519), against which Hardinge protested (Mensdorff to Aehrenthal, 14 January; A 892). Aehrenthal in turn protested against an article in the *Near East* dealing with the Emperor Francis Joseph (Aehrenthal to Mensdorff, telegram, 16 January; A 896); Hardinge declared that he had never heard of the magazine and expressed regret (Mensdorff to Aehrenthal, telegram, 18 January; A 903. Grey to Cartwright, 22 January; B 526). After this, the polemics seem to have ceased.

# CHAPTER VII

## The Abandonment of the Conference

SO LONG AS the Austro-Serbian situation remained uncertain and Turkey had not recognized the annexation, Aehrenthal could not safely abandon the position that he did not object to a conference "in principle", provided the annexation was not called in question or made the subject of discussion.[1] But he naturally left the initiative to his antagonists. Izvolsky, for his part, had to go ahead, for the idea of a conference had originated with him and it alone might permit him to escape from the many difficulties in which he found himself. On his return to St Petersburg, he gave Count Berchtold, the Austrian ambassador, a copy of the programme drawn up by himself and Grey,[2] and promptly arranged an audience of the tsar for which Berchtold had long been clamouring.[3] But since he talked in a tone of "dull resignation" and seemed "physically and morally broken", the ambassador did not take his arguments very seriously,[4] all the less so as Stolypin and Kokovtzov were inclined to be critical of their colleague.[5] That Izvolsky was indeed half-hearted about the con-

[1] Aehrenthal to Szögyény, telegram, 25 October; A 390: Goschen to Grey, telegram, 28 October; B 413.

[2] Berchtold to Aehrenthal, telegram, 30 October, and despatch, 31 October; A 462, 476. He described it as a "projet", and not as an official communication.

[3] Berchtold to Aehrenthal, private, 31 October; A 477. At the audience, which took place on 2 November, the tsar declined to talk politics, but said that he would reply shortly to the letter of Francis Joseph, as soon as certain investigations in the archives had been completed (Berchtold to Aehrenthal, telegram, 2 November; A 484). The letter, dated 22 October/4 November (A 505), reaffirmed the Russian contention that since the Austrian occupation of Bosnia and Herzegovina depended on the Treaty of Berlin, "la situation de ces deux provinces ne pourrait subir une modification qu'à la suite d'une délibération des Puissances Signataires de ce traité", and recalled the language of the London Conference of 1871, "qu'aucune Puissance ne peut se dédire des engagements d'un traité ni d'en modifier les stipulations qu'à la suite de l'assentiment des parties contractantes au moyen d'une entente amicale".

[4] Berchtold to Aehrenthal, 5 November; A 517.

[5] Berchtold to Aehrenthal, 5 November; A 518.

ference is suggested by the fact that, in spite of the rebuff which
he had received in Berlin, he transmitted to the German government a long memorandum elaborating the Russian point of view
on the nine points of the programme and inviting German adherence.[1] For the next few weeks, the Russian foreign minister
had little to say about the conference and devoted his energy to
keeping the restless Serbs in order.[2]

Instead of adhering to the Russian memorandum, the German
government, as was to have been expected, introduced serious
changes: the conference should meet "only after complete
agreement on all questions shall have been previously reached
between the Powers signatory of the Treaty of Berlin"; the
annexation was to be treated as "un fait accompli indiscutable";
and on the question of compensations, "Germany will only
agree to proposals sanctioned by Austria-Hungary". With these
and other modifications, the document was sent to Vienna for
the consideration of Aehrenthal.[3] The Austro-Hungarian foreign
minister, who was delighted by this "loyal and decisive" support,[4] in turn submitted the draft of the reply which he proposed
to make to the Russian overture,[5] and made one change at German suggestion.[6] Harmony between Berlin and Vienna having
thus been established, Aehrenthal despatched his note to

[1] G 9129, Anlage.
[2] See above, p. 74. Momentary anxiety was caused in Russia by the visit
of the German Emperor to the Emperor Francis Joseph and the Archduke
Francis Ferdinand. "We are assured", said Izvolsky, "that the military
party in Vienna is very warlike and is urging an attack upon Serbia; at the
head of this party stands the heir to the throne, but the old emperor sets
himself against all such essays. Must we not fear that the Emperor William
will support the military party?" (Izvolsky to Nelidov, Russian ambassador
in Paris, 5 November; Siebert, p. 71). To Nicolson, Izvolsky expressed himself
in less pessimistic fashion: "He [Izvolsky] did not know in what frame of mind
His Majesty was at the present moment, but if he urged Austria to take decisive
measures she might be persuaded to act on his advice. He, however, felt that
although the Emperor William was exceedingly incautious in his words, he
was prudent as to his acts, and this consideration was reassuring" (Nicolson to
Grey, 2 November; B 424). William's conversations with the Austrians seem
to have been harmless enough (William II to Bülow, telegrams, 5, 6 November;
Jenisch to Bülow, 7 November; G 9086, 9087, 9088).
[3] Schoen to Tschirschky, 31 October; G 9129.
[4] Tschirschky to foreign office, telegram, 2 November; G 9130.
[5] Aehrenthal to Flotow, 7 November; A 524.
[6] Flotow to Aehrenthal, telegram, 10 November; Aehrenthal to Flotow,
telegram, 12 November; A 545, 555.

St Petersburg, where the German comments on the Russian memorandum had already been communicated.[1]

The Austro-Hungarian note, while professing willingness to enter into an exchange of views with Russia, rejected the Russian contentions on the essential points. The independence of Bulgaria could be recognized "only when the financial questions, including that of the Oriental railway, shall have been adjusted"; there could be no question of discussing the annexation, concerning which Austria proposed to reach an understanding with the Porte; certain reservations were formulated respecting the sovereignty of Montenegro; as for "avantages à procurer à la Serbie et au Monténégro", they must be "avantages économiques".[2] The document bespoke a confidence which Aehrenthal did not hesitate to reveal privately to Berchtold, from whose report of 31 October he had learned with satisfaction that "the influential ministers" Stolypin and Kokovtzov were determined that the Serbophile current prevailing in Russia should cause no trouble. "So we can", Aehrenthal observed, "up to a certain point, reckon, as I have always done in my calculations, with Russia's need of peace and with the insight and firmness of the leading Russian ministers."[3] Aehrenthal had gauged the situa-

[1] When Pourtalès, the German ambassador, tried to discover what Russia would do if agreement about the programme of the conference was not reached by all the Powers, Izvolsky merely replied that "we shall, indeed, see whether Russia stands alone in her opinion that a situation created by an international treaty cannot be upset by a single Power in its favour". The ambassador suspected that the Russian plan was to let the conference fail and thus leave the question of the annexation open (Pourtalès to Bülow, 14 November; G 9131).

[2] A 524, zweite Beilage, and A 555. Covering note: Aehrenthal to Berchtold, 14 November; A 576.

[3] Aehrenthal to Berchtold, 14 November; A 579. Aehrenthal was of the opinion that Izvolsky had only himself to blame for his present plight; he should have thought out his policy in advance, before "he approached me with proposals on the basis of reciprocity, and should have made it clear to himself whether the compensation which he demanded of Austria-Hungary for consenting to the annexation of Bosnia and Herzegovina would be regarded as sufficient by the public opinion of his own country". Francis Ferdinand told William early in the month that "a secret mission had recently been sent to him by the Emperor Nicholas II, in which the promise was made always to maintain good friendship with Austria, and not a single man should be brought forward by Russia against Austria as a result of any present warlike complications (Serbia)" (William II to Bülow, telegram from Eckartsau, 5 November; G 9086). Nothing further is known of this mission, but it must have encouraged Aehrenthal to hold to his policy of defying Izvolsky.

tion quite accurately, for Izvolsky, when he discussed the Austrian reply with Sir Arthur Nicolson, the British ambassador, practically admitted that he did not know what rejoinder to make.[1]

The international situation at the moment was not very favourable to Russia. Great Britain had promised her diplomatic support on behalf of Serbia,[2] but when Count Benckendorff, the Russian ambassador in London, being "very indiscreet", asked Sir Edward Grey "what England would do supposing a crisis arose in the Balkans and Germany took the part of Austria as her ally?" the latter replied bluntly that "it was impossible for [him] to ask the cabinet to consider such a contingency or to come to any decision with regard to it".[3] In France the nervousness produced by the Casablanca incident had disappeared when France and Germany agreed to submit the matter to arbitration. But it soon became known that the Emperor Francis Joseph had made representations to the Emperor William in the interest of a pacific solution;[4] Pichon, the French foreign minister, was grateful for the intervention,[5] and declaring to the Austrian ambassador that "the opportunity for joint activity with us in political matters is far from being exhausted", promised that "he would urge moderation on Russia if our interests there should be injured".[6] If Izvolsky was informed of this attitude—unfortunately, no Russian documents have been published for this

[1] Nicolson to Grey, 18 November; B 453.

[2] Grey to Nicolson, telegram, 29 October; B 416. See above, p. 68. King Edward wrote a personal letter singing the praises of Izvolsky (Lee, *King Edward VII*, II, 642).

[3] Grey to Nicolson, private, 10 November; B 441.

[4] The German Emperor visited Vienna on 6–7 November. The Austrian ambassador in Paris suggested that "it would be of incalculable advantage to us if France were freed from her momentary concern by a generous intervention of our most gracious master" (Khevenhüller to Aehrenthal, telegram, 5 November; A 508). As Aehrenthal had been at pains to assert that the alliances were no barrier to "confidential relations" between Austria-Hungary and France (Aehrenthal to Khevenhüller, 5 November; A 506), and his own policy would be wrecked if Germany had to deal with France, he at once fell in with the suggestion from Paris (Aehrenthal to Khevenhüller, telegram, 7 November; A 528: Tschirschky to foreign office, telegram, 7 November; G, vol. XXIV, No. 8399).

[5] Khevenhüller to Aehrenthal, 14 November; A 572.

[6] Khevenhüller to Aehrenthal, 14 November; A 571. In a speech to the chamber of deputies on 27 November, Pichon declared that the interest of France was in the maintenance of peace and that the government was acting in this sense at Vienna, Belgrade and Constantinople.

period of the crisis—he would have all the more reason for doubting the effectiveness of the *entente* in resisting the Central Powers. The Italian government was, indeed, in favour of a conference[1] and desired that it be held in Rome;[2] but since it had also declared against territorial concessions to Serbia and Montenegro,[3] Italian support on the point which mattered most to Russia was evidently not to be expected.

Outwardly the Russian reply of 22 November maintained the Russian position intact: the conference must have full liberty of discussion and the precedent of 1871 must be respected.[4] But Izvolsky did not expect Aehrenthal to admit any discussion of the act of annexation,[5] and at the latter's objection, refrained from issuing a communiqué briefly stating the Russian point of view.[6] On both the Austrian and British ambassadors the Russian foreign minister left the impression that, in view of Russian public opinion, he would not greatly regret it if the proposal for a conference were dropped; he admitted, indeed, that matters had reached a "deadlock".[7] Since the general staff

[1] Lützow to Aehrenthal, telegrams, 25, 26, 27, and 31 October; A 400, 413, 428, 471. Tittoni declared that without a conference he would be "un homme liquidé" and would have to resign—threats which Aehrenthal calmly ignored.

[2] Monts to Bülow, 30 October; G 9082. The Austrian ambassador thought that Tittoni should be humoured on this point (Lützow to Aehrenthal, telegram, 3 November; A 492), and Aehrenthal, knowing that the German government was opposed to Rome (Szögyény to Aehrenthal, telegram, 16 November; A 585), promised to support the Italian claim (Aehrenthal to Lützow, 17 November; A 591), which was subsequently abandoned (Lützow to Aehrenthal, telegram, 5 December; A 696).

[3] Lützow to Aehrenthal, telegram, 8 November; A 533. Tittoni was, however, not above claiming territorial compensation for his own country. He kept talking about "un acte gracieux" on the part of Francis Joseph, and finally said that if an Italian university could not be established in Trent, "a frontier adjustment of a few kilometres which would give the ruins of Aquileia to Italy would create the same moral effect" (Lützow to Aehrenthal, telegram, 30 October; A 458). Aehrenthal was so indignant at this suggestion that he reproved his ambassador in Rome for transmitting it (Aehrenthal to Lützow, telegram, 3 November; A 490).

[4] *Aide-mémoire* of 9/22 November; A 626, Beilage.

[5] Nicolson to Grey, 22 November; B 457.

[6] Berchtold to Aehrenthal, 22 November; Aehrenthal to Berchtold, telegram, 25 November; Berchtold to Aehrenthal, telegram, 26 November; A 627, 646, 653.

[7] Berchtold to Aehrenthal, 22 November, and telegram, 27 November; A 626, 653. Nicolson to Grey, telegram, 27 November; B 467. Aehrenthal

had informed him, in reply to an enquiry, that "a conflict with Austria-Hungary alone would not be without chance of success, but that one with both the western neighbours must be given up from the start",[1] he was, in fact, helpless. It was an ironic commentary on the situation that the tsar addressed a personal letter to the Emperor Francis Joseph in honour of the approaching sixtieth anniversary of the latter's accession.[2]

Aehrenthal appears to have withheld his reply until the momentary high tension with Serbia had been somewhat reduced.[3] He then proceeded to press his rival to the wall. In a long and somewhat sharp letter Francis Joseph reminded the tsar that in the past Russian policy had profited from co-operation with Austria-Hungary and that "I have undertaken nothing which has not been sanctioned in advance by your predecessors and recently even by your government, which proposed to me that I extend my dominion beyond the limits which I had traced".[4] Aehrenthal himself, in the note intended for Izvolsky, recalled that the cabinet of St Petersburg had taken the initiative in the discussion about Bosnia and had promised to observe "a friendly attitude". If it wished to appeal to the principle of 1871,

the cabinet of Vienna may remark that apart from any other change in respect of the Treaty of Berlin which has come about since 1878, the Imperial government itself has believed it compatible with this principle to free itself, without an agreement between all the contracting parties, of the engagement stipulated by Article 59 concerning the port of Batum.[5]

also derived from "the tone and content" of the Russian note the impression that "Russia no longer attaches importance to the meeting of a conference" (Tschirschky to foreign office, telegram, 25 November; quoted in G 9139).
  [1] Berchtold to Aehrenthal, 22 November; A 629. Berchtold was of the opinion that only the Cadets were talking of war.
  [2] Nicholas II to Francis Joseph, 5/18 November; A 604.
  [3] See above, p. 74.
  [4] Francis Joseph to Nicholas II, 7 December; A 700.
  [5] Aide-mémoire of 3 December, accompanying despatch to Berchtold; A 705. In mentioning this matter to the German military plenipotentiary, the tsar spoke of the Austrian offer of "the freeing of Batum from the limitations of the Berlin Treaty" as "a poor compensation" for the annexation of Bosnia (Pourtalès to foreign office, telegram, 12 December; G 9180). Pourtalès interpreted this to mean that Nicholas had not read the Austrian note and been given an incorrect version by Izvolsky (Pourtalès to Bülow, 13 December; G 9183). The German and Austrian diplomatists more than once complained that the tsar was incorrectly informed by his minister of what was happening.

In any case, so a separate memorandum boldly affirmed, "the manner of procedure chosen by us in the annexation question does not justify the Russian cabinet in considering the agreement reached at Buchlau as non-existent".[1] Aehrenthal's determination not to yield is well indicated by his remark to Bülow that "I cherish no illusion about the reception which my latest memorandum will meet with from the director of Russia's foreign affairs".[2] But he had no reason to worry, for the German chancellor, speaking in the reichstag on 7 December, had used firm language. After denying that Germany had received any preliminary information about the annexation, Bülow declared that Germany fully approved the resolution of her ally and would give all necessary support. On the question of the conference, he was quite explicit:

As a natural consequence of our loyal attitude towards Austria-Hungary, I have not left the Russian foreign minister in any doubt on the matter of a conference. I told him that we shall not separate ourselves from Austria-Hungary.

The Russian foreign minister, indeed, did not find the Austrian answer to his liking.[3] But, evidently realizing his helplessness,[4] Izvolsky decided against communicating the Austrian note to the Powers, on the ground that it contained references to secret

[1] A 705, zweite Beilage.
[2] Aehrenthal to Bülow, private, 8 December; A 703; G 9145.
[3] Pourtalès to foreign office, telegram, 11 December; G 9147.
[4] The Russian minister of war assured the German military attaché that "it was out of the question for Russia to go to war on account of the Serbs". In the opinion of the attaché, "they still have enough from the last war, and the feeling that the army is not ready for war has penetrated through the press into the whole corps of officers" (report of Posadowsky-Wehner, 10 December; G 9149). On 7 December, the *Berliner Lokal-Anzeiger* published a report from its St Petersburg correspondent about an interview which Izvolsky was said to have given to the Russian journalist Schelking. At the end Izvolsky was reported to have said: "A formal alliance of England with Russia and France is imminent; it is necessary because Germany is now supporting more intensively Austria's Balkan policy." Izvolsky denied the story both to Pourtalès and in Berlin (Pourtalès to Bülow, 9 December; G 9146, and note, p. 317), but the ambassador could not refrain from once more lecturing the minister on the unwisdom of Russia's *entente* with England (Pourtalès to Bülow, 11 December; G 9152). The Austrian ambassador thought the story a "gross angelegtes Bluffmanöver" (Berchtold to Aehrenthal, telegram, 9 December; A 712).

negotiations,[1] and forthwith promised that his response would be "satisfactory", at the same time carefully avoiding any reference to Buchlau.[2] "Russia's principal concern at the moment", said Charykov, the assistant foreign minister, "was that a warlike conflict should be avoided between Austria-Hungary and the Serbian sister lands with which the interests of Russia were bound up by the tradition of more than a hundred years...the first cannon shot goes off quickly, but when will the last one sound?" Russia would therefore agree to a preliminary under-standing between the Powers and accept the conference as a registering body.[3] And the Russian note of 4/17 December, though indulging in considerable face-saving, did concede the point at issue:

> While believing that the method of procedure suggested by the cabinet of Vienna offers serious inconveniences because of its slowness, the Imperial cabinet, being desirous of giving proof on its side of a spirit of conciliation, is ready not to oppose it if the other Powers are disposed to adhere to it.

The cabinet of Vienna was accordingly invited to make known its views to the other Powers.[4]

In a conciliatory speech which he delivered in the duma on 25 December, Izvolsky tried to exculpate himself from the charges of having sacrificed the interests of Slavdom. He ex-plained that his policy had been hampered by various agreements made with Austria-Hungary since 1877; but, he contended, if Austria insisted on a change in the Berlin Treaty—and Russia could not prevent this—Russia had the moral duty to point to other articles which were disadvantageous to herself, to the Balkan states and to Turkey. Omitting any reference to the Straits, he claimed compensation for Serbia and Montenegro and made friendly reference to Bulgaria. Finally, he declared that it would be the policy of Russia to bring Bulgaria, Serbia and Montenegro together and unite them with Turkey for the

[1] Berchtold to Aehrenthal, telegram, 13 December; A 740. For this very reason, Aehrenthal had no objections to its being communicated (Aehren-thal to Berchtold, telegram, 9 December; A 711).
[2] Berchtold to Aehrenthal, telegram, 13 December; A 741.
[3] Berchtold to Aehrenthal, 15 December; A 750.
[4] *Aide-mémoire* of 4/17 December; A 769, Beilage.

protection of their national and economic independence. This statement, although accepted by the Octobrists and the Cadets, aroused no enthusiasm. Certainly there was not much reason for hoping that a Balkan league could ever be effected, and three years were to pass before it became a reality.[1]

By thus attempting to transform the dispute from an Austro-Russian controversy into an issue affecting all the Powers[2]—and a long circular setting forth the Russian point of view was at once issued[3]—Izvolsky thought to put Aehrenthal in a dilemma; for Great Britain had made her recognition of the annexation dependent on an Austro-Turkish agreement,[4] which was not yet in sight, and he appealed to Grey to urge "an equitable adjustment of the situation" on Aehrenthal.[5] But once more the Russian minister had not sufficiently reckoned with the resourcefulness of his antagonist. Aehrenthal did not relish Izvolsky's demand that Austria-Hungary explain her position to the Powers;[6] so, without asking for the latter's consent, he transmitted to the cabinets not only his own notes of 14 November and 8 December, but the Russian ones of 22 November and 17 December, adding that

it appears from these documents that the Imperial and Royal government continues to observe a sympathetic attitude with respect to the meeting of a conference on the affairs of the Balkans; the reservations which it believed that it had to formulate concerning its acceptance

---

[1] Grey thought the speech "very satisfactory", especially the emphasis on "the need for community of feeling between the Balkan states and the combination of all three of them with Turkey for defence of common interests". "I am quite in favour of this", he said, "and will encourage it whenever I can" (Grey to Nicolson, telegram, 28 December; B 493). Aehrenthal did not regard Izvolsky's hints of a Balkan league as "particularly dangerous" (Aehrenthal to Szögyény, private, 2 January; A 828), and Bülow described them as a "fanfaronade" which he had "not for one moment taken seriously" (Bülow to Aehrenthal, private, 8 January; G 9302; A 861).

[2] Izvolsky said to Pourtalès: "Ce n'est pas une question qui regarde seule l'Autriche et la Russie: c'est une question entre l'Autriche et l'Europe" (Pourtalès to Bülow, 19 December; G 9162).

[3] Izvolsky to Russian ambassadors in Berlin, Vienna, Paris, London, Rome, and Constantinople, 6/19 December; A 780; B 488, annex.

[4] Grey to Goschen, 26 October; B 407: Mensdorff to Aehrenthal, 30 October, 27 November; A 453, 661. Cf. Hardinge to Nicolson, private, 28 October; B 414.

[5] Izvolsky to Benckendorff, telegram, 21 December; B 488.

[6] Tschirschky to Bülow, 21 December; G 9163.

were dictated only by the intention to make the work of the conference as effective as possible.[1]

And when he received the Russian circular with its proposal of substituting for Article 25 of the Treaty of Berlin "a new stipulation defining in a precise manner the new situation of these two provinces", he replied with a *fin de non-recevoir*:

In the eyes of the cabinet of Vienna, this new situation can obviously be only that created for Bosnia and Herzegovina by the proclamation of his Imperial and Royal Apostolic Majesty dated 5 October.[2]

But this was not the worst of it. Since the Austrian note of 8 December stated that "the cabinet of St Petersburg had taken the initiative" in the conversations relating to Bosnia and had promised to observe "a friendly attitude", Izvolsky's reputation with the other Powers was at stake.[3]

The Russian minister did not conceal his irritation,[4] and when Aehrenthal professed not to understand this,[5] protested against the communication of the Russian note of 17 December which referred to the secret Austro-Russian agreement of 1897.[6]

[1] Circular of 23 December; A 790; B 491; G 9166.

[2] Aehrenthal to Russian chargé d'affaires in Vienna, private, 24 December; A 793.

[3] He told Nicolson that "he especially objected to [Aehrenthal's] having alluded to the pourparlers in June last in a manner which would give the other cabinets to believe that at that date the question of annexation had been debated between the two governments. He doubted if in June last, before even the revolution had occurred in Turkey, Baron d'Aehrenthal had in his mind the intention of annexing the two provinces; though now he apparently desired to make it appear as if Russia had at that date been willing to entertain such a project". Nicolson, with his usual acumen, was not misled. "The preliminary explanations which M. Izvolsky gave me did not seem to me to be quite convincing, as, so far as I could gather, the status of Bosnia and Herzegovina had been mentioned in certain discussions in June last, and it may be that M. Izvolsky committed himself a little further than he is willing to admit" (Nicolson to Grey, 2 January 1909; B 498).

[4] Fürstenberg (chargé d'affaires in St Petersburg) to Aehrenthal, telegram, 24 December; A 794: Pourtalès to foreign office, telegram, 26 December; G 9167.

[5] Aehrenthal to Fürstenberg, telegram, 27 December; A 807. Nicolson commented somewhat sardonically on Izvolsky's irritation: "There must be a considerable literature of an interesting character in the private archives of Vienna and St Petersburg; and it must be a bore when one conspirator gives away his accomplice" (H. Nicolson, *Sir Arthur Nicolson, Bart., first Lord Carnock* [London, 1930], p. 294).

[6] Fürstenberg to Aehrenthal, telegram, 28 December, and despatch, 1 January, 1909; A 813, 826. Incidentally, Izvolsky repudiated Aehrenthal's

Several days later, to the vast astonishment of the Austro-Hungarian chargé d'affaires, Izvolsky dictated a statement to the effect that the tsar had been "painfully surprised" by the action of the Austro-Hungarian minister, for he considered the agreement of 1897 "un pacte personnel entre les deux souverains", and Aehrenthal's conduct showed "un manque d'égards envers sa personne". The tsar had therefore ordered that "henceforth the Imperial cabinet should confine itself to strictly official communications with that of Vienna".[1] To make matters worse, the tsar, on the same day, despatched a letter to Francis Joseph which was a long *réquisitoire* against Aehrenthal and struck a note unusual in the correspondence of sovereigns:

> It is certainly not my business to judge whether the policy of your foreign minister has procured for your empire advantages in proportion to the troubles which it has called forth. But I have to ask myself whether this policy will stop with the perturbations which it has already caused, or whether, indeed, we are on the eve of complications still more dangerous for the general peace.[2]

The Austrian chargé could explain this extraordinary procedure only by Izvolsky's fear that Aehrenthal would resort to more revelations and that the desperate minister had brought his master into the picture in order to seek cover "behind this mighty shield".[3] And it may be noted that Izvolsky appealed to

contention that at Buchlau he had promised to observe a friendly attitude towards the annexation, declaring that he had done so "only with the reservation of his imperial master's consent, which at Buchlau he did not have", and that Aehrenthal's reference to the meeting of the Delegations had been made "only in a quite vague form".

[1] Fürstenberg to Aehrenthal, telegram, 30 December; A 820. Cf. Pourtalès to foreign office, telegram, 30 December; G 9170.

[2] Nicholas II to Francis Joseph, 17/30 December; A 822. Francis Joseph, after some delay, replied in a quiet tone, stating that Aehrenthal had acted with his approval and suggesting that the tsar was not well informed. As regards Serbia and Montenegro, he said, "I have never thought of striking at their independent existence and I cherish no design of conquest at their expense"; but he was determined to repel with the utmost energy "every aggression to which their increasing audacity may lead them" (Francis Joseph to Nicholas II, 28 January; A 935). The promise to respect the integrity of the Serb states was hardly in keeping with the plans formulated by Aehrenthal in the previous summer (see above, p. 12); but, as will be seen later, he had apparently changed his plans.

[3] Fürstenberg to Aehrenthal, 1 January; A 827.

the German government for representations in Vienna to prevent further revelations.[1]

Aehrenthal refused to be impressed by the Russian manœuvre.[2] In his reply, he hinted that he might have revealed much more than he had done, declared that he had not expected his action to be "unacceptable" to the Russian government, and authorized the chargé to put it in writing in case Izvolsky would not receive a verbal communication![3] "Indeed, after the experiences we have had, we have no desire and no interest in continuing a confidential intercourse with M. Izvolsky."[4] Once again Izvolsky had been outplayed. The only result was to cut off communication with Vienna and to encourage Aehrenthal in the conviction that a conference would not be held[5]—while he could proceed to a settlement with Turkey which would make a conference unnecessary. And, in fact, little or nothing was heard about a conference for the next two months.

Nevertheless, the long wrangle had not been brought to an end without some interesting ramifications. Early in December the German Emperor had been somewhat excited by a remark of the tsar to the German military plenipotentiary at his court, Captain von Hintze, to the effect that the aim of his policy was the opening of the Straits "by means of a conference, but not through a separate or secret agreement with the Ottoman Empire".[6]

So, perhaps because of the knowledge that Bülow was in

[1] Schoen to Tschirschky, 7 January; G 9172: Szögyény to Aehrenthal, 4 January; A 839. The German government declined the Russian request.
[2] Tschirschky to Bülow, 2 January; G 9171.
[3] Aehrenthal to Fürstenberg, telegram, 31 December; A 825.
[4] Aehrenthal to Fürstenberg, telegram, 6 January; A 851.
[5] Tschirschky to Bülow, 15 January; G 9176. Bülow had informed Aehrenthal that Germany would participate in a conference only if (1) all the signatories of the Treaty of Berlin did so; (2) complete agreement was reached beforehand between the Powers on the programme to be submitted; and (3) no capital of a great Power was chosen as the place of meeting (Bülow to Tschirschky, 12 January; G 9175: Szögyény to Aehrenthal, telegram, 14 January; A 888). The British government, on the other hand, had accepted the Russian proposals (Grey to Benckendorff, 30 December; B 495). Hardinge, however, assured the Austrian chargé that Great Britain "would make no difficulties" and urged Aehrenthal to come to terms with Turkey (Széchényi to Aehrenthal, telegram, 29 December; A 815).
[6] Pourtalès to foreign office, telegram, 12 December; G 9180.

favour of not actively opposing Russian wishes,[1] he addressed a long personal letter to the chancellor urging that since "the situation is very serious", the Central Powers should be conciliatory to Russia about the Straits: if the matter were skilfully handled, it might be possible "to bring the three imperial Powers closer together and strengthen the monarchical idea".[2] But both Bülow and Schoen, the foreign minister, judged such an overture inopportune, the former opining that Russia should try to break down the opposition of England through the mediation of France,[3] the latter because he feared that Izvolsky "will know how to represent the matter to his master that we are proceeding, not out of affection, but because his bluff has made us afraid".[4] Consequently, Hintze was instructed to speak as follows to the tsar:

It is known to the tsar that we have never made nor shall make difficulties for him in respect of the Straits. On the contrary, we shall gladly support his wishes in this matter. The difficulty lies in London. We should be willing to enter into an exchange of views with Russia on the question whether and how this difficulty is to be overcome.[5]

The tsar, when informed by Hintze, declared that he was "very happy to get such good news" and that he would "write a few lines to His Majesty".[6] And this he proceeded to do, but

[1] Bülow to William II, 1 November; G 9179—suggestions for what William should say to Francis Ferdinand and Francis Joseph, if they raised the question.

[2] William II to Bülow, 13 December; G 9181.

[3] Bülow to William II, 14 December; G 9182. The emperor's marginalia show that he was not convinced by the chancellor's arguments; in his opinion, "the principal thing is to drive a wedge between London and Izvolsky. 'Russia must get the Straits from Vienna and Berlin', those were Bismarck's and Schweinitz' words to me!"

[4] Memorandum of Schoen, 15 December; G 9184.

[5] Telegram to Pourtalès, for Hintze, 16 December; G 9184, note ***.

[6] Hintze to William II, 19 December; G 9185. From Hintze's report, it would appear that the tsar's views had changed somewhat since his first remark. "I want to settle that question legally, by negotiations with the signatories of the Berlin Treaty. Now, if there is to be a conference—I don't know whether there ever will be a conference—but I say, if there is a conference, I shouldn't like to impede, I mean, I don't want to render the heavy task of that conference still heavier by raising the question of the Straits. But in the future, in the near future, I wish this question to be dealt with, and then I shall have great pleasure in availing myself of His Majesty's help. I hope to get the consent of all the interested Powers or, at least, of most of them; of course, Turkey is the Power mostly concerned."

in such a manner as to suggest that he hoped to trade on the good will of Germany to secure pressure on Austria. After thanking William for the promised support on the Straits question and saying: "Now is not the moment for raising that affair, we have got difficulties enough, if I may say so, plenty of diplomatical food to digest for many months to come", he continued:

In my opinion the only danger of the whole political situation lies in this: will there or will there not be war between Austria and Serbia? According to our informations this real danger exists. Baron Aehrenthal, the mischiefmaker, is the only man responsible for all that has happened.... If Austria attacked any of those small countries, you can well imagine the terrible difficulty of my position, having to battle between the voice of my conscience and the heated-up passion of my people. To avoid such a calamity you can be of great help to me. I appeal to our old friendship; if you can make them understand at Vienna that a war down there is *a danger to the peace of Europe*—then war will be avoided! Excuse the frankness and warmth of these lines, but as a true friend, I felt it my duty to expose to you my views and my thoughts in these very serious days we are living through.[1]

This letter was, for obvious reasons, not appreciated by the German government and the German Emperor, and the reply of William II was rather sharp. "We were informed about Austria's intentions", he said, "*even later than you.*" But "once Austria had taken this step [the annexation] without previously consulting us, hesitation as to the course we had to follow was out of the question", for "we could not side with her opponents". He then declared to be "all nonsense" the "rumours" which represented Germany "as resenting and showing uneasiness about your agreement with England concerning Central Asia"

[1] Nicholas II to William II, 15/28 December; G 9187. Several weeks later Izvolsky once more denounced Aehrenthal as the "Störenfried in Europa", who would not make "the slightest concession to Russia" and seemingly "was willing to push matters to the point of war" [*es zum Kriege treiben wolle*]. The German ambassador was not able to reassure the Russian minister or dissuade him "from his *ceterum censeo* that Baron Aehrenthal alone bore the responsibility for everything that was now making Europe uneasy". Pourtalès was particularly struck by Izvolsky's remark: "Do not forget one thing: above all the Eastern Question cannot be solved otherwise than by a conflict" (Pourtalès to Bülow, 16 January; G 9191).

and "the visit Uncle Bertie paid you at Reval" (!). Nevertheless, he proceeded to criticize Russian policy:

It is the patent fact that for the last two years Russian policy has been gradually drawing away from us more and more; evolving always closer towards a combination of Powers unfriendly to us. A triple *entente* between France, Russia and England is being talked of by the whole world as an accomplished fact....

The tendency of Russian policy to lean on England and France was particularly noticeable in the present crisis. Your government approached mine about the Bosnian question only after a programme for the intended conference had been drawn up and agreed upon in London and Paris....

...Had Russia consulted us in the right time, matters wouldn't be in the awful muddle they are in now, nor in such a critical state. Under present circumstances, I don't quite see what I could do, except giving counsels of moderation to both sides, which I have already done.

The only consolation vouchsafed to the tsar was "the impression that your views about Austria's intentions are too pessimistic", for "we, at any rate, have not the slightest doubt that Austria is not going to attack Serbia".[1] In conclusion the emperor promised that "anything I can do in that direction [of a peaceful solution] shall certainly be done".[2]

The statement of the German Emperor that he had given counsels of moderation to both sides was true, for on the occasion of his visit to Vienna he had urged Aehrenthal to keep the

[1] The ambassador in St Petersburg was instructed, in case Izvolsky should ask what Germany would do in the event of an Austrian attack on Serbia, to say that, "we do not believe in such a possibility" and nothing more (Bülow to Pourtalès, 30 January; G 9198). As will be seen later, the German government was actually reckoning with such a possibility.

[2] William II to Nicholas II, 5 January; G 9188. The letter was drafted by the foreign office, which asked that it be sent without alterations. The emperor, however, made numerous stylistic changes. The tsar's reply simply repeated the Russian complaints and fears, but added that "we have not and do not intend settling an agreement with England of a broader scope" (Nicholas II to William II, 12/25 January; G 9194). The Germans were struck by the passage in the tsar's letter in which he said: "I venerate the Emperor [Francis Joseph] deeply; all my resentment is against his minister's reckless policy." Bülow concluded that it would be wise for William to make no answer until "a more favourable psychological moment" had come (Bülow to William II, 29 January; G 9197).

peace if possible,[1] but it did not tell the whole story of Austro-German relations. Early in December Aehrenthal wrote a long private letter to Bülow with the object of orientating the German chancellor about his future plans. He stated that "if, in the course of the next two months, the attitude of Serbia gave occasion for serious complaint, the moment will then arrive when we must come to a more decisive resolution". What that resolution might be, was indicated in the closing sentences of the letter. Stating that "all our preparations for the event of a European conflict are made, as is known, on the basis of the Triple Alliance treaty" and that he did not believe that "in the event of a Russian attack on Austria-Hungary Italy would break her word and place herself on the side of our opponents",[2] Aehrenthal remarked:

I should like to express the opinion that it would perhaps not be superfluous if in the course of the winter General von Moltke and General von Conrad could enter into a written exchange of views about such an eventuality which would take into consideration the supposition of Italian neutrality.[3]

The German chancellor was greatly pleased with Aehrenthal's communication, expressing his complete approval of the latter's policy and declaring his conviction that "the whole crisis can be brought to a good end by firmness [*Festigkeit*] towards Russia and a corresponding conciliatory attitude towards Turkey". He urged Aehrenthal not to let himself be deflected from his course by the opposition of industrial circles in Austria and Hungary,

[1] Jenisch to foreign office, telegram, 7 November; G 9088.

[2] The ambassador in Rome had expressed the opinion that in spite of the irritation with Aehrenthal's policy, Italy would not abandon the Triple Alliance, because otherwise she would become the vassal of France (Lützow to Aehrenthal, 26 October; A 414). Aehrenthal had given Tittoni assurances that Italian wishes in respect of the modification of Article 29 for the benefit of Montenegro would be respected (Aehrenthal to Lützow, telegram, 24 November; A 637). Tittoni described newspaper rumours of a Russo-Italian alliance as a "pure invention" (Lützow to Aehrenthal, telegram, 3 December; A 687).

[3] Aehrenthal to Bülow, private, 8 December; A 703, G 9127, 9145. This was suggested to Aehrenthal by Conrad von Hötzendorf, chief of the general staff, who was an advocate of war with Serbia and had been urging that it be undertaken in the following year (Conrad, *Aus meiner Dienstzeit*, I, 129, 620).

which were suffering from the Turkish boycott; under no circumstances should the Central Powers submit to Russian bluff,
for he, Bülow, was convinced that "neither Izvolsky nor any
other serious Russian statesman was thinking of war", and
France "was firmly determined to keep the peace". Thus German policy, so far from preaching moderation at Vienna, as
William had stated to Nicholas, was speaking for "Festigkeit".
Bülow'also readily agreed to the exchange of views between
Conrad and Moltke.[1] In his reply to Aehrenthal, he expressed
his "satisfaction" with the results thus far achieved, and suggested that if Izvolsky continued to misrepresent matters,
Aehrenthal might resort to further revelations.[2] Bülow and
Aehrenthal knew only too well that they had Izvolsky in a deep
hole—and they intended to keep him there.

The Austrians lost no time in taking advantage of the German
complacency. On New Year's Day, 1909, Conrad von Hötzendorf addressed a letter to General von Moltke, his opposite
number in Berlin, in which he stated that

the possibility must be reckoned with that in the event of an Austro-
Hungarian war in the Balkans Russia will enter upon warlike action
in favour of the opponents of the Monarchy, i.e. mobilize against the
Monarchy.

If Germany then stood by Austria-Hungary "in conformity
with [im Sinne] the treaty of 1879", what would be the German
plan of campaign? In particular, Conrad wished to know what
forces Germany would be able to send against Russia, for that
would determine whether Austria-Hungary might devote her
attention primarily to the Serbian campaign or must concentrate the bulk of her forces in Galicia, and he proposed "a detailed examination" of the situation.[3] What discussions this
letter may have evoked within the German government we do
not know; the only available record is Moltke's reply, in which
he revealed that the German plan would be to "launch the
principal mass of the German forces first against France" and

---

[1] Szögyény to Aehrenthal, telegram, despatch and private letter, 16
December; A 751, 752, 753. Cf. Bülow to Tschirschky, 15 December; G 9156.
[2] Bülow to Aehrenthal, private, 8 January; G 9175; A 861.
[3] Conrad to Moltke, 1 January 1909; Conrad, I, 631–4.

invited "a further exposition" of the Austrian views.[1] The
general, however, did not stop with such military technicalities,
but raised political questions of the highest import. He wrote:

It is to be anticipated that the moment may come when the patience
of the Monarchy towards the Serbian provocations will come to an
end. Then there will be hardly anything left for the Monarchy to do
but to march into Serbia.

I believe that only [*erst*] an Austrian invasion of Serbia could bring
about an eventual active intervention of Russia. This would create
the *casus fœderis* for Germany. The joint military action which would
then begin would—according to the statement of your Excellency—
rest on the basis that at first Austria can concentrate only 30 divisions
in Galicia against Russia.

At the same moment that Russia mobilizes, Germany will also
mobilize and will mobilize her entire army.[2]

This language, which Moltke stated was held with the "knowledge" (i.e. approval) of the German Emperor and his chancellor, could only mean what it said, namely, that if Austria-
Hungary, as a result of attacking Serbia, found herself at war
with Russia, Germany would come to her assistance. In the days
of Bismarck, the German government constantly warned its ally
against a policy of adventure in the Balkans which might provoke
Russia and declined responsibility for the consequences. No
doubt the situation had changed since the 'eighties: Austria's
problem in respect of Bulgaria was quite different from that
with which Serbia presented her, and Germany's position in the
constellation of European Powers was less predominant. But so
far as can be seen from Moltke's letter or other documents, the
German government did not question the wisdom of an invasion
of Serbia; it left the decision to the cabinet of Vienna, and was
prepared, in the event of that policy being adopted, to accept the
consequences. Nor was the matter a mere private understanding
between the two generals. Two days after Moltke's letter was
written, William II, commenting on a letter of Francis Joseph to

[1] As the result of a correspondence extending over several months, it
was agreed that 13 German divisions should be retained in East Prussia while
the German armies invaded France and that the Austro-Hungarian army
should invade Russia from Galicia (Conrad, I, 384–406).

[2] Moltke to Conrad, 21 January, 1909; Conrad, I, 379–84.

himself, in which the Austrian ruler had expressed his "warmest satisfaction and most sincere appreciation" of the diplomatic support of the German government,[1] stated that he would answer the letter soon and that this exchange stood in "fortunate correlation" with the letters exchanged by the chiefs of staff.[2] Aehrenthal, for his part, declared that he did not doubt that in the event of a crisis, Germany's attitude would be in conformity with the "loyal and binding declaration" given by the German Emperor, Prince Bülow and General von Moltke.[3]  In other words, the letters of the chiefs of staff constituted an official negotiation, and the Austro-Hungarian government, if it should decide on an invasion of Serbia, could count on the support of Germany to the utmost limit.[4]  Henceforth there was no reason why Aehrenthal should make any concession to Izvolsky, even if he threatened war. That "a firm block in the heart of Europe" offered "the greatest and most precious guarantee for the maintenance of peace in Europe", as William II assured Francis Joseph,[5] was true in the sense that Russia would be discouraged from resorting to arms in support of Serbia.  But in the long run, the German sanction of an invasion of Serbia was to prove as disastrous to the peace of Europe as the Russian decision to keep Serbia quiet by holding out hopes of assistance in the future.

If the combination of Austria-Hungary and Germany momentarily assured their ascendancy in Europe, the position of Italy, the third member of the Triple Alliance, had been reduced to

[1] Francis Joseph to William II, 18 January; A 900, G 9192.

[2] Szögyény to Aehrenthal, telegram, 23 January; A 920.

[3] Aehrenthal to Bülow, private, 20 February; A 1022; G 9386.

[4] In his *Denkwürdigkeiten*, II, 404-6, Bülow prided himself on having restrained Conrad and the Austrian generals from an attack on Serbia, but the official documents hardly bear out his contention. Hermann Oncken, *Das Deutsche Reich und die Vorgeschichte des.Weltkrieges* (Leipzig, 1933), II, 643-4, agrees with the interpretation given in the text above and declines to commit himself on the much-debated question whether the "exchange of views" between the two generals [*Meinungsaustausch*] should be called a "military convention", as was contended by the late Dr Heinrich Kanner and denied by most German writers and by S. B. Fay, *The origins of the World War* (New York, 1928), II, 509-10, 514. Oncken argues, however, that "*trotz der weiterreichenden Vertragsauslegung*" [my italics—B. E. S.] the German government still kept its freedom to restrain the aggressive policy of its ally, and that it did so. Certainly it did so in 1912-13—but not in 1914.

[5] William II to Francis Joseph, 26 January; G 9193; A 926.

futility. The complete lack of Italian documents[1] makes it impossible to write of Italian policy with any authoritativeness, but the passing references to the attitude and action of the Italian foreign minister[2] have shown that Tittoni's policy had been hesitant, inconsistent and equivocal. He had blown hot and cold about the conference; he had, in the main, supported the contentions of Aehrenthal, but had got nothing in return, and had therefore played with the idea of a flirtation with Russia. Unfortunately for him, he had agreed in principle to the annexation of Bosnia, but his countrymen had not. When the Austrian *coup* was announced, the latent anti-Austrian sentiments of the people flared up, and in many cities meetings were held denouncing the policy of Tittoni and demanding his resignation. The foreign minister did not dare or desire to break with the Triple Alliance; he was not strong enough to calm public opinion or to prevent a serious demonstration in Rome at the end of November. In the circumstances, it was probably natural that he should trim, but the result was that Aehrenthal treated him with polite contempt while the other Powers practically ignored him.

When parliament met on 1 December, the excitement had reached such a pitch that four "historic days" (as they were promptly dubbed) were given over to the debate on foreign affairs. The high point was the speech of Alessandro Forti, a former premier, who demanded that Austria-Hungary abandon her condescending attitude towards Italy. "The only Power", he cried, "with which war is to be feared is Austria, our ally, whose armaments are directed against Italy", and he called for an increase of Italian armaments. A tremendous demonstration greeted these defiant words; the premier, Giolitti, shook the orator's hand, and it seemed for a moment as if Tittoni's fate was sealed. But the foreign minister defended himself with vigour. The evacuation of the Sandjak and the complete independence of Montenegro were, he argued, concessions by Austria which had cost Italy nothing, and the *rapprochement*

---

[1] The important work of Francesco Tomassini, *L'Italia alla vigilia della guerra: la politica di Tommaso Tittoni* (Bologna, 1934–　), which is based on the Italian archives, has unfortunately not yet reached the period of the Bosnian crisis.

[2] See above, pp. 14, 26, 43, 60, 70.

with Russia was "an accomplished fact which will not fail to have important consequences in the future".[1] Since even the leaders of the opposition, Sonnino and Barzilai, admitted that the Triple Alliance must remain the base of Italy's foreign policy,[2] Tittoni received a vote of confidence from both houses. Nevertheless, the *malaise* which dominated Austro-Italian relations was not dissipated, for the vote also called for an increase of Italian armaments. At the moment, however, Aehrenthal had more pressing problems on his hands than Italian discontent and apparently paid no attention to it.[3]

[1] The speech is given in English translation in Baron Bernardo Quaranta di San Severino, *Italy's foreign and colonial policy: Senator Tommaso Tittoni* (London, 1914), pp. 121–51.

[2] In 1914 Barzilai was to become one of the most ardent advocates of Italian intervention in the Great War, and it was Sonnino who in 1915 denounced the Triple Alliance.

[3] At any rate there are no documents in A relating to the debate.

# CHAPTER VIII

## The Austro-Turkish Agreement

WHEN BARON AEHRENTHAL decided on the annexation of Bosnia, it was with the expectation that Turkey would not be able to offer effective resistance,[1] and in the notification addressed to the Porte he said not a word about negotiation or compensation.[2] Since at that moment he was counting on Russian support for his policy, his calculations were perhaps justified. But the Turkish government would have had to renounce a most venerable tradition if it had not taken advantage of the rift between Aehrenthal and Izvolsky to drive a hard bargain with Austria-Hungary. Furthermore, it had been informed by the Powers of the Entente that "the Treaty of Berlin cannot be modified without an agreement between the Signatory Powers".[3] So, after the first feelings of indignation had died down,[4] the Porte took the position that while it was prepared to reconcile itself with the *fait accompli* in Bosnia (without, however, recognizing the legality of the annexation), it must be compensated for the loss of the Bulgarian tribute and declared that it would assert its rights over Eastern Rumelia if necessary by military action.[5] This attitude was, to say the least, exceedingly awkward for Aehrenthal, not only because he had encouraged Bulgaria to action,[6] but also because, if a conference met to discuss the Bulgarian problem, as the Turks desired, a debate on Bosnia-Herzegovina would be difficult to avoid. He therefore hinted to Constantinople that he might no longer be able to use

---

[1] See above, pp. 16, 18.
[2] Aehrenthal to Pallavicini, 30 September, Anlage, 1; A 99.
[3] Grey to Lowther, telegram, 9 October; B 347.
[4] See above, pp. 45–6.
[5] Lowther to Grey, telegram, 12 October; B 362: Pallavicini to Aehrenthal, telegrams, 12, 14 October; A 254, 275: Marschall to foreign office, telegram, 12 October; G 9032. The Porte was also anxious that the question of the Straits should be excluded from the conference; on this point and its settlement, see above, pp. 46, 51, 53.
[6] See above, pp. 30–31.

his influence at Sofia "in favour of friendly relations with Turkey"(!).[1]

The British government, on the other hand, showed much sympathy with Turkey. Sir Edward Grey, indeed, advised the Porte not to stand on "questions of form" involving Eastern Rumelia and Crete, but he agreed that "satisfactory compensation must be given to Turkey in money indemnity" for the recognition of Bulgarian independence; he declared that whatever compensations might be accorded to Serbia and Montenegro, "they should get no advantages at the expense of Turkey", and he gave assurances that the question of the Straits would not be mentioned in the programme of the conference. He promised, in short, that "we shall do our utmost to ensure that at any conference Turkey shall get as much substance as possible".[2] He even went so far as to say that "the suggested programme still depends upon Turkey's consent".[2]

Not for a long time had the Porte been treated with such consideration, and it naturally tried to exploit the situation. While delighted by the news that the question of the Straits would not be raised,[3] it declared that the programme for a conference showed "much good will" for Turkey, but "little that was useful". Financial questions were of secondary interest; what was needed was protection against "aggressive tendencies of Bulgaria" and a territorial guarantee.[4] Since the British and German ambassadors appeared receptive to this latter idea, a Turkish counter-programme was elaborated which demanded a guarantee for "the European territories of Turkey", in order to prevent Bulgaria from raising the Macedonian question.[5] At the same time clever negotiations were strung out with the Austro-Hungarian ambassador, Marquis Pallavicini, which reduced that gentleman almost to despair.

A few days after the announcement of the annexation, the

[1] Aehrenthal to Pallavicini, telegram, 16 October; A 296.
[2] Grey to Lowther, telegrams, 13, 16 October, despatch, 15 October; B 370, 376, note 1, 388, 383.
[3] Marschall to foreign office, telegram, 16 October; G 9047. Tewfik Pasha, the foreign minister, said that Turkey would not follow up the British hint of coming to an understanding with Russia about the Straits.
[4] Marschall to foreign office, telegrams, 17, 19 October; G 9049, 9054.
[5] Marschall to foreign office, telegram, 21 October; G 9203.

Young Turks had organized a boycott of Austro-Hungarian goods and shipping, which spread rapidly throughout the country.[1] Pallavicini made repeated protests and received promises of official intervention,[2] but the boycott continued none the less.[3] He was not more successful in persuading the Porte to withdraw its protest against the annexation, even though Aehrenthal was prepared to give a declaration to the effect that Austria-Hungary "considère donc le Sandjak comme faisant—sans aucune re-striction—partie de l'Empire Ottoman dont elle désire maintenir l'intégrité de concert avec les autres Puissances".[4] The grand vizier and the foreign minister insisted on referring all sugges-tions to the council of ministers,[5] which finally rejected them.[6] Not only that: the Turkish programme for the conference, when finally communicated to Pallavicini, contained "the question of Bosnia-Herzegovina" as one of its four items![7] German insinua-tions that a conference might awaken "dangerous aspirations and appetites (those of the Serbs, Montenegrins, Greeks, per-haps even of the Italians)" and also "the desires of the Armenians and Albanians for independence"[8] were rejected with the blunt statements that "the Bulgarian question is insoluble without a conference"[9] and that Great Britain would protect Turkey from the disadvantages of a conference.[10]

[1] Eyres to Grey, 10 October; B 357. Pallavicini to Aehrenthal, telegram, 12 October; A 253. The boycott was directed exclusively against Austrian, as distinct from Hungarian, goods, with the hope of exciting Hungarian opinion against the annexation (Pallavicini to Aehrenthal, 21 October; A 354).
[2] Pallavicini to Aehrenthal, telegrams, 10, 12, 15, 16, 19 October; A 224, 254, 286, 298, 334.
[3] Pallavicini to Aehrenthal, telegram, 31 October; A 467.
[4] Aehrenthal to Pallavicini, telegram, 19 October; A 332. Aehrenthal's insistence on an exchange of notes was not approved of by Pallavicini (Marschall to foreign office, telegram, 19 October; G 9201) or by his chief of section Müller (Tschirschky to foreign office, telegram, 21 October; G 9206); Marschall also thought that Aehrenthal was asking too much (Marschall to foreign office, telegrams, 21, 22 October; G 9207, 9208).
[5] Pallavicini to Aehrenthal, telegrams, 15, 16, 17, 19, 20 October; A 285, 299, 309, 333, 343.
[6] Pallavicini to Aehrenthal, telegram, 22 October; A 363.
[7] Pallavicini to Aehrenthal, telegram, 24 October; A 384.
[8] Bülow to Marschall, telegram, 22 October; G 9205.
[9] Marschall to foreign office, telegram, 23 October; G 9209.
[10] Marschall to foreign office, telegram, 24 October; G 9212. Marschall admitted to Pallavicini that "at the moment his influence in Constantinople

The Turkish resistance was ascribed by the Austro-Hungarian and German ambassadors to British influence;[1] the British ambassador, Sir Gerald Lowther, was supposed to have promised full moral and financial support to the Porte and to have said that "the British government could not understand why Turkey was conducting direct negotiations with Austria-Hungary".[2] Sir Edward Grey denied the charge to both the Austrian and German ambassadors in London,[3] and it was, strictly speaking, unfounded, as can be seen from his instructions to his ambassador in Constantinople:

We have no desire to put obstacles in the way of a direct arrangement between Austria and Turkey, and if Austria ever make an arrangement satisfactory to Turkey I do not anticipate any difficulty in its being recognized by the Powers. But the difficulty of conciliating public opinion is one which Austria has herself created by her arbitrary procedure. It is therefore not for us to advise Turkey to condone what has been done but for Austria to smooth the path by offering what terms she can to make the agreement she desires attractive to Turkish opinion.[4]

Obviously, however, the knowledge that Great Britain was not advising an acceptance of the *fait accompli* was sufficient to stiffen the Turkish opposition. In fact, Grey was informed that "the Turkish government placed more confidence in us than in other Powers, and would certainly not come to any decisions about the present questions without taking my advice".[5] To

---

was reduced to a minimum" (Pallavicini to Aehrenthal, telegram, 24 October; A 383); personally, he favoured a conference, hoping thereby, so Pallavicini thought, to regain his influence (Pallavicini to Aehrenthal, telegram, 25 October; A 398).

[1] Pallavicini to Aehrenthal, telegram, 23 October; Szögyény to Aehrenthal, telegram, 25 October; A 373, 394: Marschall to foreign office, telegrams, 24 October; G 9211, 9212. Pallavicini subsequently modified his opinion and laid the responsibility on the declaration of the Entente Powers and Italy that all changes in the Treaty of Berlin must be ratified by the Powers (Pallavicini to Aehrenthal, telegram, 25 October, despatch, 28 October; A 405, 439).

[2] Tschirschky to foreign office, telegram, 25 October; G 9213.

[3] Grey to Goschen, 26 October; Grey to De Salis, 26 October; B 407, 408: Mensdorff to Aehrenthal, telegram, 26 October; A 408: Metternich to foreign office, telegram, 26 October; G 9219.

[4] Grey to Lowther, telegram, 24 October; B 402. Cf. Burisch, *Englands Haltung und die Annexionskrise*, pp. 26–8.

[5] Grey to Lowther, 26 October; B 406.

prove it, the grand vizier, Kiamil Pasha, who was traditionally Anglophile, actually asked Grey's opinion of a plan by which Bosnia and Herzegovina were "to be created into an independent principality, governed by a Protestant prince belonging to some neutral state, selected by the Powers and facilitated by Turkey"![1] He also proposed to make an offensive and defensive alliance with Serbia, with which state he was indeed negotiating at the moment.[2]

Against such an exaltation of spirit, Pallavicini was helpless.[3] Renewed German representations against the dangers of a conference[4] evoked the stereotyped reply that the conference offered "the only effective means of pressure" on Bulgaria,[5] and Bosnia was retained as one of the items of the Turkish programme.[6] But the Austrian ambassador had not waited for this declaration to shift his position. Convinced that the Turks would not recognize the annexation without compensation, but that at the same time they would gladly do so if compensated, he had already urged Aehrenthal to make them an offer, such as to take over a part of the Turkish state debt,[7] at which Tewfik Pasha had been hinting for some time,[8] and to enter into negotiations with the Young Turks at Salonica.[9]

The chief of the central committee of the Young Turks, Enver Bey, apparently at the request of the grand vizier himself,[10] had in fact approached the Austrian consul-general at Salonica, Rappoport, with a suggestion for an exchange of views.[11] Since Aehrenthal was still deeply involved in his controversy with Izvolsky, and Grey was maintaining his position, while the Serbs were reported to be negotiating with the Turks, it is hardly surprising that the Austrian minister, in spite of previous

---

[1] Lowther to Grey, telegram, 26 October; B 404. B does not contain Grey's reply.
[2] See above, pp. 66–7.
[3] Pallavicini to Aehrenthal, telegrams, 26 October; A 405, 407.
[4] Bülow to Marschall, telegrams, 27 October, 1 November; G 9217, 9222.
[5] Marschall to foreign office, telegram, 2 November; G 9223.
[6] Pallavicini to Aehrenthal, telegram, 1 November; A 480.
[7] Pallavicini to Aehrenthal, telegram, 25 October; A 398.
[8] Marschall to foreign office, telegram, 16 October; G 9200.
[9] Pallavicini to Aehrenthal, telegram, 27 October; A 426.
[10] Pallavicini to Aehrenthal, telegram, 28 October; A 438.
[11] Rappoport to Aehrenthal, telegram, 26 October; A 415.

refusals to negotiate, now decided to do so,[1] although he could not bring himself to offer any financial compensation.[2] Financial compensation, however, was the first item in a programme of nine points which Enver submitted to Rappoport,[3] and although the governor of Salonica, Hilmi Pasha, expressed the hope that this might be eliminated,[4] the grand vizier dispelled any doubts by saying frankly that if Austria would take over part of the state debt, "the affair would be settled at once".[5] Aehrenthal tried to parry this hint by a vague reference to "concessions to be granted in the economic field" for the development of Turkish commerce and industry,[6] and informed Rappoport that financial compensation for recognition of the annexation was "out of the question".[7] Kiamil listened politely, but did not commit himself.[8] Meanwhile the boycott continued, the Young Turk press insisting that Austria must take over part of the debt.[9]

For weeks the deadlock continued. Pallavicini was forced to admit that he had misjudged the situation, failing to foresee the intensity of the Turkish opposition; he declared that Kiamil was helpless in the matter of the boycott,[10] and urged Aehrenthal to

[1] Aehrenthal to Pallavicini, telegram, 28 October; A 437.
[2] Aehrenthal to Rappoport, telegram, 28 October; A 443.
[3] Rappoport to Aehrenthal, telegram, 30 October; A 459. The other points were: (2) renunciation of all rights in the Sandjak; (3) assumption of an obligation to insure the integrity of Turkey in Europe against any attack; favourable treatment of Moslems in Bosnia in respect of their personal status and the administration of the *vakouf*; (5) renunciation of the Austrian protectorate in Albania; (6) abolition of Austro-Hungarian post offices; (7) increase of the Turkish customs to 15 per cent.; (8) recognition of the Turkish rights to establish monopolies for matches, cards, cigarette papers and petroleum; (9) recognition of the right to introduce taxes on patents, and reservation of the right later to revise the capitulations. It will be seen that the final agreement of 26 February 1909 secured all of these except the guarantee of European Turkey.
[4] Rappoport to Aehrenthal, telegram, 31 October; A 473.
[5] Pallavicini to Aehrenthal, telegram, 2 November; A 482.
[6] Aehrenthal to Pallavicini, 4 November; A 496.
[7] Aehrenthal to Rappoport, telegram, 6 November; A 515.
[8] Pallavicini to Aehrenthal, telegram, 9 November; A 536. Pallavicini was convinced that the British and French ambassadors were preventing an Austro-Turkish agreement, but he admitted that their German colleague was also anxious to secure more compensation for Turkey (Pallavicini to Aehrenthal, private, 4 November; A 498).
[9] Pallavicini to Aehrenthal, telegrams, 12, 13, 14 November; A 557, 563, 570.
[10] Lowther (Lowther to Grey, telegram, 23 November; B 458) and Marschall (Marschall to foreign office, telegram, 23 November; G 9232) confirmed this.

take the initiative with concessions.[1] But the proud minister, though willing to discuss such economic concessions as the increase of Turkish customs and the abolition of Austrian post offices,[2] insisted that the boycott must be stopped before official negotiations could be undertaken.[3] Persuaded by the discussions at Salonica that Hilmi desired an agreement with the Monarchy,[4] Aehrenthal finally instructed Pallavicini to let the negotiations drag along until Hilmi should become grand vizier.[5] The Porte for its part rubbed in its intransigeance by despatching a circular telegram to the Powers giving its reply to the programme for a conference proposed by the Entente Powers. Point 3 was thus phrased:

> Bosnie-Herzégovine : les droits à garantir au Gouvernement Ottoman dans le cas où les Puissances jugeraient indispensable de modifier la position juridique de ces Provinces.[6]

Aehrenthal interpreted this to mean that Turkey wished Austria to take over a part of the state debt,[7] but the grand vizier explained to the German ambassador that he wished Bosnia-Herzegovina to become an autonomous province "under a vali named by the Powers and confirmed by the Sultan".[8] In general, the Turkish tactics were to let Tewfik seem ready to make concessions, which Kiamil subsequently withdrew, a game they could play the more safely because, while Marschall went

---

[1] Pallavicini to Aehrenthal, telegrams, 16, 19, 22 November, private letter, 18 November; A 586, 621, 624, 600. He threatened Kiamil that he would go on leave if the boycott were not stopped, and asked Aehrenthal's approval of this course (Pallavicini to Aehrenthal, telegrams, 23, 25 November; A 632, 642): but the German foreign office advised against such a step (Szögyény to Aehrenthal, telegram, 27 November; A 657), and the irate ambassador agreed to remain at his post, in view of the negotiations at Salonica, although he thought the time had come for " serious measures " (Pallavicini to Aehrenthal, telegrams, 27, 28 November; A 657, 667).

[2] Aehrenthal to Pallavicini, 19 November; A 606, 607.

[3] Aehrenthal to Pallavicini, telegrams, 14, 21 November; A 569, 621.

[4] Rappoport to Aehrenthal, telegrams, 17, 28 November; A 593, 671, 672.

[5] Aehrenthal to Pallavicini, telegram, 30 November; A 679.

[6] Telegram of 18 November; A 601. Summary in Grey to Bertie, telegram, 20 November; B 456.

[7] Aehrenthal to Pallavicini, telegram, 21 November; A 620. Cf. Tschirschky to Bülow, 30 November; G 9235.

[8] Marschall to foreign office, telegram, 23 November; G 9232: Szögyény to Aehrenthal, telegram, 24 November; A 634.

through the form of supporting Pallavicini's protests against the boycott, they knew that he sympathized with them and wished them to get compensation.

Aehrenthal held out until early in December, when he finally recognized that circumstances were too strong for him. The boycott was maintained and extended, and it became clear that the Young Turks, whom Aehrenthal expected to play off against Kiamil, were using this means as a lever for greater concessions.[1] Kiamil, as usual, promised action,[2] but the police could or would do nothing.[3] Pallavicini, instructed to get in touch with Hilmi Pasha, who had become minister of the interior,[4] found that gentleman full of fair promises;[5] but the ambassador was convinced that Hilmi could do nothing until he became grand vizier.[6] After a last desperate effort to impress the Porte by sending his dragoman instead of calling personally on the grand vizier,[7] the ambassador had to report that the situation was hopeless. In a single day 5000 new members had joined the boycott organization. The press was saying that Austria was about to capitulate, for Pallavicini's failure to leave after threatening to do so was interpreted as a sign of weakness. Things would change only "wenn wir Ernst zeigen", and he therefore asked permission to depart on 9 December and to make clear that this was intended as "a first step towards the rupture of relations".[8]

At the moment, Aehrenthal was toying with the idea of claiming damages from Turkey for the losses resulting from the boycott,[9] and he informed Bülow that he intended to resist the

[1] Giesl to Pallavicini, 28 November (an interesting report by the military attaché of a conversation with the organizers of the boycott); Pallavicini to Aehrenthal, 4 December; A 680, 688.
[2] Pallavicini to Aehrenthal, telegram, 1 December; A 683.
[3] Pallavicini to Aehrenthal, telegram, 3 December; A 686.
[4] Aehrenthal to Pallavicini, telegram, 3 December; A 685.
[5] Pallavicini to Aehrenthal, telegram, 7 December; A 699.
[6] Pallavicini to Aehrenthal, private, 4 December; A 690.
[7] Pallavicini to Aehrenthal, telegrams, 5 December; A 693, 694.
[8] Pallavicini to Aehrenthal, telegram, 6 December; A 698.
[9] Aehrenthal to Pallavicini, telegram, 8 December; A 704. The claim was to be based on article 6 of the Austro-Turkish commercial treaty of 1862, which provided that Austrian goods and produce "seront admis comme antérieurement dans toutes les parties de l'Empire Ottoman sans aucune exception". During the boycott it had been impossible to land goods from Austrian ships.

demand for compensation, believing that "the leading Young Turkish groups will have to become reasonable as soon as they see that we shall not let ourselves be intimidated".[1] Nevertheless, without waiting to hear Pallavicini's opinion on the advisability of claiming damages, on the following day, 9 December, he modified his instructions and declared that, although he would maintain his position in respect of the boycott, he was ready to negotiate "for the purpose of reaching a general understanding".[2] Evidently the minister felt it useless to resist the pressure being exerted on him from two sides, silently from London, actively from Berlin.

At the end of October, Count Mensdorff, the ambassador in London, had been unable to move Grey from the position that "compensation should be offered Turkey and the new regime for the 'moral injury' suffered",[3] and at the beginning of December he had to report that "Grey will not depart" from this position, adding, however, that the British government was not inciting Turkey and would be glad if an agreement could be reached.[4] Grey offered no advice to Aehrenthal, but the fact that King Edward avoided talking with Mensdorff about the question[5] was more eloquent than formal representations. How effective these tactics were can be gauged from the intense irritation which Aehrenthal was presently to display. It is worth noting that the sharp criticism of the Turkish attitude addressed by Bülow to the British ambassador in Berlin, with which was coupled a suggestion that Great Britain "should advise Ottoman

[1] Aehrenthal to Bülow, private, 8 December; A 703; G 9243.
[2] Aehrenthal to Pallavicini, telegram, 9 December; A 708. Pallavicini replied that the Belgian minister had protested to the Porte against the refusal to unload Belgian goods from Austrian ships and received the answer that the Porte had no responsibility for the unloading of ships. The ambassador therefore thought that an Austrian demand would have to be "a kind of ultimatum", unless Austria were willing to take over part of the state debt—in which case "the question of the annexation would be solved immediately and also the boycott would come to an end" (Pallavicini to Aehrenthal, telegram, 9 December; A 709).
[3] Mensdorff to Aehrenthal, 30 October; A 453.
[4] Mensdorff to Aehrenthal, private, 5 December; A 695. Cf. Mensdorff to Aehrenthal, 27 November; A 661.
[5] Mensdorff to Aehrenthal, 3 November; A 489.

government to be more reasonable",[1] only led Grey to reaffirm his position.[2]

But if the German government took a strong line with Great Britain, it was beginning apparently to be worried by Aehrenthal's attitude. Marschall reported from Constantinople that the departure of Pallavicini would not intimidate the Turks, but only embitter them; "Young Turkish circles are talking of a war with Austria, as if the chances were in favour of Turkey", for they were counting on the British fleet to protect the coasts on a Balkan rising. If, said the ambassador, Aehrenthal clung to his notion of "no negotiations without previous stopping of the boycott", then he was surely heading for a rupture and "incalculable complications".[3] Marschall's telegram was transmitted to Vienna, his observations being declared "quite worth considering", Aehrenthal was definitely advised to come to terms with Turkey, and the suggestion was made that compensation might be granted to Turkey on the ground that the revenues of Bosnia had now been "definitively" acquired by Austria.[4] The Austrian minister admitted that it was necessary "d'entrer dans des pourparlers" with the Turks and promised to think over the instructions which were being drafted for Pallavicini.[5] On the

[1] Goschen (transferred from Vienna to Berlin early in November) to Grey, telegram, 25 November; B 460. Cf. Kiderlen to Metternich, 30 November; G 9223.

[2] Grey to Goschen, telegram, 26 November; B 465. Aehrenthal had also learned that no help was to be expected from France. Relying on the service rendered at the time of the Casablanca incident (Aehrenthal to Khevenhüller, private, 19 November; A 611), when Francis Joseph had urged William II not to press matters too far, the Austrian minister requested that French influence be used in Constantinople to stop the boycott (Aehrenthal to Khevenhüller, telegram, 24 November; A 636). In view of the French sympathy with Turkey and the advantage which the French were taking of the boycott, Khevenhüller refrained from making an official request (Khevenhüller to Aehrenthal, 28 November; A 670), but Crozier, the French ambassador in Vienna, expressed to Aehrenthal the opinion that the boycott would cease if the plan for a conference were accepted! (Aehrenthal to Khevenhüller, telegram, 29 November; A 674). The German ambassador, in reporting to Berlin the failure of this attempt to "win over France and draw her away from England", remarked that Aehrenthal's conduct of affairs was evoking discontent "in the widest circles" (Tschirschky to Bülow, 29 November; G 9234). [3] Marschall to foreign office, telegram, 5 December; G 9239.

[4] Schoen to Tschirschky, 6 December; Bülow to Tschirschky, 6 December; G 9240 and note **. Cf. a memorandum of Kiderlen, 8 December; G 9241.

[5] Tschirschky to Bülow, 8 December; G 9242.

following day, as already noted, Pallavicini was authorized to begin negotiations,[1] although Aehrenthal still held out against pecuniary compensation.[2] Thus in the course of two months the minister who had expected to crush the opposition of Turkey by affecting to minimize or ignore it had been beaten by those tactics of passive resistance traditionally employed by the Porte, tactics which were obviously approved by Great Britain and probably also by the German ambassador in Constantinople.

In order to effect his change of front with as little loss of face as possible, Aehrenthal sent to Constantinople an elaborate note setting forth the Austrian case for damages on the basis of the commercial treaty of 1862 and containing this passage:

> Si donc le Gouvernement Impérial ne savait, pour une raison ou pour une autre, assurer l'exécution pleine et entière de cette obligation dont il reconnaît lui-même le bien-fondé,[3] le Gouvernement I. et R. se verrait contraint à s'en tenir au Gouvernement I. Ottoman et à le rendre responsable des dommages et préjudices que les ressortissants autrichiens et hongrois ainsi que le trafic et la navigation des deux États de la Monarchie ont eu à souffrir à la suite du boycottage.[4]

When handing over the note, however, Pallavicini was to declare that he was empowered to begin negotiations for a settlement of the political questions; in other words, the two issues were to be treated simultaneously but separately. While the *démarche* would have to be made to Kiamil, contact was to be maintained with Hilmi, with whom, it was hoped, the negotiations would finally be concluded.[5] As regards the debt, the ambassador was instructed to discourage any raising of the question, on the ground that Austria would have to put forward counter-demands, such as the cost of maintaining her troops in the Sandjak for thirty years and of assisting the Bosnian refugees of 1878; but he was not to decline a discussion. Aehrenthal was also prepared to

[1] Aehrenthal to Pallavicini, telegram, 9 December; A 708.
[2] Tschirschky to foreign office, telegram, 10 December; G 9245.
[3] On 28 November, the Turkish chargé in Vienna transmitted a note stating that the Porte had issued orders to the effect that "no obstacle was to be put in the way of operations affecting Austrian merchandise" and that it was taking steps "wherever this is possible and within the limits of the law, with a view to stopping the boycott"; A 669.
[4] Draft of a note intended for the Porte; A 717, Beilage.
[5] Aehrenthal to Pallavicini, 10 December; A 717.

make concessions in the matter of the increase of the Turkish customs dues.[1] Finally, Pallavicini was empowered to make use of Achmed Riza, one of a delegation of Young Turks who had approached Khevenhüller in Paris with hints that their party desired a settlement.[2]

The Turkish reception of Aehrenthal's offer was not very encouraging. Kiamil pointed out that the Austrian readiness to increase the Turkish customs was useless unless the other Powers were also willing and bluntly demanded that Austria assume £4,000,000 of Turkish debt,[3] which Pallavicini once more urged Aehrenthal to do.[4] Tewfik indeed expressed the hope that the boycott would cease, now that the principle of negotiations had been accepted, but the leaders of the movement refused to act "so long as Austria-Hungary had not recognized the demands of Turkey".[5] Moreover, the prospect of Hilmi becoming grand vizier was now remote, for Kiamil had the support of the new parliament which was about to meet.[6] The only encouraging symptom was that Kiamil had rejected the Serbian offer of an alliance.[7]

Aehrenthal was not yet ready to give up the fight, and pro-

[1] Aehrenthal to Pallavicini, private, 10 December; A 718.
[2] Aehrenthal to Pallavicini, telegram, 11 December; Khevenhüller to Aehrenthal, 12 December; A 722, 729. In a letter to Back von Surány, a Hungarian who had acted as intermediary between Khevenhüller and the delegation, the ambassador stated that Aehrenthal "verrait avec plaisir que le Comité délègue une ou deux personnes pour entrer en pourparlers avec Monsieur le Marquis de Pallavicini" (A 729, Beilage); he appeared also to have given assurances that Aehrenthal would offer some kind of financial compensation (Pallavicini to Aehrenthal, telegram, 26 December; A 800). Pallavicini was embarrassed by the conflict between the letter to Back and Aehrenthal's instructions to himself, and asked whether he was really to negotiate with the Young Turks (Pallavicini to Aehrenthal, telegram, 27 December; A 806). Aehrenthal repudiated the promise of Khevenhüller (Aehrenthal to Pallavicini, telegram, 28 December; A 809) and reproved the latter (Aehrenthal to Khevenhüller, 31 December; A 824).
[3] Pallavicini to Aehrenthal, telegram, 13 December; A 738. Cf. Marschall to foreign office, telegram, 14 December; G 9246.
[4] Pallavicini to Aehrenthal, private, 14 December; A 743. He had already warned Aehrenthal that the new offer would fall flat without the promise of pecuniary compensation, suggesting 50,000,000 francs (Pallavicini to Aehrenthal, telegram, 11 December; A 723).
[5] Pallavicini to Aehrenthal, telegram, 15 December; A 749.
[6] Pallavicini to Aehrenthal, telegram, 13 December; A 739.
[7] Pallavicini to Aehrenthal, telegram, 14 December; A 742.

ceeded to raise, as he had threatened, the question of Austrian counter-claims for compensation for expenses incurred in Bosnia.[1] But he also sent to Constantinople the draft of an economic agreement supplementing the existing commercial treaty in three respects,[2] and though he once more rejected the demand for an assumption of state debt, he admitted that financial compensation might be given in another form, such as a loan to be guaranteed by the Great Powers.[3] Pallavicini was instructed to spin out the negotiations, with the hope that the situation might change after the meeting of parliament[4] (although the Young Turks were urging a prompt settlement),[5] the intention being to try to win over members to the Austrian point of view by bribery.[6]

This manœuvre was as futile as the preceding ones. Even before receiving the detailed instructions, Pallavicini roundly declared once more that no understanding was possible until Austria agreed to "an effective pecuniary compensation",[7] and when, on the following day, 18 December, the sultan in his speech at the opening of parliament referred to the "attacks" on Turkey and the injury to her "rights", the ambassador asserted that either he must leave his post or "we must yield on the matter of a material satisfaction"; he therefore urged Aehrenthal to offer the Porte £2,000,000 "quite without regard to the [other] concessions promised".[8] If anything more were needed

[1] Aehrenthal to Pallavicini, telegram, 16 December; A 754.
[2] A 762, Beilage. The three points were: (1) An increase of the Turkish customs to 15 per cent., with certain exceptions; (2) the Porte might levy an excise on certain articles of consumption and establish certain monopolies (matches, cigarette papers and playing cards), on which the old duty of 11 per cent. would continue to be paid; suppression of the Austrian post offices.
[3] Aehrenthal to Pallavicini, 17 December; A 763.
[4] Aehrenthal to Pallavicini, private, 17 December; A 764. Aehrenthal argued that assumption of the state debt for Bosnia would create a precedent unfavourable to Bulgaria, to whom assurances had been given that she would be protected against a similar Turkish claim (Aehrenthal to Thurn, telegram 12 December; A 734).
[5] Pallavicini to Aehrenthal, telegram, 16 December; A 756.
[6] Aehrenthal to Pallavicini, 16 December; A 755. Pallavicini advised against this (Pallavicini to Aehrenthal, 23 December; A 789).
[7] Pallavicini to Aehrenthal, telegram, 17 December; A 765. He also pointed out that Russia would demand compensation for consenting to an increase of the Turkish customs, which deprived Aehrenthal's offer of much value.
[8] Pallavicini to Aehrenthal, telegrams, 18 December; S 773, 774.

to make the minister's cup full, it was a note from the Porte replying to Aehrenthal's claim for compensation for losses arising out of the boycott, which laid the responsibility for the boycott on the "conflit provoqué par le gouvernement austro-hongrois" and the refusal of Pallavicini to enter upon negotiations, considerations which might be submitted, if necessary, "à la juste appréciation de l'opinion européenne".[1]

At this time Aehrenthal "let himself go" in a manner which bespoke his intense irritation and nervousness. Long convinced that the resistance of the Porte was to be explained only by British approval of the Turkish claims, he was greatly annoyed by the conduct of Sir Fairfax Cartwright, the new British ambassador, who arrived in Vienna on 10 December. The ambassador, apparently with the approval of his government, proposed to issue a *communiqué* (in German) to the press concerning the address he would make when presenting his credentials to the emperor, with the object of enlightening the Austrian public about the sentiment of England; Aehrenthal declared that speeches were not made on such occasions, and Cartwright had to forego his plan.[2] Without, however, waiting to be presented, the ambassador called on Aehrenthal and, according to the latter's account, began by referring to "the great uneasiness which he could state existed in England and France because of our attitude in the present crisis". The Austrian minister insisted on treating the conversation as of a private character. Aehrenthal indeed listened to and subsequently adopted a suggestion of Cartwright that Austria might participate in a guaranteed loan to Turkey;[3] but he took occasion to ventilate his grievances against the British press—"he was very careful to state [Cartwright reported] that he had no official complaints to make against His Majesty's government, whose attitude, he was ready to confess, had been perfectly correct"— and at the same time to give the impression that he would not let himself be moved by its threats. He seems, in short, to have

---

[1] Note verbale of Tewfik Pasha, 17 December; A 766, Beilage.

[2] Cartwright thought that Aehrenthal vetoed the plan because he did not wish "to calm the hostility of public opinion against us here" (Cartwright to Grey, private, 7 January 1909; B 508).

[3] See above, p. 112.

taken a considerable dislike to the new ambassador.[1] When, a few days later, Aehrenthal learned from Mensdorff that Grey repudiated any responsibility for the British press and was still complaining about the manner of the annexation (although he would welcome an Austro-Turkish understanding),[2] Aehrenthal wrote a long and bitter letter to his ambassador denouncing both the official British policy, which though outwardly correct was secretly hostile,[3] and the alleged machinations of British travellers in the Balkans. In his opinion,

Either England's policy is an inexplicable bad drunk [*ein unerklär-licher böser Rausch*], or it is only too explicable, but also at the same time very hazardous. For a hostile policy directed against a Great Power against which no direct charge can reasonably be brought, is in the long run to be carried through only by means which are calculated to engender the maximum in bad blood. It cannot and dare not be open, it must display *mala fides* at every turn.[4]

[1] Aehrenthal to Mensdorff, private, 17 December; A 767. Cartwright to Grey, telegram and despatch, 11 December; B 483, 484. Cartwright derived the impression that Aehrenthal would brook no intervention in his dispute with Serbia and Russia, but that "as regards Turkey...he is sincerely desirous of coming to some arrangement". Aehrenthal gave the German ambassador a long account of the interview (Tschirschky to Bülow, 16 December; G 9159); the German foreign minister said that the reports of the Prussian representatives in Munich, Stuttgart and Darmstadt, where Cartwright had been stationed before his transfer to Vienna, left no doubt that he was "an outspoken enemy of Germany" who shared all the prejudices of the British press (Szögyény to Aehrenthal, private, 22 December; A 785).
[2] Mensdorff to Aehrenthal, telegram, 16 December; A 758. Cf. Grey to Cartwright, private, 16 December; B 487. When informing Tschirschky of this, Aehrenthal said: "And in the meantime England is doing everything in Constantinople to make our negotiations difficult" (Tschirschky to Bülow, 17 December; G 9161).
[3] He cited a remark which King Edward was reported to have dropped when receiving Achmed Riza, the Young Turk leader: "Capital trick, your boycott; go on!" Achmed Riza told the story in Paris (Khevenhüller to Aehrenthal, private, 12 December; A 730).
[4] Aehrenthal to Mensdorff, private, 17 December; A 768. Mensdorff zealously defended British policy from Aehrenthal's charges, declaring that Grey, for all his irritation with Aehrenthal's methods, sincerely desired an Austro-Turkish agreement and the maintenance of peace. He thought it unlikely that King Edward had made the remark attributed to him. Incidentally, he quoted his German colleague Metternich in support of his views (Mensdorff to Aehrenthal, private, 20 December; A 781). Several weeks later, Metternich wrote to Bülow in much the same strain and denied that Grey was trying to separate Austria from Germany (Metternich to Bülow, 7 January 1909; G 9190). Ernst Kabisch, "England und die Annexionskrise 1908-9", *Berliner Monatshefte*, VIII (1930), 915-32, is highly critical of Aehrenthal,

It was not surprising that the French ambassador in Vienna "had it from well-informed sources, but not directly from Baron d'Aehrenthal, that a strong suspicion exists here that His Majesty's government at heart desires to bring about a European war".[1] So long as he was in this frame of mind, Aehrenthal was not likely to listen to suggestions coming from London; at the same time, there was obviously no hope of changing the British view that Turkey was entitled to real financial compensation.

Moreover, the German government had once more urged a settlement. In a long conversation with the Austrian ambassador, Prince Bülow had reviewed the entire European situation—at the moment, Austro-Russian relations were exceedingly tense[2]—and had expressed the conviction that "the whole crisis can be brought to a good end by firmness towards Russia and a corresponding attitude of conciliation towards Turkey".[3] If the German chancellor did not go beyond suggesting an Austrian loan to Turkey in which the German market might share, he did definitely advise Austria-Hungary "to show herself as accommodating as possible in economic matters and in questions affecting the state finances".[4] Evidently Germany expected her ally to make a serious move.

Nevertheless Aehrenthal made a last effort to avoid surrender by ordering Pallavicini to take act of a remark of Kiamil that if the economic concessions offered by Austria went far enough, the demand for an assumption of part of the state debt would be dropped.[5] But the shrewd old grand vizier made his invariable reply: though professing to appreciate the "great advantages"

who had persuaded himself that the British attitude was dictated by the fact that Austria was Germany's ally and refused to pay attention to Mensdorff's explanations.

[1] Cartwright to Grey, telegram, 21 December; B, p. 830. Grey replied: "Suspicion is absurd and preposterous: it is entirely opposed to the policy of H.M. government and alien to the feeling of this country. It is not too much to say that readiness of Turkey to negotiate with Austria is to some extent due to our influence. In no single instance have we instigated or stiffened the opposition of Turkey, Serbia or Montenegro" (Grey to Cartwright, telegram, 23 December; B, p. 830).

[2] See above, pp. 84-6.

[3] Szögyény to Aehrenthal, telegram, 16 December; A 751.

[4] Szögyény to Aehrenthal, 16 December; A 752.

[5] Aehrenthal to Pallavicini, telegram, 19 December; A 779.

of the proposed new commercial treaty, he argued that they could be realized only with the consent of all the Powers and once more demanded pecuniary compensation.[1] Kiamil's refusal apparently convinced Aehrenthal that further jockeying was useless. At any rate he proceeded to consult the governor of the Bodenkreditanstalt about "a payment to Turkey" and then took up the matter with the Austrian and Hungarian premiers and the joint minister of finance, who was also entrusted with Bosnian affairs. Although the ministers were of opinion that it was not compatible with the dignity of the Monarchy to "buy" [abkaufen] Turkish good will,[2] Aehrenthal himself was convinced that there was no other course,[3] an opinion in which he was doubtless confirmed by the intensification of the boycott,[4] the damaging of the Austro-Hungarian arms on an establishment in Beirut, and the demand of Achmed Riza for the restoration of the status quo ante on the ground that financial compensation would be "only humiliating" for Turkey![5] For the moment, because of the opposition of the two premiers, he could not do more than offer an Austro-Hungarian loan of 50–60,000,000 francs; but since he thereby professed to meet Kiamil's demand for "a material concession on the part of the Monarchy which could be made effective and available independently of the consent of the other signatory Powers",[6] he did at long last concede the principle asserted by the Porte from the beginning.

This offer, however, was never presented to the Porte. Pallavicini had already complained that successive but inadequate overtures merely strengthened the Turkish resistance,[7] behind which he suspected Russian intrigues.[8] He now took the position

[1] Pallavicini to Aehrenthal, telegram, 21 December; A 784.
[2] Tschirschky to foreign office, telegram, 23 December; G 9249.
[3] Aehrenthal to Szögyény, private, 7 January 1909; A 855.
[4] Marschall to foreign office, telegram, 26 December; G 9250.
[5] Pallavicini to Aehrenthal, 30 December; A 819. The Young Turks had passed the word that "the negotiations with the government would lead to nothing as long as the committee did not give its consent" (Pallavicini to Aehrenthal, telegram, 26 December; A 800).
[6] Aehrenthal to Pallavicini, telegram, 31 December; A 823.
[7] Pallavicini to Aehrenthal, 30 December; A 818. He condemned the activities of Khevenhüller in Paris and Rappoport in Salonica on the ground that "viele Köche versalzen die Suppe".
[8] Pallavicini to Aehrenthal, telegram, 2 January; A 829.

that when he presented the new offer, after the feast of Beiram, he must give it the form of a ten days' ultimatum which should demand effective measures for the unloading of Austrian ships and the stoppage of the boycott: he calculated that by the end of the time limit, "the Porte will be pretty well dried up financially and cannot think of serious resistance"; the "Hauptsache" at the moment was, he said, to cure the Turks of the "illusion" that "we must come to an agreement with Turkey at any price".[1] Aehrenthal himself had been considering a rupture,[2] but the German government advised against such a measure, which "would be a vain gesture and would at first only please the diplomatically unskilled Young Turks".[3] Now or never, the Austro-Hungarian minister had to take decisive action. Action was indeed the more necessary because the relations between Austria and Serbia had again become tense, thanks to a provocative speech delivered by the Serbian foreign minister on New Year's Day.[4]

As it happened, hints had been conveyed to Aehrenthal by the Turkish ambassador in Vienna and by the grand vizier that if Austria objected to the assumption of part of the state debt demanded by Turkey, financial compensation might be granted for the loss of sovereignty over Bosnia-Herzegovina.[5] Perhaps it was this play with form which enabled Aehrenthal to overcome the opposition of the Austrian and Hungarian premiers.[6] Be that as it may, his reply to Pallavicini's proposal of an ultimatum was to ask the ambassador whether he thought that the Turks would accept £T2,500,000[7] as compensation for the crown lands in

[1] Pallavicini to Aehrenthal, telegram, 4 January; A 842. He actually used the word "war" in his conversations with Tewfik (Marschall to foreign office, telegram, 4 January; G 9256) and Achmed Riza (Pallavicini to Aehrenthal, telegram, 5 January; A 844).

[2] Tschirschky to foreign office, telegram, 23 December; G 9249.

[3] Bülow to Tschirschky, telegram, 31 December; G 9253. Germany was urging the Porte not to insist on an indemnity (Bülow to Marschall, telegram, 29 December; memorandum of Schoen, 1 January; G 9252, 9255).

[4] This problem will be treated in a later chapter.

[5] Aehrenthal to Pallavicini, telegram, 28 December; Pallavicini to Aehrenthal, telegram, 28 December; A 810, 811.

[6] Aehrenthal to Szögyény, private, 7 January; A 855, G 9259

[7] This sum had been twice suggested by Sir Charles Hardinge, the permanent under-secretary of the British foreign office (Széchényi to Aehrenthal, telegram, 29 December; Mensdorff to Aehrenthal, telegram, 2 January; A 815, 830).

Bosnia, after an arranged arbitration had decided that these lands belonged to the Turkish state rather than to the annexed provinces.[1] Since Pallavicini offered only technical objections to the form of the arbitration,[2] which Aehrenthal easily overcame, he was authorized to make the formal offer to the Porte, which was asked for a prompt answer.[3] The offer was also transmitted to the Powers,[4] and the British government, which had "repeatedly" recommended "a material compensation" as "the most suitable means" of settlement, was asked to appreciate "the spirit of conciliation" thus shown and "to take account of it in its judgment of the general political situation".[5]

The British government expressed its satisfaction with the Austrian proposals,[6] and recommended them to the Porte.[7] Italy approved.[8] The German government naturally rejoiced, and instructed Marschall to support Pallavicini, "without regard to any Russian sensitiveness".[9] But apparently the Russian government raised no objections,[10] for its ambassador at Constantinople personally advised the Porte not to reject the Austrian offer.[11] Aehrenthal might therefore reasonably expect that his difficulties had at last been overcome and that the negotiations would be rapidly concluded.

Once again, however, he was doomed to be disappointed. Kiamil personally at once accepted the Austrian offer, on condition that no counter-claims were advanced for damages resulting

[1] Aehrenthal to Pallavicini, telegram, 6 January; A 850. The Porte was of course to recognize the annexation, either in a conference if one were held or otherwise; the offer of a new commercial treaty was also allowed to stand.

[2] Pallavicini to Aehrenthal, telegram, 7 January; A 860.

[3] Aehrenthal to Pallavicini, telegram, 8 January; A 862.

[4] Circular telegram, 9 January; A 868.

[5] *Mémoire* communicated by Mensdorff, 11 January; B 516, enclosure.

[6] Mensdorff to Aehrenthal, telegrams, 11 January; A 875, 876: Cartwright to Aehrenthal, 12 January; Grey to Cartwright, 16 January; B 527, enclosure 1, 516.

[7] Metternich to foreign office, telegram, 12 January; G 9258, note *: Szögyény to Aehrenthal, telegram, 13 January; A 884.

[8] Lützow to Aehrenthal, telegram, 10 January; A 871.

[9] Schoen to Marschall, telegram, 10 January; G 9260.

[10] Because of Izvolsky's decision to exchange only written communications with Aehrenthal, Berchtold sent no reports from St Petersburg at this time; at least, none are printed in A, so that Izvolsky's reactions to Aehrenthal's offer are not known.

[11] Pallavicini to Aehrenthal, telegram, 15 January; A 894.

from the boycott, which, he agreed, must cease,[1] and after consultation with the ministers, on 12 January, communicated an
official acceptance to Pallavicini, proposing a protocol in six
points. These may be summarized as follows:

(1) Renunciation by Austria-Hungary of all rights in the Sandjak
of Novi Bazar.
(2) Formal consent to the economic concessions offered.[2]
(3) Assurance of full religious freedom and equality for the Moslem
population of Bosnia-Herzegovina.
(4) A declaration by Austria-Hungary of readiness to negotiate
concerning the protectorate over the Catholics of Albania.
(5) Payment by the Monarchy of £T2,500,000 for the crown lands
in the provinces.
(6) Recognition of the annexation by Turkey.

Finally, Kiamil expressed the hope that "since we have now
come to an understanding, Baron Aehrenthal will help me in the
negotiations with Bulgaria".[3] Aehrenthal at once approved of
this plan,[4] and the negotiations got under way. But it was not
until 26 February that the agreement was finally signed! The
delay was due in part to the change of grand viziers, Hilmi
finally supplanting Kiamil on 14 February, partly to Turkish
insistence on an extra concession by which Austria promised her
"full and sincere support" when the Porte opened negotiations
with the Powers for the abolition of the capitulations.[5] This, the
Turkish government managed to secure by allowing the boycott
to continue, in spite of repeated promises to stop it.[6] At the

[1] Pallavicini to Aehrenthal, telegram, 9 January; A 865.
[2] Germany had already agreed to this, and Kiamil asked whether Great
Britain would agree also (Lowther to Grey, telegram, 11 January; B 510).
[3] Pallavicini to Aehrenthal, telegram, 12 January; A 880.
[4] Aehrenthal to Pallavicini, telegram, 13 January; A 885.
[5] For the details of the negotiations, which were largely technical, relating
to the text of the protocol, see K. und k. Ministerium des Aussern,
*Diplomatische Aktenstücke betreffend Bosnien und die Herzegowina 1908 bis
1909* (Vienna, 1909), Nos. 96, 102, 104, 105, 171, 191. Convenient summary
in Pallavicini to Aehrenthal, 26 February; A 1062. Text of the protocol in
*British and foreign state papers*, CII, 180–2; and in A 1522 and B 622.
[6] Pallavicini to Aehrenthal, telegrams, 14, 20, 27, 30 January, 1, 8, 15
February; A 890, 908, 930, 941, 950, 974, 993. Aehrenthal's threat that unless
the boycott were stopped, the Austrian and Hungarian parliaments would not
ratify the protocol (Aehrenthal to Pallavicini, telegram, 22 January; A 915)
was calmly ignored.

same time, the Porte further complicated matters by conducting parallel negotiations on another question.

When accepting the Austrian proposal for financial compensation, the Porte revealed that Serbia had threatened to satisfy her own ambitions by seizing the Sandjak and stirring up trouble in Macedonia if Turkey came to an understanding with Austria.[1] As Kiamil kept recurring to this danger, and finally asked if Austria-Hungary would not give a guarantee for the Sandjak in some form,[2] Aehrenthal suggested an exchange of notes, intending thereby to pave the way for reopening the project of a railway through the Sandjak.[3] The draft Austrian note recited that the Austrian interest in the maintenance of Turkish sovereignty in Novi Bazar "is quite as great to-day as it was in the thirty years" of Austrian occupation. Therefore

> Le cabinet de Vienne qui repousse toute idée d'accorder à la Serbie ou au Monténégro des compensations territoriales, comprend parfaitement que la Sublime Porte se place au même point de vue quant aux empiètements possibles desdits États sur le territoire du Sandjak.
>
> Il existe donc à ce sujet un parallélisme parfait entre les intérêts de l'Autriche-Hongrie et de la Turquie.
>
> Persuadés que la Sublime Porte observera en présence des aspirations serbes et monténégrines visant le territoire austro-hongrois une attitude sympathique à notre égard, nous nous déclarons prêts à donner à la Sublime Porte notre appui en conférence ou autrement pour contrecarrer les desseins que la Serbie ou le Monténégro pourraient former à l'endroit du Sandjak du Novibazar.

The guarantee was to run for three years, during which Turkey was to "fortify her strategic position" in the Sandjak. In return, she was promised "active and friendly support" in the financial and technical questions relating to the Uvats-Mitrovitsa railway.[4]

---

[1] Pallavicini to Aehrenthal, 9 January; A 865.

[2] Pallavicini to Aehrenthal, despatch, 20 January, and telegram, 23 January; A 907, 921. Kiamil said that a three years' guarantee would be sufficient, "for Turkey would then be strong enough to protect her territory even against an eventual league of the three Slavic Balkan states", and that although the declaration must be kept secret, he could then declare in parliament that "Turkey had nothing to fear for the Sandjak of Novi Bazar".

[3] Aehrenthal to Pallavicini, 31 January; A 948.

[4] A 948, Beilage.

Although Pallavicini let the Porte know that he had received satisfactory instructions about the matter,[1] he waited to make the formal overture until Hilmi had become grand vizier; the Turks, for their part, exhibited no curiosity until the negotiations over the protocol were practically completed, and their subsequent tactics raise doubts as to whether they were ever in earnest about the matter. Before Pallavicini was able to see Hilmi, Aehrenthal had stipulated that the transport of war material for Serbia through Turkish territory must be stopped[2] (Austro-Serbian relations having become tense again). The grand vizier, when finally approached, found this condition reasonable, saying that a shipment of fifteen tons of dynamite had already been held up.[3] But he desired an addition to the note which would assure "material support" to Turkey in the event of an attack on the Sandjak, and when Pallavicini rejected this,[4] suggested various changes in the note; the most important being the substitution of "tout appui" for "notre appui en conférence ou autrement".[5] Aehrenthal's reply was to the effect that the "tout appui" would be given only "sur le terrain diplomatique" and that the notes could not be published, as the new foreign minister desired; furthermore, he insisted on a binding and written promise to stop the Serbian war material.[6]

The situation was evidently developing in a way not to the liking of the Turks, who had been disagreeably impressed by Pallavicini's insistence that, in return for the guarantee of the Sandjak, they must proceed with the Uvats-Mitrovitsa railway.[7] So they began to seek a way of excape. Hilmi's discovery that

[1] Pallavicini to Aehrenthal, 10 February; A 982.
[2] Aehrenthal to Pallavicini, telegram, 22 February; A 1035.
[3] Pallavicini to Aehrenthal, telegram, 24 February; A 1046.
[4] Aehrenthal's instructions made clear that the "appui" offered would be diplomatic only. He emphasized this in a conversation with the new Turkish foreign minister who passed through Vienna at this time (memorandum of conversation with Rifaat Pasha, 27 February; A 1069).
[5] Pallavicini to Aehrenthal, despatch, 26 February, telegram, 27 February; A 1063, 1070).
[6] Aehrenthal to Pallavicini, 4 March; A 1104. As a move to induce the Turks to accept his proposal, Aehrenthal passed on to Constantinople a secret report from Budapest, according to which Serbia and Montenegro were preparing a *coup de main* in the Sandjak (Aehrenthal to Pallavicini, telegram, 2 March; A 1086).
[7] Pallavicini to Aehrenthal, 4 March; A 1105.

Kiamil had promised the Serbs to allow the passage of war materials[1] provided the grand vizier with a lever for further negotiations, especially as the British and French ambassadors were demanding that a considerable quantity of dynamite *en route* to Salonica should be shipped to some mining companies operating in Serbia,[2] while their Russian colleague was insisting on the passage of 100,000 Belgian rifles and 50,000,000 cartridges.[3] In spite, therefore, of vigorous representations from Pallavicini,[4] backed up by strong language from Aehrenthal,[5] it was not until 20 March, four weeks after the Austrian government had demanded this concession, that the Porte finally gave the written declaration,[6] and then only with certain reservations which annoyed Aehrenthal.[7]

Meanwhile the *pourparlers* over the Sandjak had come to a standstill. Although the German government had advised Aehrenthal to offer "serious—not merely diplomatic support" to Turkey,[8] the Austrian minister would not agree to the phrase "tout appui" without some sort of qualification;[9] as a last concession, when the Porte threatened to make parliamentary difficulties over the ratification of the protocol,[10] he suggested "tout son appui et son concours efficace".[11] The Turks professed to be satisfied, but evidently they had lost interest. Having received assurances, at first verbal and then written, from Serbia with respect to the Sandjak,[12] and having been advised by the

[1] Pallavicini to Aehrenthal, 4 March; A 1106.
[2] Pallavicini to Aehrenthal, telegram, 9 March; A 1154.
[3] Marschall to foreign office, telegram, 11 March; G 9272.
[4] Pallavicini to Aehrenthal, telegrams, 8, 11, 13 March; A 1144, 1184, 1201.
[5] Aehrenthal to Pallavicini, telegrams, 10, 11, 12, 17 March; A 1168, 1183, 1192, 1250.
[6] Pallavicini to Aehrenthal, telegram, 20 March; A 1293. Text in A 1338, Beilage.
[7] Aehrenthal to Pallavicini, telegram, 21 March; A 1300.
[8] Marginal note of Zimmermann, 17 March, on memorandum of 9 March; G 9271. The German Emperor advised the Porte to conclude a military convention with Austria-Hungary (Szögyény to Aehrenthal, 16 March; A 1233).
[9] Pallavicini to Aehrenthal, telegram, 25 March; Aehrenthal to Pallavicini, telegram, 17 March; A 1217, 1249.
[10] Pallavicini to Aehrenthal, telegrams, 19, 20 March; A 1277, 1291.
[11] Aehrenthal to Pallavicini, telegram, 22 March; A 1311.
[12] Pallavicini to Aehrenthal, telegrams, 18, 23 March; A 1265, 1321.

British ambassador that he personally thought an agreement about the Sandjak "unnecessary and undesirable",[1] they asked that the exchange of notes be postponed until the protocol had been ratified and until Rifaat, the foreign minister, had returned from abroad.[2] They even talked of submitting a new programme for the conference,[3] to which Aehrenthal naturally objected.[4]

Rifaat, before returning to Constantinople, stopped in Vienna to see Aehrenthal. He explained that the Porte would no longer insist on publication of the notes to be exchanged about the Sandjak because "Serbia and Montenegro might find, in the existence of an Austro-Hungarian-Turkish agreement, a proof of the weakness of the Ottoman Empire in that region and an encouragement for their territorial aspirations".[5] But this was probably only a device to gain time, for after his return to Constantinople, he said nothing about the notes to Pallavicini and the grand vizier was evasive,[6] although the protocol of 26 February had at last, on 5 April, been ratified. Aehrenthal drew the conclusion that the Porte had given up the plan, "which had sprung from its own initiative", and instructed Pallavicini not to raise the question; but he was evidently disappointed by his failure.[7]

From the beginning to the end of the long negotiations, the Turks had outplayed the Austro-Hungarian minister. To be sure, he was greatly handicapped by having at the same time to deal with Russia and Serbia and to a certain extent with Great Britain, nor was there, so far as can be seen, any way by which he could have broken the boycott without the cash payment

[1] Lowther to Grey, telegram, 21 March; B 730.
[2] Pallavicini to Aehrenthal, telegram, 23 March; A 1320.
[3] Pallavicini to Aehrenthal, telegram, 26 March; A 1363.
[4] Aehrenthal to Pallavicini, telegram, 27 March; A 1377. The Porte explained that its purpose was to secure through a conference the consent of the Powers to the economic concessions already offered by Austria (Pallavicini to Aehrenthal, telegram, 30 March; A 1420). Aehrenthal refused, but agreed that Articles 23 and 61 of the Berlin Treaty, which the Porte was also anxious to bring before a conference, might be eliminated by an exchange of notes (Aehrenthal to Pallavicini, telegram, 3 April; A 1449). In the end, Turkey gave up the plan for a conference (Pallavicini to Aehrenthal, 7 April; A 1488).
[5] Aehrenthal to Pallavicini, 1 April; A 1433.
[6] Pallavicini to Aehrenthal, 7 April; A 1489.
[7] Aehrenthal to Pallavicini, 15 April; A 1521.

to which he was ultimately driven. But he exhibited unusual *naïveté* in accepting Turkish assurances of their special friendliness for the Monarchy, of their desire to stop the boycott, of their anxiety about the Sandjak, etc. Such threats as he allowed himself to make in Constantinople were weighed and found wanting; Hilmi, whom Aehrenthal professed to trust, played with him as successfully as Kiamil, whom he disliked. In the end, the Turks got nearly everything which they desired. More than that, as we shall next see, they practically ignored Austria-Hungary in their negotiations with Bulgaria, in spite of Aehrenthal's desire to have a hand in them and thus keep Bulgaria within the Austrian sphere of influence.

# CHAPTER IX

# The Turco-Bulgarian Settlement

I T HAD BEEN part of Aehrenthal's calculations that the proclamation of Bulgarian independence, which antedated by one day the annexation of Bosnia-Herzegovina and was as much a violation of the Treaty of Berlin as the latter act, would divert some attention from his own proceedings;[1] he also expected to assist Bulgaria in coming to terms with Turkey and thus bind the new kingdom more closely to Austro-Hungarian policy. As matters turned out, the Bulgarian problem was largely lost sight of in the excitement produced by the issues already discussed, and, in the end, it was Russia, not the Habsburg Monarchy, which negotiated the settlement between Sofia and Constantinople and reaped the fruits of this success.

As soon as the independence of Bulgaria was proclaimed, Aehrenthal reminded Izvolsky that at Buchlau they had "reckoned with the possibility of this event" and proposed recognition of the new state;[2] at the same time he notified the Bulgarian government that he had taken up the matter with the Powers, adding that he expected Bulgaria to settle the question of the Oriental Railway as a "matter of honour".[3] But the Russian government, which resented the proclamation of Bulgarian independence under the aegis of Austria-Hungary, rebuffed the overture,[4] and the Bulgarians showed no disposition to settle the question of the Oriental Railway, that is, to return the line to the Austro-Hungarian company which had previously operated it. Aehrenthal therefore dropped the matter—he had his hands sufficiently full with the Porte, the Serbs, Izvolsky and Grey!—except to send to Sofia assurances of a "friendly

---

[1] See above, p. 31.

[2] Aehrenthal to Berchtold, telegram, 5 October; A 143.

[3] Aehrenthal to Thurn, telegram, 6 October; A 161. The German attitude was identical (memorandum of Schoen, 9 October; telegram to Tschirschky, 9 October; G 9275, 8975, note ***). The Italian representative in Sofia, on the other hand, was instructed to refrain from any action "which could be interpreted as recognition by Italy of the new situation proclaimed in Bulgaria" (memorandum of conversation with Avarna, 8 October; A 194).

[4] Berchtold to Aehrenthal, telegram, 6 October; A 160: Nicolson to Grey, telegram, 7 October; B 327.

attitude" in the event of Turco-Bulgarian complications.[1] Thus the Powers of the Entente were free to assume the initiative if they so desired.

Meanwhile the Turks had protested to the Powers against the "illegal and arbitrary act" of Bulgaria, demanded the re-establishement of "the legal order" in Bulgaria and Eastern Rumelia[2] and declared their intentions not only of retaining their rights over Eastern Rumelia, but if necessary of asserting them "by military force". If that province ceased to be a buffer state, the grand vizier argued, "Bulgaria will inevitably have designs on Macedonia, which would lead to a great conflagration".[3] A suggestion, emanating apparently from the British ambassador, of "a guarantee from the Powers that Macedonia should not be allowed to fall into the hands of Bulgaria"[4] was rejected as worthless in view of Turkey's "recent experience".[5] The Bulgarian government was equally intransigent, declaring in the *Vreme* that "if Turkey wants concessions, let her come and take them"![6] Alarmed by rumours of Turkish mobilization, it began to talk of counter-measures; whereupon the Porte denied such intentions and appealed to the Powers to keep Bulgaria quiet.[7] Although the German government acted promptly, received the necessary assurances, and passed them on to Constantinople,[8] they were received there with scepticism.[9]

[1] Aehrenthal to Thurn, telegram, 17 October; A 319.
[2] Turkish circular, 7 October; A 173; G 8973.
[3] Lowther to Grey, telegram, 12 October; B 362.
[4] Lowther to Grey, private, 13 October; B 375.
[5] Lowther to Grey, telegram, 15 October; B 382. Grey replied that the "true safeguard was good government and a strong Turkish army" (Grey to Lowther, telegram, 13 October; B 370) and that "proposals for guarantee of Eastern Rumelia and occupation of Crete are quite impracticable" (Grey to Lowther, telegram, 16 October; B 388). He urged Turkey to "secure largest possible pecuniary compensation from Bulgaria".
[6] Romberg to foreign office, telegram, 15 October; G 9276.
[7] Schoen to Romberg, telegram, 16 October; G 9277.
[8] Schoen to Marschall, telegram, 17 October; G 9278. The Bulgarian government gave assurances in London that "Bulgaria will take every step that is possible to avoid a war with Turkey". The British foreign office urged the utmost prudence on Bulgaria and to "give no provocation" (Grey to Buchanan, 19 October; B 396).
[9] Marschall to foreign office, telegram, 18 October; G 9280. Marschall, strongly pro-Turkish, advised against any attempt at mediation, "in view of the absolute unreliability of Bulgaria".

This situation, which was all the more dangerous because of the high tension between Austria and Russia and between Austria and Serbia, was saved by the action of France. To a French threat that the Powers would demand the surrender of Eastern Rumelia if he went to war, Prince Ferdinand replied by assuring President Fallières that he would keep the peace and that his government would compensate Turkey for the "material interests" which she possessed in Bulgaria.[1] Not only did this assurance induce the Turks to stop their mobilization,[2] but also, when, at the further suggestion of France, a Bulgarian agent, Dimitrov, was despatched to Constantinople,[3] the way was opened for a bargain. The Turks, evidently following British advice to seek substance rather than to insist on form, contented themselves with demanding compensation for the Oriental Railway and the capitalization of the Eastern Rumelian tribute.[4] When Bulgaria showed some hesitation, being willing only to pay the interest on the Eastern Rumelian share of the Turkish debt, the Powers of the Entente made a formal *démarche* in Sofia demanding a binding declaration that warlike preparations would be avoided and advising negotiations with the Porte.[5] With this lever in hand, together with hints that the French banks would not make a loan until the difficulties with Turkey were adjusted,[6] Ferdinand was able to overcome the resistance of his ministers.[7] The required assurances were given, the Turkish demands were accepted in principle, and the minister of commerce, Liapchev, was sent to Constantinople to conduct the negotiations.[8]

It was soon evident, however, that a settlement would be very difficult. The Turkish demands were: (1) capitalization of the

[1] Radolin to foreign office, telegram, 20 October; G 9281.
[2] Statement of the French ambassador in Vienna, 21 October; A 356.
[3] Radolin to foreign office, telegram, 21 October; G 9282.
[4] Thurn to Aehrenthal, telegram, 23 October; A 377.
[5] Romberg to foreign office, telegram, 29 October; G 9284.
[6] Romberg to foreign office, telegram, 1 October; G 9286.
[7] The German minister discreetly supported the representations of the Entente, whereas his Austrian colleague remained passive (Romberg to Bülow, 2 November; G 9288). Aehrenthal had instructed Thurn to avoid anything which would involve formal recognition of the new kingdom, but otherwise to maintain "as friendly an attitude as possible" (Aehrenthal to Thurn, telegram, 27 October; A 434).
[8] Marschall to foreign office, telegram, 31 October; G 9285.

Eastern Rumelian tribute; (2) capitalization of the Bulgarian tribute (which had never been paid); and (3) assumption of part of the Turkish state debt. The Bulgarians were ready to pay 40 million francs for the Oriental Railway and 60 million francs in lieu of the Eastern Rumelian tribute; in addition, they wished the Bulgarian Exarch maintained at Constantinople and claimed "protection" for the Bulgarians of Macedonia. Declaring the Turkish demands unacceptable, the Bulgarian government appealed to the Powers for help, at the same time threatening to order mobilization if the Porte proved stubborn.[1] This gave Aehrenthal a chance to point out to the Entente Powers that Bulgaria had desisted from her military preparations at their advice, adding that he was ready to support their mediation at Constantinople,[2] and the suggestion appealed sufficiently to Izvolsky for him to transmit it to London and to ask for the opinion of the British government.[3] But Grey, remaining true to the principle that Turkey was entitled to substantial compensation, thought that Bulgaria ought to pay "something between 5 and 10 millions", i.e. between 125 and 250 million francs; he suggested consulting the French government, which was interested in both Turkish and Bulgarian finance and possessed intimate knowledge of both.[4] Consequently no Entente representations appear to have been made at Constantinople.

In consequence, the Turco-Bulgarian negotiations had reached

[1] Marschall to foreign office, telegram, 4 November; memorandum of Griesinger, 6 November; G 9287, 9289. Thurn to Aehrenthal, telegram, 5 November; A 511.

[2] Aehrenthal to Berchtold, Khevenhüller and Mensdorff, telegrams, 5 November; A 516. Aehrenthal, notifying the Bulgarian government of his action, advised it to observe "a conciliatory, yet firm attitude" in its negotiations with the Porte (Aehrenthal to Thurn, telegram, 6 November; A 521). The British agent in Sofia was of the opinion that Bulgaria desired "close understanding if not alliance with Turkey", being "preoccupied with idea of an Austrian advance next spring". He heard that "Austria is making advances by offering to facilitate passage of Bulgarian war material"; but since Prince Ferdinand was an opportunist, "only in the event of Turkey rejecting his overtures and leaving him isolated is he likely to make common cause with Austria-Hungary" (Buchanan to Grey, telegram, 4 November; B 427). There is no indication in the Austrian documents of an offer to Bulgaria in respect of war material, but it may have been conveyed through military channels.

[3] Benckendorff to Hardinge, 9 November; B 439.

[4] Grey to Nicolson, telegram, 13 November; B 442.

a deadlock by the end of November, and Liapchev returned to Sofia. The Turks were no more impressed by the arguments of Baron von Marschall that by delaying to agree with Austria-Hungary, they had delayed the conference and thereby given Bulgaria a chance to raise her demands,[1] than were the Bulgarians by Grey's advice to take advantage of the Turkish willingness to negotiate on a strictly financial basis without political conditions and to offer a "liberal" lump sum in payment of all claims.[2] Aehrenthal, for his part, was unwilling to do anything for Bulgaria until she had settled for the Oriental Railway.[3] So it was left for the German government to try its hand, and it did so by advising its ally to work for an Austro-Bulgarian understanding on the basis of allowing Bulgaria a slice of Serbian territory in the event of her co-operation in an Austro-Serbian war.[4] Perhaps it was Bülow's hint that a Bulgarian "indiscretion" would have a calming effect on Serbia, Turkey and Russia which induced the hard-pressed Austrian minister to listen to this suggestion,[5] and to ask his minister in Sofia for an opinion as to what persons in Bulgaria could be best approached.[6]

Count Thurn's reports were rather pessimistic. The feeling in Bulgaria, he said, was that "at present the Monarchy was in a difficult and rather isolated position", that "no practical result" was to be expected from its intervention, and that both Prince Ferdinand and his government were more and more convinced that "salvation could come only through Russia".[7]

[1] Marschall to foreign office, telegrams, 26, 30 November; G 9290, 9291.
[2] Grey to Lowther, telegram, 3 December; B 473.
[3] Aehrenthal to Thurn, 26 November; A 655.
[4] Bülow to Tschirschky, 30 November; G 9292: Szögyény to Aehrenthal, telegram, 30 November; A 678.
[5] Tschirschky to Bülow, 3 December; G 9294. Bülow seems to have been not entirely satisfied with Aehrenthal's response, for he returned to the charge several weeks later, arguing that "Austria should bind Bulgaria to herself closely and firmly, not only on account of her own Slavs, but because any action by Russia against Austria-Hungary would thereby be made more difficult" (Bülow to Tschirschky, 12 December; G 9295).
[6] Aehrenthal to Thurn, telegram, 5 December; A 697.
[7] Thurn to Aehrenthal, telegram, 7 December; A 702. Thurn said that the "tsar" himself was the only person with whom negotiations could be conducted, though he thought that perhaps military circles might be won to the idea of co-operation against Turkey and Serbia.

Not only that, but Russia was trying to reconcile Bulgaria with Serbia and Montenegro,[1] and was ready to support her aspirations in Macedonia "in case Bulgaria were submissive to her wishes".[2] Nevertheless, Aehrenthal tried to keep the matter open by declaring that Austria would not set a precedent by assuming part of the Turkish debt[3] and by urging that an alliance with Serbia or Turkey would not correspond with the real interests of Bulgaria, "for in a conflict with Austria-Hungary the advantages can well be imagined which Serbia or Turkey might get, but not the profit which Bulgaria could receive therefrom".[4]

A new circumstance enabled the Austro-Hungarian minister to proceed with his plan, as it seemed. When the Bulgarian government, irritated by the passage in the sultan's speech opening the Turkish parliament in which he referred to the connection between the proclamation of Bulgarian independence and the annexation of Bosnia,[5] protested to the Powers,[6] Aehrenthal invited the other cabinets to join with him in representations to the Porte "et de lui recommander à nouveau de faire preuve de sentiments bienveillants et de sage modération dans les négociations avec la Bulgarie".[7] But Izvolsky, who had not taken the Bulgarian note very seriously and was of the opinion that "some Power should propose a fixed amount" for Bulgaria to pay,[8] was "perplexed and perturbed" by Aehrenthal's

[1] Thurn to Aehrenthal, telegram, 11 December; A 726.
[2] Thurn to Aehrenthal, telegram, 12 December; A 736.
[3] Aehrenthal to Thurn, telegram, 12 December; A 734.
[4] Aehrenthal to Thurn, telegram, 12 December; A 735. The prince's secretary, Dobrovich, assured Thurn that "so long as King Ferdinand was king of Bulgaria", Bulgaria would not join with Serbia or Turkey (Thurn to Aehrenthal, telegram, 14 December; A 746). The Bulgarian minister of war, General Nicolayev, speaking with the Austrian military attaché, Major Hranilovich, tried to minimize the effects of the Russian activity in Bulgaria and expressed himself enthusiastically in favour of an Austro-Bulgarian understanding (Thurn to Aehrenthal, 17 December; Hranilovich to Conrad, 17 December; A 770, 771).
[5] Thurn to Aehrenthal, telegram, 22 December; A 786.
[6] The Bulgarian circular is given in Schulthess, *Europäische Geschichtskalender, 1908*, p. 420.
[7] Circular telegram of Aehrenthal, 26 December; A 797.
[8] Nicolson to Grey, 27 December; B 492. Bulgaria was willing to pay 82,000,000 francs.

proposal, thinking that there was "some prearranged plan", since "as matters stand Austria is the last Power to suggest representations at Constantinople". In spite of the fact that the Bulgarian minister in St Petersburg was affirming that "we would prefer war to going beyond our last offer", Izvolsky was for saying that "all necessary advice had been given at Constantinople and there was no need of any further steps". But he asked for the opinion of the British and French governments.[1] Once more Grey stood by Turkey. He agreed with Izvolsky's proposal, provided the amount named "should certainly not be less than 125 million francs",[2] and he rebuffed Aehrenthal with the blunt statement that "Turkey had shown a more conciliatory spirit so far than Bulgaria" and that "in view of the moderating advice which [His Majesty's government] had already given to Turkey, there was no reason why they should avail themselves of the opportunity of the Bulgarian circular note to make renewed representations to her".[3] Thus the Austrian plan to curry favour with Bulgaria through the assistance of the Entente failed miserably.

With the turn of the year, the Porte requested Bulgaria to reopen the negotiations.[4] For a moment, the Bulgarian government seemed ready to do so,[5] but it finally begged the Entente Powers to advise Turkey to negotiate, "not only on a purely pecuniary basis, but on the good results which would issue from an *entente* with Bulgaria".[6] Acting on this request Sir Edward Grey proposed that the British, French, Russian and

[1] Nicolson to Grey, telegram and despatch, 30 December; B 494, 496.
[2] Grey to Nicolson, telegram, 4 January 1909; B 499.
[3] Grey to Cartwright, 6 January; B 502. Cf. also Grey to Cartwright, 4 January, and Hardinge to Nicolson, private, 4 January; B 500 and ed. note.
[4] Romberg to Bülow, 9 January; G 9303.
[5] Buchanan to Grey, telegram, 6 January; B 511, ed. note.
[6] Bertie to Grey, telegram, 8 January; B 511, note. The Turkish ambassador in Vienna told his British colleague that his government "would attach great value to conclusion of offensive and defensive alliance with Bulgaria" (Cartwright to Grey, telegram, 13 January; B 513)—the negotiations with Serbia having been abandoned—but he thought that the offer should "come spontaneously from Bulgarian side" (Cartwright to Grey, telegram, 17 January; B 517). Grey approved, suggesting that the alliance might compensate Turkey for the insufficiency of Bulgaria's financial offers (Grey to Cartwright, telegram, 16 January; B 515). Nothing more, however, seems to have been heard of the idea.

possibly Italian governments should urge Bulgaria to pay 125 million francs and at the same time secure the consent of Turkey to the junction of the railways between Kumanova and Kustendil,[1] which would greatly improve the Bulgarian communications with Macedonia. Izvolsky, however, contended that Bulgaria could not pay more than 100 million francs,[2] and, in spite of Grey's refusal to recommend this sum to the Porte,[3] stuck to this figure, expressing the fear that by insisting on a larger sum, "we shall throw Bulgaria into the arms of Austria and Germany".[4]

This fear was not unjustified, so far as Austro-German desires were concerned. For Prince Bülow, impressed by Izvolsky's reference, in his speech to the duma on 25 December, to a Balkan league, including Turkey, for the defence of their national and economic independence,[5] had "urgently" recommended to Aehrenthal to reach an understanding with Bulgaria "as soon as possible",[6] and the latter, encouraged perhaps by a report of Bulgarian irritation with Russia,[7] made a definite bid by instructing his minister in Sofia to seek an audience of Prince

[1] Grey to Nicolson, 11 January; B 511.
[2] Nicolson to Grey, telegram, 20 January; B 523. For a time the Russian minister was worried by rumours of an Austrian loan to Bulgaria, which, however, were discounted after French inquiries had been made in Vienna (Nicolson to Grey, telegrams, 17, 20 December; B 518, 522).
[3] Grey to Nicolson, telegram, ? 23 January; B 529, note.
[4] Nicolson to Grey, telegram, 24 January; B 529. The French minister in Sofia suggested a *démarche* in Sofia by the six Powers to induce Bulgaria to resume negotiations with the Porte (Romberg to Bülow, 23 January; G 9306).
[5] Memorandum of Bülow, 27 December; G 9297. See above, p. 86.
[6] Bülow to Tschirschky, 28 December; G 9298: Szögyény to Aehrenthal, telegram, 30 December; A 817. At the same time, Marschall was instructed to persuade the Porte to be conciliatory towards Bulgaria (Schoen to Marschall, 29 December; G 9300. Aehrenthal explained to Bülow that he had hitherto hesitated in this course because of the unreliability of Prince Ferdinand, but that he expected "the practical sense of the Bulgarian people" would make them see the "parallelism of interests" between themselves and the Monarchy (Aehrenthal to Szögyény, private, 2 January; A 828: Tschirschky to Bülow, 30 December; G 9301). Bülow was delighted, and instructed the German minister to Sofia to see Prince Ferdinand in support of the Austrian proposals (Bülow to Aehrenthal, private, 8 January; Bülow to Romberg, private, 14 January; G 9302 and note *).
[7] Fürstenberg to Aehrenthal, telegram from St Petersburg, 30 December; A 821.

Ferdinand and read to him a specially prepared "notice".[1] The cabinet of Vienna, this document stated, accepted the view that Bulgaria was liable to pay only for the Oriental Railway and the tribute of Eastern Rumelia and promised to support this "in the conference". Bulgaria would probably not take "an active part" in an Austro-Serbian war. But in the event of a conflict between Bulgaria and Turkey,

L'Autriche-Hongrie ne pourrait guère y intervenir au commencement de l'action; elle n'hésiterait cependant pas dans le cas d'une agression de la part de la Turquie à assumer l'obligation de ne pas tolérer que la Serbie prenne une attitude menaçante ou belliqueuse vis-à-vis de la Bulgarie.

It was also suggested that an exchange of views would be useful "sur la base d'une entente destinée à assurer aux deux pays un appui mutuel en présence d'une action combinée de la Serbie et de la Turquie".[2] Thurn was also to explain verbally that in the latter case, "we should have no objection to an aggrandisement of Bulgaria in the direction of Pirot" and to promise Ferdinand "full understanding and protection" of his dynastic interests. Without waiting to hear the result of his overture, Aehrenthal sought to make it more attractive by adding that it had reference "not only to the present situation, but also to more distant developments".[3]

Prince Ferdinand showed himself not unreceptive to the Austrian suggestions, but asked if territorial aggrandisement could be expected "only" in the direction of Pirot; while promising to consider the matter, he requested Thurn to consult the premier and the war minister, MM. Malinov and Nicolayev.[4] The latter thought the moment "highly opportune" for a bargain and even talked of a military convention.[5] But the Bulgarians could not rid themselves of the idea that the Monarchy had its own designs on Macedonia,[6] and the wily prince insisted

---

[1] Aehrenthal to Thurn, 3 January; A 835.
[2] A 835, Beilage.
[3] Aehrenthal to Thurn, telegram, 11 January; A 878.
[4] Thurn to Aehrenthal, telegram, 11 January, and despatch, 12 January; A 879, 882.
[5] Thurn to Aehrenthal, telegram, 13 January; A 887.
[6] Thurn to Aehrenthal, 15 January; A 895.

that not he, but his government, must make the decision.[1] When Thurn was finally able to discuss the matter officially, the prime minister boldly asked what Austria would do in the event of a rupture between Bulgaria and Turkey, while Liapchev declared that the best proof of the parallelism between Austrian and Bulgarian interests would be Austrian pressure at Constantinople to secure "the actual conclusion of an agreement",[2] which was, of course, out of the question at the moment, for, as Aehrenthal pointed out, the Austro-Turkish agreement was not yet concluded. All the Austrian minister could do was to give assurances about Bulgarian aspirations in Macedonia and the possible danger from Turkey.[3]

While the Powers were thus skirmishing, the Bulgarians, evidently weary of Turkish resistance, decided to act: taking advantage of a Turkish proposal for a frontier rectification, they mobilized two divisions.[4] Aehrenthal at once suggested a *démarche* to the Porte against any demand for an adjustment of frontier,[5] but Izvolsky proposed representations at both Sofia and Constantinople, to which Grey agreed,[6] adding that Germany and Austria should be associated with the action.[7] The Russian

[1] Thurn to Aehrenthal, telegram, 18 January; A 904. Paléologue, the French minister, told Thurn that Bulgaria had hinted to the French government about a military convention with Austria, but he refused to believe that Austria would make such an agreement with the "unreliable" Ferdinand; it was "un chantage politique comme les Bulgaries aiment à le faire" (Thurn to Aehrenthal, private, 18 January; A 905). Rumours of such a convention, however, continued to circulate for some time (A 995, 1041).

[2] Thurn to Aehrenthal, telegram, 22 January; A 917.

[3] Aehrenthal to Thurn, telegram, 25 January; A 923. Aehrenthal informed Bülow that "the affair appears to be progressing well", for "three of the most influential ministers had been initiated and won for the plan" (Tschirschky to Bülow, 24 January; G 9307). The German minister in Sofia reported, however, that Ferdinand was not free from distrust of Austria and would not hear of an understanding. Romberg was thereupon instructed to make renewed efforts to bring about the *rapprochement* (G 9302, note).

[4] Buchanan to Grey, telegram, 24 January; B 531: Romberg to foreign office, telegram, 25 January; G 9308. The grand vizier denied that the question of frontiers had been officially raised, but admitted that military circles desired a slight rectification near Mustapha Pasha and in the mountains; if agreed to by Bulgaria, the Porte would accept an indemnity of £5,000,000 (Marschall to foreign office, telegram, 26 January; G 9308, note *).

[5] Circular telegram of Aehrenthal (London omitted), 27 January; A 929.

[6] Grey to Lowther and Buchanan, telegrams, 25 January; B 538, note 1.

[7] Grey to Nicolson, telegram, 25 January; B 532.

minister accordingly invited the Powers to advise both Turkey and Bulgaria to "abstain from any measures that might be interpreted as provocative", including the raising of frontier claims.[1] The Austrian foreign minister, consulted by Berlin,[2] raised no objections, provided the communication were so worded as not to involve the withdrawal of Bulgarian troops,[3] and sent instructions to his representatives in the two capitals, but with a hint to Sofia that the *démarche* was not to be taken seriously.[4] Pallavicini, however, refused to act, on the ground that no Turkish military measures had been taken on the Bulgarian frontier and that the frontier question had not been raised, and Marschall, who had been instructed to follow the example of his Austrian colleague,[5] likewise made no move.[6]

In the meantime, there had been two new developments. In the first place, the French government having declared that Bulgaria could not pay more than 100,000,000 francs,[7] Izvolsky came forward with a scheme by which Russia would advance the sum necessary to satisfy Turkey (120,000,000 francs), which Bulgaria would repay to Russia over a period of fifty years at a lower rate of interest than she would have to pay for 100,000,000 francs borrowed in Paris.[8] Secondly, Bulgaria presented the Russian government with a near-ultimatum which caused Izvolsky to sit up half the night revamping his proposal. In its new form it provided that Russia would find 82,000,000 francs for Bulgaria "on easy terms" and settle with Turkey for the remainder of the Turkish demand, his plan being that Russia should renounce twenty annuities of the Turkish war indemnity

[1] Circular telegram of Izvolsky, ?28 January; A 938.
[2] Schoen to Tschirschky, telegram, 28 January G 9309.
[3] Tschirschky to foreign office, telegram, 29 January; G 9310.
[4] Aehrenthal to Pallavicini and Thurn, telegrams, 30 January; A 940.
[5] Schoen to Marschall, telegram, 31 January; G 9312.
[6] Marschall to foreign office, telegram, 2 February; G 9313.
[7] Khevenhüller to Aehrenthal, telegram, 28 January; A 934: Grey to Bertie, 28 January; B 540.
[8] Memorandum of Benckendorff, 27 January; B 536. Grey doubted if the plan was "practicable" (Grey to Nicolson, telegram, 27 January; B 535) and suggested that, if the proposal fell through, the six Powers should fix the sum to be paid by Bulgaria (memorandum to Benckendorff, 28 January; B 539).

of 1879 which, if capitalized, would amount to 150,000,000 francs.[1] This Grey accepted,[2] and it was communicated to Bulgaria and to the other Powers and, verbally, to the Porte.[3]

The German government did not like the plan, and made an evasive answer.[4] Aehrenthal not only refused to support the proposal, but warned Sofia of the consequences which acceptance of the Russian scheme would have "in the future for Bulgaria's economic and political freedom ",[5] adding a threat that he would not continue the negotiations under way for a general understanding if the proposal were accepted.[6]

But the Bulgarians proved too quick for the Austrian minister, for they at once accepted the Russian proposal in principle,[7] before Thurn had received Aehrenthal's instructions.[8] They did, it is true, let the idea spread that if Turkey did not also accept, Bulgaria would go to war or at any rate mobilize.[9] When, however, the representatives of the Powers were finally able to make the *démarche* agreed upon,[10] General Paprikov, the foreign minister, assured them that Bulgaria had "no aggressive designs against Turkey" and that if Turkey accepted the Russian proposals, the reservists could be disbanded "within

---

[1] Nicolson to Grey, 30 January; B 542.

[2] Grey to Nicolson, telegram, 30 January; B 541. In London "the real reason" for Russia's action was thought to be that "she wishes to detach Bulgaria from Austria and attach her to Russia" (Grey to Nicolson, private, 2 February; B 551).

[3] Sverbeyev to Aehrenthal, 30 January; Fürstenberg to Aehrenthal, telegram, 31 January; A 943, 949: Pourtalès to foreign office, telegram, 31 January; Marschall to foreign office, telegram, 2 February; G 9314, 9317: Nicolson to Grey, telegram, 31 January; B 543.

[4] Schoen to William II, 1 February; G 9315. The emperor commented: "In this way Bulgaria will come completely into financial dependence on Russia and will be drawn away from Austria. Nothing doing! [*Geht also nicht!*]". Russia was informed that Bulgaria would have to give guarantees for the payment of the Eastern Rumelian tribute and of the indemnity due to the Oriental Railway (memorandum of Kiderlen, 5 February; G 9322). Izvolsky tried, not very successfully, to reproach the German government for its attitude (Pourtalès to Bülow, 10 February; G 9329).

[5] Aehrenthal to Thurn, telegram, 1 February; A 953.

[6] Aehrenthal to Thurn, telegram, 1 February; A 954.

[7] Thurn to Aehrenthal, telegram, 1 February; A 955.

[8] Thurn to Aehrenthal, telegram, 2 February; A 958: Tautphoeus to foreign office, telegram, 2 February; G 9319.

[9] Buchanan to Grey, telegram, 2 February; B 546.

[10] See above, p. 134.

a few days ".[1] Aehrenthal presented a good face on his discomfiture:

For him [he said] it was all clever bluff on the part of Bulgaria. By mobilizing a division Turkey was frightened into abandoning the idea of rectification of frontier, and now, by loud talk of war at Sophia, impecunious Russia had suddenly devised a scheme for providing pecuniary indemnity for Turkey.

Which was perhaps true. Nevertheless, the Austrian minister was, as the British ambassador suspected, "greatly irritated ",[2] and instructed his minister in Sofia that if the Bulgarians tried to reopen the negotiations for an understanding, they were first to be asked if they still enjoyed "complete liberty of action ".[3]

Could the Entente Powers also induce the Porte to accept? At first the Turks were not greatly impressed: they would get nothing from Bulgaria[4] and were therefore disposed to decline.[5] But after Grey had pointed out the hopelessness of trying to get more than 100,000,000 francs from Bulgaria and had urged consideration of the Russian scheme,[6] the Turkish government thought better of the proposal and decided to

---

[1] Buchanan to Grey, telegram, 2 February, and despatch, 3 February; B 549, 556.

[2] Cartwright to Grey, telegram, 3 February; B 554. For Aehrenthal's irritation see his letter to Szögyény, private, 8 February; A 972, and Tschirschky to foreign office, telegram, 3 February; Romberg to Bülow, 12 February; G 9321, 9332.

[3] Aehrenthal to Thurn, telegram, 3 February, A 960. Grey discounted the idea that "a yearly payment of interest to Russia will put Bulgaria in political leading strings. She grows more independent every year and, rather than become subservient to Russia, would herself raise a loan and pay off the debt" (Grey to Lowther, telegram, 6 February; B 561).

[4] Marschall to foreign office, telegram, 2 February; G 9317. The grand vizier wanted 100,000,000 francs at once and 25,000,000 later (B 548, note).

[5] Marschall to foreign office, telegram, 3 February; G 9320.

[6] Grey to Lowther, telegram and despatch, 2 February; B 548, 552. Grey declared himself "all in favour of the Russian proposals", but reminded Izvolsky of the necessity of not raising the question of the Straits (Grey to Nicolson, private, 2 February; B 551). Izvolsky at once sent the necessary assurances to Constantinople (Nicolson to Grey, 4 February; B 558). British approval of the Russian scheme was made known to Germany (Metternich to foreign office, telegram, 2 February; Kühlmann to Bülow, 5 February; G 9318, 9325) and to Austria (Mensdorff to Aehrenthal, telegram, 3 February; A 959).

accept it in principle.[1] At the same time a counter-proposal was submitted: the Turkish claims, which were put at 150,000,000 francs, would be met by capitalizing the annual Turkish payment of £T350,000 on the indemnity of 1879, still due for seventy-four years, which would come to 149,500,000 francs, and by the remission of the indemnity.[2] As Russia was willing to cancel the indemnity to the amount of 120,000,000 francs[3] and the Porte reduced its claims to 125,000,000 francs,[4] an agreement was seemingly in sight.

Before it was actually reached,[5] a new complication was introduced by a proposal of the Entente representatives in Sofia that their governments should be the first to recognize Ferdinand as King of Bulgaria[6] and by the visit of that prince to St Petersburg. Grey at once vetoed the proposal, pointing out that if the Entente acted without inviting Germany, Austria and Italy to join, "we shall be exposed to charge of altering Treaty of Berlin without consent of other Treaty Powers, the very thing which we have reprobated in the action of Austria".[7] Ferdinand's

---

[1] In view of the Turkish acceptance, the Russian government requested that Bulgaria should be asked to cancel her mobilization (Sverbeyev to Aehrenthal, 9 February; A 980: Tschirschky to foreign office, telegram, 9 February; G 9327). Aehrenthal refused, on the ground that Bulgaria had already decided to dismiss her reservists (Aehrenthal to Sverbeyev, 10 February; A 985).

[2] Lowther to Grey, 6 February; B 562: Marschall to foreign office, telegram, 6 February, and despatch, 11 February; G 9324, 9331.

[3] Marschall to foreign office, telegram, 9 February; G 9328: Lowther to Grey, telegram, 19 February; B 589.

[4] Lowther to Grey, telegram, 19 February; B 590.

[5] From this point, the British, German and Austrian documents throw little light on the negotiations.

[6] Buchanan to Grey, telegram, 9 February; B 563.

[7] Grey to Bertie, telegram, 9 February; B 564. Aehrenthal learned of the suggestion and proposed a counter-stroke: he would remind Bulgaria of his statement immediately after the proclamation of independence that Austria was ready to recognize the new kingdom (Aehrenthal to Szögyény, telegram, 14 February; A 991: memorandum of Schoen, 15 February; G 9333). The German government agreed, but declared that it saw no way of preventing the Entente Powers from acting—which, however, would avail them nothing, as the consent of all the Powers was required (memorandum of Kiderlen, 15 February; G 9334: Szögyény to Aehrenthal, telegram, 16 February; A 999). The hopelessness of the situation from the Austrian point of view was reflected in the statement of General Nicolayev that he had not been able to speak to the prince about the Austro-Bulgarian understanding and that in the event of an Austro-Serbian war, "an active participation by Bulgaria was,

visit to the Russian capital presented real difficulties. The prince had expressed the desire to attend the funeral of the Grand Duke Vladimir.

This request could not possibly be refused [Izvolsky explained] and the Russian government could not receive him otherwise than as a king and give him sovereign honours...if the prince were not received as a king it would be an affront to Bulgaria and would throw that country into the arms of Austria and would also run counter to public sentiment here.[1]

Izvolsky offered apologies to the Turkish ambassador in St Petersburg, requested the German government to take act of the "Zwangslage" in which Russia found herself,[2] and sought Aehrenthal's assistance in expediting the Russo-Turkish negotiations at Constantinople, the success of which would make possible the formal recognition of Bulgaria. The Austrian minister, already annoyed by the rumour that the Entente Powers had recognized Bulgaria,[3] consulted Berlin before replying,[4] and on receiving assurances that Germany would not grant recognition until the conditions long ago formulated had been fulfilled,[5] sent a curt refusal of the Russian suggestion.[6] The British government decided that they "must just stand aside" and directed Sir Arthur Nicolson "to avoid at the funeral any position likely to compromise them".[7] In French eyes, "no change in the situation" was effected by the courtesies of Russia to its guest.[8] Izvolsky was thus left to deal with Ferdinand as best he could.

in the present circumstances, pretty well out of the question" (Hranilovich to Conrad, 18 February; A 1012)—and by this time, as will be seen in a later chapter, an Austro-Serbian war was not out of the question.
[1] Nicolson to Grey, telegram, 19 February; B 584. The forthcoming reception was announced in Sofia and represented as signifying recognition of the new kingdom by the Entente Powers (Thurn to Aehrenthal, telegram, 19 February; A 1019).
[2] Bülow to William II, 19 February; G 9335.
[3] Aehrenthal to Szögyény, telegram, 19 February; A 1013.
[4] Aehrenthal to Szögyény, telegram, 21 February; A 1029.
[5] Szögyény to Aehrenthal, telegram, 22 February; A 1034. Cf. Schoen to Tschirschky, 25 February; G 9341.
[6] Aehrenthal to Szögyény, telegram, 23 February; A 1037.
[7] Minute of Grey on B 584 and note 1.
[8] Romberg to foreign office, telegram, 21 February; G 9337.

The prince, arriving in St Petersburg on 21 February, was received at the station by the Grand Duke Constantine, a retinue of generals, and a guard of honour, which gave cheers for "your tsarist majesty". At the funeral service, he entered the church last of the visiting princes and, pretending (as was thought) not to be able to find a seat, stood by the side of the tsar. On the following day a dinner in his honour was given by the tsar. In the press, the affair was spoken of as the "recognition of the Kingdom of Bulgaria", since Izvolsky refrained from making clear that it was only an "act of courtesy".[1] The prince gave both the tsar and Izvolsky "solemn assurances that there was no understanding of any kind between Austria and Bulgaria", to which Izvolsky replied that "of course if His Royal Highness said so he was bound to believe him, but that many had believed otherwise".[2] Ferdinand also declared that in the event of a conflict between Austria and Serbia, "Bulgaria would take no action against the latter country". Speaking to Nicolson, Izvolsky declared that he did not have "absolute confidence" in these assurances, but he thought that "for a time at least His Royal Highness would act in accordance with them";[3] probably a correct reading of the enigmatic prince's character.[4] Whether, as the grand vizier of Turkey claimed to know, a far-reaching

[1] Pourtalès to foreign office, telegram, 21 February, and despatch, 23 February; G 9338, 9340.

[2] Nicolson to Grey, telegram, 27 February; B 620.

[3] Nicolson to Grey, 28 February; B 625.

[4] On the way home, Ferdinand travelled via Vienna and sought to see Aehrenthal, who was willing to receive him privately, but not as king (Aehrenthal to Thurn, private, 5 March; A 1119). The prince, who had understood from his minister in Vienna, Sarafov, that Aehrenthal had declined an interview, was greatly irritated (Thurn to Aehrenthal, telegrams, 7 March; A 1139, 1150), whereupon Aehrenthal declared that Sarafov had misrepresented his language and demanded the minister's recall (Aehrenthal to Thurn, telegram, 8 March; A 1147). Ferdinand professed to be satisfied by Aehrenthal's explanations (Thurn to Aehrenthal, telegram, 10 March; A 1175), but he snubbed Thurn by refusing to speak with him at a diplomatic reception, which led the latter to ask for his own recall (Thurn to Aehrenthal, private, 11, 22 March; A 1187, 1318). Aehrenthal was, however, reluctant to give Ferdinand this satisfaction and tried to console his representative by pointing out that his predecessors had had similar experiences with Ferdinand (Aehrenthal to Thurn, private, 1 April; A 1440). Cf. Romberg to Bülow, 10 March; G 9347.

political agreement was reached between Ferdinand and the Russian government,[1] cannot at present be determined.[2]

After this comedy was concluded, the Turkish foreign minister repaired to St Petersburg at the beginning of March. An agreement was soon reached in principle,[3] but Izvolsky proposed an additional article in the protocol, the effect of which was that "now that the compensation question had been settled Turkey declared she expressly recognized the new political order of things in Bulgaria".[4] As a result of British protests,[5] a declaration signed by Izvolsky was substituted to the effect that the abandonment by Russia of the indemnity annuities should not come into force until Turkey had informed the Signatory Powers that she no longer opposed recognition of the new situation in Bulgaria.[6] On this basis, the Russo-Turkish agreement was

[1] Pallavicini to Aehrenthal, telegrams, 13, 15 March; A 1202, 1219: Lowther to Grey, telegram, 18 March; B 708. The terms of the supposed agreement, as indicated to Lowther, are quite different from those of the military convention about which there were negotiations between Russia and Bulgaria later in the year (cf. E. Laloy, *Les documents secrets des archives du ministère des affaires étrangères de Russie publiés par les Bolchéviks* [Paris, 1919], pp. 52–8; M. Bogitshevich, *Causes of the war* [London, 1920], pp. 89–93).

[2] Nicolson thought it unwise to sound Izvolsky on the matter, because "he informed me on a previous occasion that nothing of any interest passed in the two interviews which he had with His Royal Highness and he would naturally repeat this statement were I again to allude to the matter". The fact, however, that the agreement was so much in favour of Bulgaria gave, in the ambassador's mind, "some colour to the presumption that the main conditions may be authentic" (Nicolson to Grey, 21 March; B 734). General Nicolayev denied that the prince had undertaken any engagement at St Petersburg with respect to the attitude of Bulgaria in an Austro-Serbian conflict (Thurn to Aehrenthal, telegram, 21 March; A 1306).

[3] Pourtalès to Bülow, 6 March; G 9344. The German government tried to upset the transaction by declaring the Russian proposal in respect of the Oriental Railway unsatisfactory and by appealing to France for assistance (Schoen to Radolin, 7 March; G 9345) but was rebuffed (Radolin to foreign office, telegram, 10 March; G 9346). The French government later asserted that the German request had come too late (Radolin to Bülow, 17 March; G 9350). Berlin was doubtless trying to take advantage of the new situation created between France and Germany by the Moroccan agreement of 8 February.

[4] Nicolson to Grey, telegram, 13 March; B 677.

[5] Nicolson to Grey, telegram, 13 March; Grey to Nicolson, telegram, 15 March; B 678, 684.

[6] Nicolson to Grey, telegram, 16 March; B 696. The British government did not like this any better than the proposed additional article; "our position will in any case remain the same", noted Hardinge and Grey.

signed *ad referendum* on 15 March. The Russian government renounced forty annuities of war indemnities, and the Porte secured the right to capitalize the other thirty-four at four per cent. Of the 125,000,000 francs realized by this arrangement, 40,000,000 were allowed for the tribute of Eastern Rumelia, the same amount for the Oriental Railway, 2,000,000 for a minor line, and 43,000,000 for the crown lands in Eastern Rumelia and Bulgaria; the Porte renounced all claims to the Bulgarian tribute and its original demand that Bulgaria should take over part of the Ottoman public debt. Turkey was not to receive any cash, but ultimately she would profit to the amount which the British Government had suggested as an equitable compensation.[1]

The bargain was so profitable for Turkey that the German government naturally advised the Porte to accept it.[2] Bulgaria, on the other hand, was not altogether pleased. The price to be paid for the Turkish crown lands was deemed too high, the provision was resented which required Bulgaria to pay the tribute of Eastern Rumelia from the proclamation of independence to the final adjustment, and likewise the stipulation that Bulgaria would still have to settle with the Oriental Railway Company,[3] without which German and Austrian recognition would not be granted.[4] General Paprikov, the foreign minister, repaired to St Petersburg to secure better terms,[5] and Liapchev returned to Constantinople. The counter-revolution which took place in Constantinople on 13 April so alarmed the Bulgarians that they considered mobilization, but, on the advice of Liapchev, postponed it for a few days. The hint was sufficient for the Turks, and the agreement was finally signed on 19 April.[6]

---

[1] Text in B 696, ed. note.
[2] Schoen to Marschall, telegram, 20 March; G 9351.
[3] Romberg to Bülow, 19 March; G 9352.
[4] Liapchev gave assurances to the German minister that the claims of the Oriental Railway would be adjusted (Romberg to Bülow, 25 March; G 9353). The German government denied in St Petersburg the insinuations of the Russian minister in Sofia that its insistence on these claims being satisfied was dictated by hostility to Russia (Schoen to Pourtalès, telegram, 10 April; G 9355).
[5] The Russian minister in Sofia, Sementovsky, strongly supported the Bulgarian point of view (Romberg to Bülow, 24 April; G 9359), as did also Sir George Buchanan, the British agent (Sir G. W. Buchanan, *My mission to Russia* [London, 1923], I, 79).    [6] Buchanan to Grey, 28 April; B 857.

Instead of having to pay the Eastern Rumelian tribute from 5 October, Bulgaria was let off with the payment of interest on it, and she further secured that the compensation to the Oriental Railway should be made out of the 40,000,000 francs earmarked for the line in the Russo-Turkish protocol.[1]

Russia was the first to recognize the new kingdom,[2] the tsar telegraphing congratulations to " His Majesty King Ferdinand I ". Great Britain followed suit immediately.[3] Germany and Austria-Hungary waited until they received assurances from the Bulgarian government that the Oriental Railway Company would be compensated.[4] As a kind of offset to the success which the Triple Entente had undoubtedly scored in bringing about the settlement, the representatives of the Triple Alliance in Sofia presented their recognition collectively, in order to demonstrate their solidarity.[5] In point of time, this was the last problem of the long crisis to find a solution. Probably the delay was due in part to the fact that for weeks the Powers had to give their more immediate attention and energy to the questions of Serbia and Montenegro, which will next be discussed.

[1] Text in B 853, enclosure. Bulgaria had to make certain small direct payments for postal materials, lighthouses and sanitary services. The question of the *vakoufs* was settled in a separate protocol. Bulgaria promised full liberty of worship to Moslems, and the name of the sultan was still to be pronounced in the public prayers.

[2] This was apparently suggested by the British government (Grey to Nicolson, 27 April; B 854).

[3] Grey to Buchanan, telegram, 23 April; B 851.

[4] Bülow to William II, 20 April; Schoen to Romberg, 26 April; G 9356, 9361: Aehrenthal to Thurn, telegrams, 21, 26 April; A 1554, 1569: Cartwright to Grey, telegram, 21 April; B 849.

[5] Romberg to foreign office, telegram, 27 April; G 9362. Buchanan to Grey, 28 April; B 857.

# CHAPTER X

## The Question of Serbia: Russia's Retreat

THE AUSTRO-TURKISH agreement of 26 February 1909[1] and the Turco-Bulgarian settlement arranged through the good offices of Russia[2] disposed of the two questions involving an alteration in the Treaty of Berlin which were raised in October 1908 by the Austrian annexation of Bosnia-Herzegovina and the proclamation of Bulgarian independence. Nevertheless, the European crisis was not resolved by these two transactions, for the crisis had arisen not so much from the cavalier treatment of Turkey by Austria and Bulgaria as from the protest of Serbia against the action of Austria and the support extended to Serbia by Russia and Great Britain. In spite of having no *locus standi* in the Bosnian matter, the Serbian government not only protested against the annexation but demanded territorial compensation at the expense of Austria-Hungary, and the Russian and British governments refused to recognize the annexation. By the middle of December 1908 the relations of Austria and Serbia were primed with dangerous possibilities,[3] and the relations of Austria and Russia had become so strained that intercourse between the two governments had been reduced to written communications.[4] For the moment Izvolsky and Aehrenthal were equally nonplussed.[5] In such circumstances anything might happen.

[1] See above, p. 119.  [2] See above, pp. 141–2.
[3] See above, pp. 76–8.  [4] See above, pp. 89–90.
[5] Aehrenthal inquired of his representative in Belgrade what would be the effect on Serbia if the Austrian or Hungarian parliament were to reject the pending commercial treaty between the Monarchy and Serbia (Aehrenthal to Forgách, 19 December; A 777). Forgách replied that rejection could not increase the tension between the two countries and that acceptance would not modify it (Forgách to Aehrenthal, telegram, 21 December; A 782). When the British minister in Belgrade sounded Forgách on the possibility of economic concessions by Austria to Serbia, particularly in railway matters, Forgách replied that the time was not yet "ripe" (Forgách to Aehrenthal, 17 January 1909; A 897: Whitehead to Grey, 18 January; B 520), and Aehrenthal agreed with him (Aehrenthal to Forgách, 23 January, 7 February, A 919, 969). Izvolsky admitted that "he feared the question of finding an adequate compensation for Serbia was almost insoluble" and that "he could not devise any way out of the difficulty" (Nicolson to Grey, telegram, 24 January; B 530).

The danger of the situation was thrown into sharp relief by the action of Serbia. Towards the end of December the skupshtina voted additional war credits which brought the total up to 34 millions of dinars.[1] Then on 2 January 1909 Milovanovich, the foreign minister, delivered a sensational speech in which he declared that Bosnia must receive autonomy and that Austria must recognize the Save and the Danube as her southern boundary; in addition he asserted that the effect of Austrian policy had been to "make slaves out of the people of the two Serbian lands". Aehrenthal, who had a high regard for Milovanovich personally, was most indignant,[2] and immediately demanded a disavowal.[3] The Serbian statesman at once explained that "make slaves of" was an inaccurate translation of the Serbian word *zarobiti*, which meant "subjugate", and declared that the Serbian aspirations did not extend to the Serb provinces of Austria; in Forgách's opinion, the speech was intended for internal consumption and "not much importance" was to be attached to it.[4] Nevertheless, Aehrenthal insisted on an apology, of which he formulated the text,[5] and notified the Powers and the other Balkan capitals.[6] Milovanovich sparred for time,[7] but finally agreed to the publication of a written apology,[8] with which Aehrenthal declared himself satisfied.[9]

[1] Forgách to Aehrenthal, telegram, 23 December; A 787. The minister of war was supposed to have said that 40 millions were needed to make the army ready for war.

[2] Cartwright to Grey, telegram, 5 January; B 501. Aehrenthal assured Cartwright, the British ambassador, that "he did not wish for war; in fact, Austria-Hungary was perfectly well aware that no glory and no satisfaction could be obtained from fighting Serbia"; but the incident "showed the necessity for Austria-Hungary to demand solid guarantees from any new Serbian government which might now be formed to the effect that they abandoned all exaggerated chauvinistic pretensions" (Cartwright to Grey, 6 January; B 504).

[3] Aehrenthal to Forgách, telegram, 3 January; A 832.

[4] Forgách to Aehrenthal, telegram, 5 January; A 837.

[5] Aehrenthal to Forgách, telegram, 5 January; A 843.

[6] Circular telegram of Aehrenthal, 5 January; A 845.

[7] Forgách to Aehrenthal, telegram, 6 January; A 846.

[8] Forgách to Aehrenthal, telegrams, 7 January; A 853, 854.

[9] Aehrenthal to Forgách, telegram, 7 January; A 852. Forgách discounted the assertions of the Vienna press that Milovanovich had dared to make his speech only because of the "appui moral" which Serbia received from England; but he thought that the British minister, Whitehead, who derived his income from the family torpedo factory at Fiume, manifested his Serbian sympathies

If the incident was thus happily closed, the general situation remained none the less dangerous. The calling up of the new Serbian recruits at the end of January, instead of in May, seemed to indicate the Serbian conviction that "war was to be regarded as certain and unavoidable in the spring".[1]

Both the Russian and the British governments began to grow uneasy. Izvolsky feared that, with the Austro-Turkish agreement in his pocket, Aehrenthal would show himself "all the more intransigent" towards Serbia, and he would not be convinced that Austria did not cherish far-reaching ambitions in respect of Serbia.[2] Grey was perhaps more concerned over the situation between Austria and Turkey than about the

in an unfortunate manner (Forgách to Aehrenthal, 10 January; A 870). Grey was of the opinion that "Mr Whitehead is doing very well" (minute on B 520).

[1] Forgách to Aehrenthal, 20 January; A 906. The Serbian government proposed to send a note to the Powers demanding, in keeping with Milovanovich's speech, autonomy for Bosnia (Forgách to Aehrenthal, telegrams, 18, 22 January; A 899, 913). Aehrenthal declared forthwith that he would not accept such a note (Aehrenthal to Forgách, telegram, 23 January; A 918). It was therefore postponed (Forgách to Aehrenthal, telegram, 27 January; A 928) and submitted to Russia and Great Britain, both of whom expressed strong disapproval (Nicolson to Grey, telegram, 31 January; Grey to Whitehead, telegram, 2 February; B 544, 545: Forgách to Aehrenthal, telegram, 6 February; A 967: Gruyich to foreign office, 9 February; S 50). Consequently the note was not circulated (Forgách to Aehrenthal, telegram, 8 February; A 970).

[2] Pourtalès to Bülow, 15 January; G 9346. According to Descos, the French minister in Belgrade, who claimed to have it from the French ambassador in St Petersburg, there were two conflicting tendencies in Russian policy. Izvolsky, who regarded Serbia and Montenegro as valuable allies for a later reckoning with Austria, wished to drag out the Bosnian question, keeping the two Slav states quiet for the moment but not satisfying them. On the other hand, Charykov, who was sympathetic with Neo-Slavism, was anxious to obtain a large autonomy for Bosnia (Forgách to Aehrenthal, 26 January; A 925). Charykov told the Serbian minister in St Petersburg that "in the matter of territorial compensation, Russia will do everything for us that is possible" (Popovich to foreign office, 25 January; S 44). General Taube, the former military attaché in Belgrade, said that Russia was reorganizing her army so as to be able to pursue a policy "which corresponds to her tradition and greatness"; "Serbia must take this into account and wait for a more favourable time" (Popovich to foreign office, 27 January; S 46). The British ambassador did not think it "very wise on the part of Russia to have gone so far in the way of assurances to Serbia... The meaning of these assurances will doubtless be amplified in Belgrade, and may give rise to hopes which it will be difficult to realize" (Nicolson to Grey, private, 21 January; B 525).

Austro-Serbian problem, but, he noted, "the situation is getting so ominous that in the interests of peace whatever settlement first appears practicable should be encouraged", and "if a conflict were to take place between Austria and Turkey it would be a very rash assumption to suppose that it would be limited, as far as continental nations are concerned, to Austria and Turkey alone".[1] But conscious as they were of the distrust with which they were regarded by Aehrenthal, both ministers evidently felt the futility of offering any suggestions to the Austrian government.[2]

Italy and France were, however, freer to act, and they inquired whether the German government would be disposed to join with the Western Powers in mediation. When Schoen, the German foreign minister, replied evasively, Jules Cambon, the French ambassador, suggested that Germany might inquire in Vienna and France in St Petersburg whether they could be of use,[3] and was supported by his Italian colleague.[4] The German Emperor, who thought the suggestion "academic",

[1] Minute on B 506; Grey to Rodd, 8 January; B 509.

[2] Mensdorff told Grey that in Austria the suspicion prevailed that "we were siding against Austria because she was a friend of Germany". Grey dismissed this as "quite absurd". "As a matter of fact," he continued, "I had carefully abstained from any attempt on any occasion to make mischief between Austria and Germany. Had I ever attempted to do that, we should have been exposed to the charge of attempting to isolate Germany: a charge which was often made, but for which there was no justification. The balance of power in Europe was preserved by the present grouping, and I should not think of wishing to disturb it" (Grey to Cartwright, private, 6 January; B 505).

[3] Memorandum of Schoen, 20 January; G 9365. The idea seems to have originated with Italy (Goschen to Grey, 7 January; B 507). The French apparently had in mind reviving the idea of a conference, but were not sure of the Russian attitude and wished Grey to sound Benckendorff on the matter (Bertie to Grey, telegram, 21 January; B 524). Grey appears to have telegraphed to Nicolson, for the latter stated that Izvolsky had some "misgiving", on the ground that "France will be inclined to support Austria, and that England will be disposed to associate herself with France, and thus leave Russia isolated if she presses for compensation for Serbia and Montenegro" (note on B 528). (This lack of harmony between France and Russia was to be more in evidence later on.) Grey replied: "I have already assured the Russian government of my diplomatic support in the question of compensation to Serbia and Montenegro with a view to arriving at a peaceful solution, and you may assure M. Izvolsky that I have not modified my intention" (Grey to Nicolson, telegram, 23 January; B 528).

[4] Memorandum of Stemrich, 22 January; G 9366.

expressed to Szögyény, the Austrian ambassador in Berlin, his "full approval" of Aehrenthal's policy,[1] and the German foreign office could see no reason "for helping M. Izvolsky out of his unpleasant situation".[2] So, in spite of a second attempt by Cambon, nothing came of this plan.[3]

The next opportunity for launching some kind of mediation or for a decisive discussion was provided by the visit of the British royal pair to Berlin early in February, but the conversations of Sir Charles Hardinge, the permanent under-secretary of state, who accompanied King Edward, were singularly barren. Bülow, the German chancellor, confined himself to saying that he had not approved of Aehrenthal's method in dealing with the Bosnian question, but had been compelled to support him; Hardinge did not, as Aehrenthal had greatly feared that he would,[4] raise the question of autonomy for the annexed provinces. The German chancellor thought that Serbia might be satisfied by a commercial treaty and some railway concessions, but warned that Austria was "becoming exasperated by the provocative attitude of the Serbian government". When Hardinge pointed out that if war unhappily resulted, it would be "very desirable" for Austria to promise to respect the independence and integrity of Serbia and asked if Germany would make representations to Vienna, Bülow replied that "it

[1] Szögyény to Aehrenthal, private, 21 January: A 912.
[2] Memorandum of Kiderlen, 23 January; G 9367.
[3] Bülow to Tschirschky, 6 February; G 9372. In Bülow's opinion, the French were suspicious of Izvolsky's policy, but were reluctant to make isolated representations at St Petersburg, lest they irritate their ally; which was all the more reason why Germany should not help pull the chestnuts out of the fire. Since Izvolsky continued to fear an Austrian attack on Serbia (Pourtalès to foreign office, telegram, 25 January; G 9368), the German government declared that "according to our information Austria-Hungary does not desire war and if, nevertheless, it should be forced upon her, will neither infringe the independence of Serbia nor seek Serbian territory" (Schoen to Pourtalès, telegram, 25 January; G 9369). The German assurances were based on knowledge of a letter which Francis Joseph intended to write to the tsar and which was finally sent on 28 January (A 935; see above, p. 89).
[4] Aehrenthal to Szögyény, 8 February; A 971. The German government replied that it did not expect the question to be raised, but that it would refuse to discuss it (memorandum of Schoen, 9 February; G 9373: Szögyény to Aehrenthal, telegram, 9 February; A 976).

would be difficult for Germany to act alone".[1] But both states-men believed that since Russia was in no position to go to war and Great Britain, Germany and France all desired to see war avoided, the peace was not likely to be disturbed. Bülow received the impression that Great Britain had abandoned the idea of a conference; at any rate Hardinge said that it could not be held without a previous understanding on all disputed points, and that if such agreement were reached, a conference would be unnecessary (Hardinge's memorandum is silent on this point).[2] Thus no advance was made towards a solution of the Austro-Serbian problem.[3]

A few days after Hardinge had returned from Berlin, however, the British government decided to intervene.[4] On 13 February it learned that Izvolsky had information "from a good source"

[1] Hardinge repeated this warning several days later to Stumm, who, however, insisted that Austria cherished no aggressive intentions against Serbia (memorandum of Stumm, 13 February; G 9375).

[2] Memorandum of Hardinge, 11 February; B, pp. 608–9: memorandum of Bülow, 10 February; G 9330. Cf. Szögyény to Aehrenthal, telegrams, 12, 14 February; A 989, 992. Szögyény reported that King Edward was friendly and did not indulge in harsh criticism of Austrian policy (Szögyény to Aehrenthal, 17 February; A 1003).

[3] Izvolsky was much annoyed by the official communiqué issued in Berlin on the British visit, which stated that there was "a complete understanding between Great Britain and Germany". He said: "This means Great Britain has joined Germany and Austria in Near Eastern policy. France has come into better relations with Germany [the Franco-German agreement about Morocco of 9 February], and Russia has been isolated." Nicolson protested vainly against this interpretation (Nicolson to Grey, telegram, 13 February; and despatch, 14 February; B 567, 570). Although Grey was absent, Hardinge at once telegraphed in his name that "there is no foundation whatever for the suspicions of M. Izvolsky...and there will be no modification whatever in the policy of His Majesty's government which is based on close co-operation with Russia and they will continue to give him their full diplomatic support in securing a peaceful solution of the Balkan questions" (Grey to Nicolson, telegram, 14 February; B 568). Hardinge sent to Izvolsky his own account of his conversation with Bülow, and remarked: "It is really very trying that he [Izvolsky] should, after all we have done and are doing for him, not realize the loyalty of our attitude" (Hardinge to Nicolson, private, 16 February; B, pp. 596–7). Izvolsky declared himself "much gratified" by these "frank assurances", and "quite convinced of the loyalty of His Majesty's government" (Nicolson to Grey, telegram, 15 February; B 571).

[4] Less than a week before Grey had refused to make any suggestions to Serbia for a settlement (Grey to Whitehead, 9 February; B 566). He had also declined to advise Serbia on the question whether she should conclude an alliance with Bulgaria (Whitehead to Grey, telegram, 3 February; Grey to Whitehead, telegram, 6 February; B 553, 560).

that "Austria intends to present shortly an ultimatum to Serbia, which, if not obeyed, will probably be followed by a punitive expedition, or execution, as it is termed".[1] Two days later the Russian chargé in London and the French ambassador presented "information...as to the Austrian intentions towards Serbia which has made us very apprehensive".[2] Perhaps most significant of all was a veiled threat from Izvolsky:

If Russia [Nicolson reported] were compelled by force of circumstances to passively assist at an Austrian occupation or invasion of Serbia, it would mean the complete collapse of her present policy, and question would of necessity arise whether she ought not to change entirely her course and abandon her alliance and *entente*....From Berlin there had been frequent hints that Russia was steering a wrong course and making combinations which at a critical moment would prove of no value.[3]

Since from the very beginning of the crisis it had been British policy to maintain the *entente* with Russia, the time had now come to act. Moreover, inasmuch as Bülow had expressed to Hardinge his desire that England, France and Germany should co-operate in the Near East, there was a chance to test the value of his professions: "If Bülow should refuse to join with France and ourselves, then we shall know exactly where we are."[4]

Accordingly a telegram was drafted which, if approved by the French and Russian governments, was to be sent to the British ambassador in Vienna for presentation to Aehrenthal, and Germany was to be asked to join in the proposed action.[5] The

[1] Nicolson to Grey, telegram, 13 February; B 567.

[2] Hardinge to Nicolson, private, 16 February; B, p. 597. No light is thrown on what this information was; probably it was the same as Nicolson reported from St Petersburg. On 11 February Aehrenthal informed Forgách that he was doubtful whether it would be possible to renew the commercial *modus vivendi* with Serbia which would expire on 31 March, that Austria could not indefinitely tolerate the provocative attitude of Serbia, and that if Serbia persisted, "a clarification of the situation certainly cannot be avoided". Forgách was instructed to hint to his colleagues that the continuation of Serbian military preparations might compel Austria to abandon her rôle of "expectant and observing spectator" (Aehrenthal to Forgách, 11 February; A 987). Some of this may well have filtered through to the Entente capitals, although there is no record of it in the published documents.

[3] Nicolson to Grey, telegram, confidential, 15 February; B 572.

[4] Hardinge to Nicolson, private, 16 February; B, p. 597.

[5] Grey to Nicolson, telegram, 16 February; B 573. Izvolsky was asked to indicate "the terms for Serbia and Montenegro which he considers reasonable".

telegram began by saying that the British government was "very seriously disturbed by report that Austria feels she may be compelled to take active measures against Serbia in the near future, and is already contemplating them", and expressed the doubt "whether any assurances could induce Russia to regard such a situation with equanimity". The telegram then continued:

We are not aware that Serbia has taken any offensive steps or given any new provocation beyond general excitement at home. We hoped she was waiting, and intended to wait, till the Powers discussed her affairs.[1] You should explain this view to Baron d'Aehrenthal, and ask whether there is any definite action on the part of Serbia of which Austria complains, or whether she has reason to apprehend such action. In this event you should assure him that we will do our best at Belgrade, as we have done before successfully, to remove such cause of complaint, for we are most anxious, for reasons given above, to avert by every means in our power the contingency of seeing Austria compelled to take active measures against Serbia.[2]

To secure peace it seems undesirable to delay any longer discussion amongst the Powers of what settlement can be arrived at with regard to Serbian and Montenegrin interests. To initiate this discussion we would suggest that Austria should state confidentially to us what concessions she is prepared to make, for we have always understood that she is prepared to make concessions under Article 29 of the Treaty of Berlin, and to offer some other advantages in addition.[3]

The approval of the French and Russian governments having been secured,[4] the telegram was communicated to the German government,[5] and the adhesion of Italy invited.[6]

---

[1] Grey had insisted to Mensdorff that the problem of Serbia should be postponed until the Turkish and Bulgarian questions had been settled (Mensdorff to Aehrenthal, telegrams, 3, 10 February; A 959, 983). Cf. Gruyich to foreign office, 9 February; S 50.

[2] A week before, Grey had refused to discuss the Serbian demand for the autonomy of Bosnia, and while declaring his readiness to support "reasonable" Serbian demands, had insisted that his whole policy was directed to "the maintenance of peace" (Gruyich to foreign office, 9 February; S 50).

[3] B 585.

[4] Bertie to Grey, telegram, 18 February; Nicolson to Grey, telegram, 18 February; B 578, 581.

[5] B 573, ed. note. The telegram was also shown to the German ambassador in London, who expressed to his government his approval of the course proposed (Metternich to foreign office, telegram, 18 February; G 9376).

[6] Grey to Rodd, telegram, 19 February; B 587. Grey's explanations of his action are not without interest. To the French ambassador he said that while he welcomed the Franco-German agreement over Morocco, he "thought it

The French government, with but scant political interest in Serbia,[1] alarmed by rumours of an Austrian ultimatum,[2] and pressed by Great Britain,[3] warmly supported the proposed *démarche*,[4] even though the French ambassador in Vienna did not think that the representations would lead to any practical result.[5] Actually the representations were never made. For Bülow, immediately on receipt of the draft telegram, submitted

desirable to keep the *entente* between France and England as fresh and vigorous in the sunshine as it had been during the storms of the Algeciras Conference and on the other occasions ". If, as Cambon suggested, Germany at the moment "required a friendly foreign policy ", then "we should assist her to display a *façade d'amitié* ", for "only if Germany would co-operate with us in advising at Vienna a policy of moderation and peace that our efforts could be made effective " (Grey to Bertie, 16 February; B 574). To the German ambassador Grey explained that if Bülow had declared that "it would be difficult for Germany to act alone ", likewise "it was difficult for Russia to approach Austria direct with regard to the Serbian question ". Although "relations between Austria and Italy were also rather delicate ", he hoped that Italy would join in the proposed step, for "he thought it would have an excellent effect if these four Powers were shown to be working together for peace " (Grey to Goschen, 18 February; B 583). Later, when made aware that his proposal was resented by Aehrenthal (Cartwright to Grey, telegram, 20 February; B 592), he explained to Mensdorff that he had used the phrase "to avert the contingency of seeing Austria compelled to take active measures against Serbia " and not "prevent ". The object of the proposal had been "(1) to give Austria an opportunity for stating whether she wished us to counsel moderation at Belgrade, and if so, on what grounds to base our representation;... (2) we wished to bring within the sphere of negotiation the concessions which Austria was understood to be prepared to offer ". If Austria would make her concessions known, "the other Powers could then reinforce their counsels of moderation at Belgrade by saying that negotiations were beginning, and that Serbia must not do anything to disturb the peace or to give provocation while the negotiations were being carried on " (Grey to Cartwright, 24 February; B 604). Mensdorff's version is phrased somewhat differently (Mensdorff to Aehrenthal, telegram, 24 February; A 1047).

[1] Khevenhüller to Aehrenthal, 20 February; A 1027. The French ambassador in Vienna told his Serbian colleague, Simich, that "France, who was well known to have great economic and financial interests in Serbia and was her principal creditor, naturally wished to see war avoided between the Monarchy and Serbia " (memorandum of Gagern, Aehrenthal's *chef de cabinet*, 22 February; A 1036).

[2] Khevenhüller to Aehrenthal, telegram, 19 February, and despatch, 20 February; A 1017, 1028.

[3] Grey to Bertie, telegram, 19 February; B 591.

[4] Radolin to foreign office, telegrams, 19, 20 February; G 9377, 9380.

[5] Cartwright to Grey, telegram, 20 February; B 592. Aehrenthal had informed Crozier that "newspaper reports about an ultimatum to Serbia were entirely unfounded ", and that if the French government were alarmed, "it should convince the Serbian government of the folly of the policy it had hitherto pursued " (Aehrenthal to Szögyény, telegram, 20 February; A 1020).

to the emperor a long memorandum urging rejection of the
proposal, on the ground that Austria had patiently borne the
provocations of Serbia, and declaring that any diplomatic action
should be taken in Belgrade rather than in Vienna.[1] On the
following day, 20 February, it was learned that Aehrenthal
would not take kindly to the suggested step.[2] The British and
French ambassadors[3] were therefore put off with evasive answers
until a formal reply could be drafted. It was only on 22 February
that this document was communicated to Sir Edward Goschen
and Jules Cambon. The German government declared itself
"in entire accord" with the pacific intentions of the Anglo-
French proposal, but found it impossible to adhere to the
suggested form of procedure, for it would expose Austria-
Hungary "to the appearance of having given way to external
pressure". The suggestion was, however, made that "steps
should be taken at Belgrade to request the Serbian government
to guarantee that its provocative attitude will no longer be
maintained", and the opinion was offered that "an action at
Belgrade would be rendered all the more efficacious if all the
Powers, and particularly Russia, would participate in it". This
idea was immediately seized upon by Jules Cambon as "a way
in which the common action desired by His Majesty's government could still be secured", and, as will be seen presently,
was subsequently developed into official action.

One paragraph of the German reply stated:

Austria-Hungary has declared on several occasions that she did not
wish to attack Serbia. She has proved the sincerity of this declaration,
and her steadfast intention of adhering to it by her long sufferance
and by the imperturbability which she has hitherto retained, in spite
of numerous provocations on the part of Serbia.

The implication assuredly was, as the next sentence affirmed,
that "peace and order are endangered by Serbia alone". Yet

[1] Bülow to William II, 19 February; G 9379.
[2] Bülow to William II, 20 February; Tschirschky to foreign office, telegram,
20 February; G 9381, 9382: Aehrenthal to Szögyény, telegram, 20 February;
A 1020. For Aehrenthal's formal refusal, see Aehrenthal to Szögyény,
telegram, 23 February; A 1038.
[3] The Russian ambassador, being ill, deputed Jules Cambon to speak for
him. The Italian ambassador did not receive instructions until the following
day, when he vigorously supported the proposal.

the German government knew that Aehrenthal was now contemplating "a clearing-up of the relationship with Serbia, probably in March",[1] that he was indeed preparing to issue an ultimatum if Serbia did not come to heel and recognize the annexation.[2] If the German government could hardly be expected to reveal Aehrenthal's plans to the Entente Powers, yet its implied assurances of Austria's pacific intentions were scarcely justified.[3]

In face of this rebuff, the British government moved very cautiously. Though professing to "reciprocate cordially the sentiments expressed in the opening sentences of German reply", it pointed out to Berlin that "action at Belgrade is hardly likely to be efficacious unless Russia participates, and we doubt whether she can do so without some knowledge of terms, which Austria is likely to concede".[4] If, as reported from Paris, Herr von Kiderlen, now acting German foreign minister, was coming forward with a specific proposal, it would, in Grey's opinion, be necessary to make sure that the proposition "would really be carried through by the emperor and the German government".[5] As for a conference, which Tittoni, the Italian foreign minister, was once more urging, Grey "did not see what else could be

[1] Tschirschky to foreign office, telegram, 20 February; G 9382.

[2] Aehrenthal to Bülow, private, 20 February, received 22 February; A 1022; G 9386. Aehrenthal stated that he intended to offer Serbia a renewal of the existing commercial arrangement, provided Serbia would abandon her claims to territorial compensation or the demand for autonomy of Bosnia. Failing direct negotiations on these points, he would resort to an ultimatum. According to Baernreither, *Fragmente eines politischen Tagebuches*, p. 106 (entry of 21 February), Aehrenthal " is planning a *sommation* and an ultimatum to Serbia at the beginning of March: disarmament, dissolution of the committee, etc. If submission follows, good—if not, better, invasion [*Einmarsch*], another dynasty, customs union". The customs union was being thought of as "a kind of economic straight-jacket".

[3] The account of the proceedings in Berlin is taken from Goschen to Grey, 26 February; B 615. Cf. also his telegrams of 22, 23 February; B 595, 596, 597. For what was told the Austrians, cf. Szögyény to Aehrenthal, telegrams, 20, 22, 23 February; A 1023, 1024, 1033. Text of the German reply in G 9383.

[4] Grey to Goschen, telegram, 24 February; B 599.

[5] Grey to Bertie, 25 February; B 611. Bülow appealed to Grey to support the plan (Bülow to Metternich, telegram, 25 February; G 9394). Grey replied non-committally that he "was very glad to hear that a proposal was coming" and would be "delighted to receive it" (Grey to Goschen, 26 February; B 616). Actually, the proposal, which proved to be stillborn, was never communicated to Grey.

suggested", but he did not think that "any conference could be arranged unless Germany proposed it or unless it was ascertained through Germany that Austria would be willing to come into it".[1] In other words, the initiative for mediation must for the moment be left to others.[2] Grey confined himself to remarking to Metternich, when the ambassador asserted that "if Austria fought Serbia, Russia would not be threatened", that such things "were questions of race feeling, which had to be dealt with as matters of fact, and which had been the cause of many wars in history";[3] and to Mensdorff, the Austrian ambassador, that "it would be much easier to counsel patience at Belgrade when we had something to go upon", and that "if Austria was not prepared to hold any communication with the other Powers about the Serbian difficulty and meant to take matters into her own hands without giving any opportunity for mediation, the situation might become very serious".[4]

There was indeed good reason to regard the situation as "very serious". The British minister in Belgrade had reported a conversation with his Austrian colleague:

He told me yesterday that Austria would demand not only immediate cessation of military armaments,[5] but also guarantees that

[1] Grey to Rodd, 24 February; B 607. Cf. Lützow to Aehrenthal, telegram, 24 February; A 1050. Aehrenthal told the British ambassador in Vienna that "the prospect that the Serbian question might be raised there in an acute form might compel Austria-Hungary to abstain from taking part in the conference" (Cartwright to Grey, telegram, 24 February; B 603).

[2] Hardinge, noting that "our efforts to get Germany to co-operate with us and France have failed" and that "it appears from the telegrams which reach us that the situation daily grows worse and that an ultimatum from Austria to Serbia may be expected in the near future", suggested that the British and French governments should make representations to the Austrian ambassadors in London and Paris, by which Aehrenthal would be asked to indicate the economic concessions which he was willing to make to Serbia; these concessions would then be notified to Russia for an expression of opinion. If Austria would not indicate her intentions, then England and France should propose a conference "to settle this and other outstanding questions" (Minute on B 598). Grey did not adopt the suggestion.

[3] Grey to Goschen, 14 February; B 606. Cf. Metternich to foreign office, telegram, 24 February; G 9393.

[4] Grey to Cartwright, 24 February; B 604. Cf. Mensdorff to Aehrenthal, telegram, 24 February; A 1048.

[5] Aehrenthal had recently complained that "the military preparations which Serbia was making now were of a very serious character, and were giving rise to great disquietude here" (Whitehead to Grey, telegram, 17

the Serbian government would stop all further intrigues and propaganda in Bosnia and Croatia. He confirmed this to-day by saying that Austria would require Serbia to reverse her policy completely.

In Whitehead's opinion, no Serbian government could yield to this demand "except under pressure from all the Powers, including Russia".[1] Grey was no longer under any illusions: "the only way to avoid war", he told Paul Cambon, the French ambassador, "was for Serbia to renounce her territorial claims". But he was unwilling to give this advice to Serbia without the consent of Russia, for he had promised Izvolsky diplomatic support for the Serbian claims, though not to the point of war, nor could he ask Russia to give this advice in Belgrade "unless we could convince the Russian government that if Serbia were induced to renounce her territorial claims Germany would then do her part in supporting economic concessions".[2] The dilemma was real. Fortunately Aehrenthal had intimated that if Serbia would accept the Austro-Turkish protocol about to be signed and at the same time issue a declaration to the effect that she desired to cultivate peaceful relations with Austria-Hungary, the way would be opened for direct negotiations between Vienna and Belgrade. "If, after that, the Serbian government put forward their economic and commercial grievances in moderate language, they would be met by Austria-Hungary in a friendly

February; B 575). This statement being referred to Belgrade, the British minister reported that the second (ban) cavalry reservists to the number of about 2500 were being given three weeks' training; that while the legal peace footing of the army was 36,000 men, about 25,000 were with the colours; on the other hand, that the winter strength in recent years had rarely exceeded 15,000 (Whitehead to Grey, telegram, 19 February; B 588).

[1] Whitehead to Grey, telegram, 22 February; B 597. Cf. Aehrenthal to Forgách, 11 February; A 987 (footnote 30). On the other hand, the Austrian ambassador in Rome was reported as saying that "there had never been any question of an ultimatum to Serbia" (Rodd to Grey, telegram, 22 February; B 594).

[2] Grey to Bertie, 25 February; B 611. The Russian chargé in London was impressed by the "great uneasiness" prevailing there "because the negotiations between the Powers for the prevention of an Austro-Serbian conflict make no progress". He quoted the personal opinion of Hardinge that Russia should advise Serbia to abandon her claims for territorial compensation or the autonomy of Bosnia (Poklevsky to Izvolsky, telegrams, 24, 27 February; Siebert, pp. 75–6).

spirit."[1] Moreover, the Serbian government had just issued a memorandum giving pacific assurances and declaring its intention to await quietly the decision of the Powers.[2]

Grey therefore decided that the time had come to act, not at Vienna, but at St Petersburg. In a long telegram, he said:

...Nothing except economic concessions can be obtained for Serbia without a successful war. Unless Serbia renounces territorial claims there will be war. I understood from M. Izvolsky in October that these claims would probably have to be abandoned in the end: I made clear that we would support Russia in getting what could be obtained by diplomatic support, but that we could not press things to the point of war....

German ambassador informed me yesterday that some proposal was coming from Germany to us and France. I have not received it, but I think it will be to the effect that if Serbia will renounce territorial claims Austria should be invited to consider favourably economic concessions.

I have already expressed to French government opinion that Russian advice to Serbia to renounce territorial concessions cannot be expected unless there is firm assurance from Germany of support to obtain economic concessions at Vienna. To this I adhere. Time has now come when Russia should decide whether she means to give Serbia armed support to obtain territorial concessions or to tell her at the critical moment that in the interest of peace these demands cannot be supported. If Russia feels it difficult for her to be first to explain to Serbia the logic of the situation we and France might do so in the interests of peace, but we must first ourselves know what Russia intends to do.

We are of opinion that to risk Serbian territorial claims a war which

[1] Cartwright to Grey, telegram, 24 February; B 601. Cf. circular telegram of Aehrenthal, 24 February; A 1053, and Tschirschky to foreign office, telegram, 24 February; G 9391.
[2] Text in B 610. Izvolsky proposed that this memorandum should be communicated immediately to Vienna, and asked that "instructions should be sent to the British, Russian, French, and possibly Italian ambassadors at Berlin to take steps with the German government in this sense". Grey consented to the latter step if the other Powers agreed (Grey to Nicolson, telegram, 25 February; B 609). Several days later Serbia presented a new memorandum "of a less satisfactory nature, which [Izvolsky] hesitated to use as a basis for addressing Berlin" (Nicolson to Grey, telegram, 26 February; B 614). Grey advised the Serbian government to withdraw the document, in which he was supported by Hardinge in a conversation with the Serbian minister in London (Grey to Whitehead, 27 February; B 623: Gruyich to foreign office, 27 February; S 60).

might eventually involve the greater part of the continent of Europe must even from the Russian point of view be out of all proportion to the interests at stake.[1]

Great Britain thus abandoned the position she had maintained since October, that is, she withdrew her diplomatic support of the Serbian pretensions, and she advised Russia to do likewise. As a matter of fact, Russia had already advised Serbia in the sense desired, as will be seen presently, but this was not known in London. In taking such a strong line, Grey may well have been influenced by the knowledge that the French government had already urged practically the same course on its ally.[2]

When receiving, on 22 February, the note of the German government refusing to join in the proposed representations at Vienna,[3] the French ambassador had suggested that Germany might be willing to join in representations at Belgrade and also associate herself with the other Powers in conveying such assurances as they might receive from the Serbian government to Vienna. Kiderlen agreed to submit the proposal to the emperor if Cambon could secure the approval of his government; the Austrian ambassador thought it acceptable and was willing to guarantee that his government would not issue an ultimatum to Serbia "for a fortnight or three weeks";[4] the Russian ambassador declared that his government was "quite disposed to join the other Powers in making representations at Belgrade".[5] Bülow was delighted. He informed the emperor that "now that we have firmly and openly placed ourselves on the side of Austria, France will be forced, with or without England, to give peaceful counsels in St Petersburg", for "France for various reasons did not desire war",[6] and he suggested leaving any further action in St Petersburg to the French, with which William agreed.[7]

---

[1] Grey to Nicolson, telegram, 27 February; B 621.
[2] Nicolson to Grey, telegram, 26 February; B 612.
[3] See above, p. 153.
[4] Cf. Szögyény to Aehrenthal, telegram, 24 February; A 1044.
[5] Goschen to Grey, 26 February; B 615.
[6] Bülow to William II, 22 February; G 9388.
[7] Bülow to William II, 25 February; G 9395. The emperor was at first of a different mind. "In view of the seriousness of the situation," he wrote (comment on a telegram from Tschirschky, 24 February; G 9391), "it is necessary that we get in touch *immediately* with Paris and demand of France

We know nothing about the communications between Cambon and his government,[1] but on 26 February he informed Kiderlen that the French foreign minister, Pichon, was personally ready to recommend in London and St Petersburg the following procedure: France, England and Russia should advise Serbia to drop her territorial claims and refrain from all provocation of Austria. She should also be asked to indicate what economic concessions she desired, and the Powers would then inquire in Vienna whether Austria was prepared to negotiate on this basis.[2] Cambon undertook to draft with Kiderlen an identic note for presentation in Belgrade embodying these ideas, and he was confident that Russia would yield to French pressure.[3] This plan was, of course, quite different from what the British had in mind, for Grey insisted that before Serbia could be advised to

that she exert pressure jointly with us on Russia which will force this country to take a clear position with respect to Serbia (co-operate in the pressure on Belgrade). It must be made clear to France that in the event of Russian intervention against Austria, the *casus fœderis* will instantly and immediately arise for us, that is, mobilization. France must be asked for a clear, binding declaration that in this event she above all *will not make war on us*. Neither at the beginning of the war nor later. A declaration of neutrality will not suffice. If France refuses this declaration, it is to be interpreted by us as a *casus belli*, and the Reichstag as well as the world is to be informed that in spite of our request to go with us along the only possible way to maintain the peace of Europe, France has refused, and therefore has *willed the war*.

" A clarification in this form is necessary, so that we can at first exploit our mobilization against France and then refrain from it. In no circumstances can the army be placed in a situation, in which half of it is engaged against Russia, while half stands as covering against an uncertain France. We must use everything against the West or everything against the East. In the first case, if France refuses to give the declaration not to intervene in the Russo-Austro-German war. In the second case, if France is ready to exert pressure on Russia along with us to keep the peace and, in case of Russian refusal, not to attack us, by working together with Austria against Russia. Immediate execution in Paris. The chief of the general staff agrees." Bülow promptly squashed this imperial vagary, but it is worth noting that the emperor's suggestion foreshadowed the procedure used in 1914.

[1] The French diplomatic documents for the period are not yet available, and our scant knowledge of French policy is derived from the documents of other governments. Obviously France, having recently (9 February) concluded with Germany what seemed to be an advantageous agreement concerning Morocco, wished to avoid new difficulties with her over the Near East. Moreover, the then premier, Clemenceau, was always haunted by the fear that France would be dragged into war because of Anglo-German rivalry and would have to bear the brunt of the German offensive.

[2] Memorandum of Kiderlen, 26 February; G 9397.

[3] Memorandum of Kiderlen, 26 February; G 9398.

renounce her claims, assurances must be obtained from Aehrenthal that Austria would offer economic concessions.[1] The
French proposal reversed the order of action.

To secure its acceptance, the French government presented
a strongly worded note in St Petersburg:

The feeling of France for Russia [it ran], her adherence to the
indissoluble alliance which unites the two countries and the responsibility which France assumes in these circumstances, make it her duty
to enter upon an exchange of views with the Russian government
without delay in order to examine with it that line of policy which,
with due consideration of the higher interests of both countries, must
be maintained. The Russian government will surely agree with the
French government that both must do everything possible to prevent
the danger of an armed conflict in a question in which the vital
interests of Russia are not involved. French public opinion would be
unable to comprehend that such a question could lead to a war in
which the French and the Russian army would have to participate. . . .

The Russian ministry of foreign affairs publicly declared last
October that Russia, whatever might be her feelings regarding the
causes of the present crisis, could not see in them a *casus belli*. . . .

In connection with the Serbian demands—which, as is generally
recognized, are difficult to justify—we have expressed our doubt
whether it would be possible to realize them. But we have joined
with the Russian government in demanding that the question be
submitted to a conference. In reality, this is the only difficulty, for
which another solution must be found than that which the cabinet of
Belgrade demands with regard to its claims for territorial compensations. The moment has therefore arrived for Russia and France to
examine this question in common. We beg the Russian government
to communicate its opinion to us, in the firm conviction that the general
discussion of the question by both governments will permit the present
crisis to be solved under conditions which will be equally satisfactory
to France and to Russia.[2]

_____

[1] Grey to Goschen, 24 February; B 606: Metternich to foreign office,
telegram, 24 February; G 9393: Mensdorff to Aehrenthal, telegrams, 24, 25
February; A 1048, 1056. See above, p. 156.

[2] Note of the French embassy to the Russian government, 26 February;
Siebert, pp. 74–5. The rumour circulated in Paris that the Russian ambassador
had asked Pichon what would be the attitude of France if Russia went to
war on account of Serbia, and that the French foreign minister had been very
cool (Khevenhüller to Aehrenthal, telegram, 25 February, and despatch,
6 March; A 1058, 1127).

Izvolsky was in a greater dilemma than Grey. In his opinion the conduct of Serbia had not been provocative, at least recently; yet he was convinced, as he kept repeating to the British and German ambassadors, that in March, as soon as the Austro-Turkish agreement had been signed, Austria would proceed to military action against Serbia. The economic concessions, in return for which Serbia might be asked to abandon her territorial claims, he qualified as "illusory", for "Austria, as she had done in the past, would block Serbian trade whenever she thought it desirable to do so". Yet when pressed to state what concessions he thought might satisfy Serbia, he was unable to do so.[1] Izvolsky's fears were increased when, as he had expected,[2] Germany refused to join in representations at Vienna. If Austria moved against Serbia, declared the premier, Stolypin, "there would be such a movement in Russia which would be warmly supported by all parties without distinction, in favour of the government taking measures to assist Serbia in resisting Austrian aggression, that it would be quite impossible for the government to resist it".[3] But Russia was in no position to go to war; the

---

[1] Pourtalès to Bülow, 30 January, 20, 24 February; G 9364, 9387, 9403: Nicolson to Grey, 13, 14, 15, 17, 18, 24, 26 February; B 568, 570, 571, 577, 581, 582, 600, 612.

[2] Nicolson to Grey, telegram, 24 February; B 600. The German embassy in St Petersburg accused Nicolson of misrepresenting the nature of the German reply to Grey's proposals for a *démarche* in Vienna: Germany was pictured as following Aehrenthal implicitly, and he as bent at any price on exploiting the present situation and weakness of Russia in order to make Austrian preponderance felt in the Balkans. Bülow protested to London that this was not consonant with Grey's promise to co-operate in any proposals likely to promote peace (Bülow to Metternich, telegram, 27 March; G 9401). Grey transmitted the protest to Nicolson, adding that he had told Metternich that "it was quite incredible that any such language had been disseminated by British embassy" (Grey to Nicolson, telegram, 1 March; B 629). Nicolson denied that he had encouraged Izvolsky "in an anti-German and anti-Austrian line of policy", and said that there was "soreness in German and Austrian circles that Izvolsky leans more towards us than to them" (Nicolson to Grey, private, 9 March; B 660). Metternich never reported on the matter to Berlin, so far as the German documents show.

[3] Nicolson to Grey, 17 February; B 576. The British ambassador shared this view. "It is almost a certainty that, if Austria does attack Serbia," he reported, "Russian government will be compelled to take up arms" (Nicolson to Grey, telegram, 18 February; B 581). A week later he wrote: "There is an exceedingly bitter and angry feeling against Austria here, which mounts crescendo. . . . If Austrian troops begin to shoot down Serbs and Montenegrins, there will in all probability be a great outburst here" (Nicolson to Grey,

military chiefs thought that from three to five years would be needed to prepare the army, and the army itself was opposed to war.[1] In other words, Russia, on her own estimate of the situation, had either to abandon Serbia or go to war in unfavourable circumstances.

This was the situation when the French proposal was presented. Izvolsky was furious. The proposal as presented—the "Kiderlen proposal", he called it—was quite different from that suggested by Jules Cambon, which was "to ask for friendly declarations at Belgrade and to forward these to Vienna" and which he had accepted. The new proposal, "apparently inspired at Vienna and approved by Pichon", was intended "to substitute a direct agreement between Vienna and Belgrade for the joint action of the Powers, after the model of the Austro-Turkish settlement". The effect would be "to deliver Serbia to the mercy of an Austria armed to the teeth", whereas point 7 of the original programme for the conference had stipulated that the concessions to Serbia were to be determined by the Powers. No Serbian government could agree to the proposal; it "would call forth universal indignation in Russia, nor would it prevent a conflict".[2] He therefore rejected the proposal, although he did not object in principle to a *démarche* in Belgrade.[3] "France", he complained to Nicolson, "had gone over bag and baggage to Austria", and the game of Austria and Germany "was to put forward proposals to which they knew Russia would probably give a negative reply, and would thereby put Russia in the position either of being the obstacle to peace or of abandoning

private, 24 February; B 605). This belief was shared by the Austrian ambassador. "It must be definitely expected", he wrote, "that in the event that an offensive is undertaken on our part without Serbia having been guilty of a violation of the frontier, a storm will sweep through the country which will denounce our action as a deliberately prepared humiliation of a helpless kindred people" (Berchtold to Aehrenthal, 15 February; A 997).

[1] Berchtold to Aehrenthal, 15, 24 February; A 997, 1051. Berchtold discounted a rumour which had reached Aehrenthal (Aehrenthal to Berchtold, private, 19 February; A 1018) that a Russian mobilization was under consideration; a certain shifting of troops, which he admitted, was only a sign of the general "nervousness".

[2] Izvolsky to Nelidov, telegram, 27 February; Siebert, p. 76. Cf. Pourtalès to foreign office, telegram, 27 February; G 9406.

[3] Memorandum of Schoen on conversation with Jules Cambon, 28 February; G 9409.

the cause of a Slav state in the most humiliating manner ".[1]
In conversation with the French ambassador, Admiral Touchard,
Izvolsky " contrasted the loyal attitude of [the British] government, the friends of Russia, with that of Russia's ally and pointed
out...that in the Casablanca incident Russia had expressed her
readiness to remain faithful to the alliance in all eventualities ".[2]
But indignation did not solve the problem before him. And
so Izvolsky, like Grey, was driven by the logic of the situation
to the conclusion that the Serbian territorial claims must be abandoned. Accordingly on 27 February he telegraphed to Belgrade:

We hear with satisfaction that the Serbian government remains
true to its resolution not to depart from the peaceful standpoint which
it has assumed, to avoid everything which might lead to an armed
conflict between Serbia and Austria and to carry out no military
measures on the frontier.[3] We are convinced that the vital interests

[1] Nicolson to Grey, telegram, 26 February; B 612. Nicolson took advantage
of the moment to remark that " territorial compensation to Serbia or autonomy
of the two provinces in the sense she desired were evidently impossible to
obtain ". When he asked what concessions Izvolsky thought Serbia could
obtain, the latter had to reply that " he did not know " (Nicolson to Grey,
telegram, 26 February; B 613).

[2] Nicolson to Grey, telegram, 27 February; B 617. Touchard tried to
persuade Izvolsky that " the French government in no way desired to force
hands of Russian government or to ask them to take any steps which were
displeasing to them "; he also urged his government " not to press Kiderlen
proposal ". Pichon declared that there had been a " misunderstanding ": he
had " neither accepted nor recommended this proposal ", but " simply communicated it to London and Paris in order to ascertain the opinion of both
cabinets ", and he declared that " he himself found the form and manner of
the procedure unacceptable, especially the proposed *tête-à-tête* between
Austria and Serbia " (Nelidov to Izvolsky, telegram, 28 February; Siebert,
p. 79). Pichon also defended himself vigorously against the reproach of
lukewarmness about the alliance. " He has not ceased to let the cabinet of
Berlin thoroughly understand that France is supporting the policy of the
Russian government in this crisis on all points, and that it will uphold the
treaty of alliance which binds her to Russia in the most loyal manner."
But, he explained to the Russian ambassador, this policy " creates an extra-
ordinarily difficult situation for the two countries, neither of which wishes
war ", and he had therefore " sought means by which this danger might be
forestalled ". Nelidov was convinced that " if France failed Russia, this would
mean, so far as the British were concerned, the end of the Anglo-French
entente ", and therefore France could be relied upon; but he warned his
government that " the possibility of a war is regarded with very mixed feelings
by the press and public opinion here " (Nelidov to Izvolsky, 3 March;
Siebert, p. 81).

[3] Cf. the Serbian memorandum of 25 February (B 610, and p. 157 above).
On 27 February this promise was confirmed by the Serbian foreign minister

of Serbia, for whom we have always felt the greatest sympathy, necessarily impose on her this line of policy, which is also the only one that takes account of the general situation at the moment.

We have been able to convince ourselves through various sources that the Powers are not disposed to support the idea of a territorial aggrandisement of Serbia. The Royal government must deduce from this that all efforts to move the Powers to support such demands would remain futile and that Serbia can be assured of the sympathies of the Powers only if she refrains from insisting on demands which must lead to an armed conflict with Austria. We deem it necessary to warn the Royal government against adopting any attitude which might expose it to such a danger. We hope that Serbia, as she has just declared, will remain true to her commitments to follow the advice of the Great Powers. At the same time, we believe that the Serbian government must, in the prevailing circumstances, clearly declare to these Powers that it does not insist on its territorial demands and that it will rely upon the decisions of the Powers in all pending questions. These could then devote all their efforts to protecting the interests of Serbia.[1]

Thus Russia made the great surrender in the interests of peace. The decision was notified the same day to the Serbian minister[2] and the British ambassador,[3] and to France;[4] it was

to the British and German ministers in Belgrade. Milovanovich declared that Serbia would be guided by the advice of the Powers, but that she could not negotiate directly with Austria (Ratibor to foreign office, telegram, 27 February; G 9405: Whitehead to Grey, telegram, 27 February; B 618). A memorandum to this effect was communicated to the British foreign office on the same day, but since it contained a phrase describing the dilemma in which Serbia would be placed by the Austrian press campaign, Hardinge told the Serbian minister that "such language could serve no useful purpose and would prevent His Majesty's government from communicating the memorandum to the Austro-Hungarian government as a serious guarantee of Serbia's pacific intentions" (Grey to Whitehead, 1 March; B 634).

[1] Izvolsky to Sergeyev, telegram, 27 February; Siebert, p. 77. In a second telegram (Siebert, p. 78) Izvolsky declared that the Russian point of view was "the same as before", that "the annexation will not be formally recognized" and that "Pashich's wish will be fulfilled".

[2] Nicolson to Grey, telegram, 28 February; B 624. The minister told Nicolson that "now that Russia had abandoned Serbia he did not know what his government could or would do"; he was "most disheartened and uneasy".

[3] Nicolson to Grey, telegram, 27 February; B 619. Nicolson said that he thought the step "an admirable one" and he "was sure it would be pleasing to [his] government". Later, when Nicolson had received Grey's telegram of the same date (B 621) advising Russia to take this step, he read parts of it to Izvolsky, who was "pleased" by it and said he had heard that his step "had made a good effect in London" (Nicolson to Grey, telegram, 1 March; B 631).

[4] Izvolsky to Nelidov, telegram, 27 February; Siebert, p. 76.

also communicated to the German and Austrian governments.[1] It was, naturally, greeted with approval in London.[2] But the decision did not necessarily ensure an immediate settlement of the Serbian question. Izvolsky was careful to state that he was "strongly against any direct negotiations between Austria and Serbia",[4] Grey likewise "strongly deprecated idea of Serbia being left to settle with Austria alone", and promised his support "in securing best settlement that could be obtained by diplomatic means".[1] On the other hand, Aehrenthal was standing out for direct negotiations with Serbia on economic questions,[5] and this position had the support of Germany, as the Russian government was duly notified.[6] In face of this divergence of views, the negotiations between Kiderlen and Jules Cambon for a formula which the Powers might use for a *démarche* in Belgrade were abandoned,[7] and the crisis entered upon a new and stormier phase.

[1] Memorandum of Schoen, 28 February; G 9408: Sverbeyev to Aehrenthal, 1 March; A 1084.

[2] Grey to Nicolson, telegrams, 1 March; B 626, 627. Grey said that he "much appreciated the statesmanlike step which Izvolsky had taken; that [he] knew how difficult it was for him to advise Serbia to renounce territorial claims". Nicolson reported that "it has been a cause of sincere satisfaction to M. Izvolsky that not only have you [Grey] promised him the valuable diplomatic support of His Majesty's government, but that you have recognized the sacrifice he had made in boldly counselling Serbia to abandon claims to which she had closely clung and which were cordially supported by public opinion in Russia. He knew that he would be rebuked and upbraided by the press of his country, and would lose much in public esteem; but he deliberately faced this situation in his earnest desire to do what he could towards securing a pacific solution" (Nicolson to Grey, 3 March; B 646).

[3] Nicolson to Grey, telegram 27 February; B 619. Several days later he repeated that he was "most anxious that Serbia should not be induced to enter into direct negotiations with Austria" (Nicolson to Grey, telegram, 1 March; B 631). Izvolsky took the same position with the German ambassador (Pourtalès to foreign office, telegram, 2 March; G 9413: Berchtold to Aehrenthal, telegram, 1 March; A 1083).

[4] Grey to Nicolson, telegram, 1 March, and despatch, 1 March; B 627, 635. The French government took the same position (Nelidov to Izvolsky, telegram, 28 February; Siebert, p. 79).

[5] Aehrenthal to Szögyény, 26 February; A 1060; G 9404.

[6] Bülow to Pourtalès, telegram, 28 February; G 9407.

[7] On 28 February a new formula was devised in Berlin which began by referring to the Austro-Turkish agreement of 26 February. It then continued: "The German, British, French, Italian and Russian governments call the attention of the Serbian government to the new situation created by this arrangement between the parties principally interested, and they venture to hope that the Serbian government, renouncing all territorial aspirations

beyond the frontiers of the kingdom, will abstain from every action which might disturb the tranquillity of the neighbouring Monarchy, *and for which the full responsibility would fall upon Serbia*, and will follow a course of pacific action which will procure for her the economic advantages which Austria-Hungary has declared herself ready to grant to Serbia *on the basis of a direct agreement between the two Powers.*" The French government objected to the phrases in italics. Izvolsky declared that the Powers could not officially inform Serbia of an agreement of which they had no official knowledge, and that "the endeavour to obtain from Serbia an assurance that she would have no territorial aspirations outside her present frontiers was going too far". If Serbia accepted the Russian advice to abandon her territorial claims no formula was needed; with which view the British agreed. The proposal was then quietly dropped (Nelidov to Izvolsky, telegram, 28 February; Siebert, p. 79: Nicolson to Grey, telegram, 1 March; B 632: Bülow to William II, 2 March; G 9411: Szögyény to Aehrenthal, 3 March; A 1093, 1094).

# CHAPTER XI

# *The Approach of the Crisis*

THE RUSSIAN advice to Serbia to abandon her territorial claims against Austria-Hungary and to submit to the decision of the Powers[1] was intended to pave the way for a solution of the crisis which had hung over Europe for five months. As a next step, Izvolsky proposed that the Serbian reply to his *démarche*, in the event of its being satisfactory, should be brought to the notice of the Austrian government, "who should be asked what were their intentions".[2] At the moment, the prospects of a satisfactory reply were favourable. On 24 February a new government had been formed in Serbia, a coalition cabinet which would be strong enough to impose its will on the excited and distracted country,[3] and it had promptly, before receiving the Russian communication, assured the Powers that Serbia would place herself in their hands.[4] On 2 March, the Russian minister in Belgrade, Sergeyev, conveyed the advice of the Russian government to the Serbian foreign minister. Milovanovich gave a personal reply which he hoped, he said, to be able to confirm after consultation with the cabinet. Sergeyev interpreted the reply in this manner:

Serbia has no intention of making any categorical demands of a territorial or economic nature, so that it is, consequently, not at all necessary to give up the first. Serbia places her fate entirely in the hands of the Great Powers and accepts their decision in advance, leaving them to determine whether the Serbo-Bosnian question should be settled at once or whether this question should be postponed to a more favourable moment. He [Milovanovich] does not

[1] See above, p. 163.
[2] Nicolson to Grey, telegram, 27 February; B 619.
[3] Novakovich became premier in place of Velimirovich; Pashich, the Radical leader, was appointed minister of public works; Milovanovich remained foreign minister.
[4] Ratibor to foreign office, telegram, 27 February; G 9405: Whitehead to Grey, telegram, 27 February; B 618. A memorandum to this effect was presented to the British foreign office (enclosure in B 634).

consider it advisable to take up negotiations with Austria at this early date.[1]

With much difficulty, Milovanovich persuaded his colleagues to accept his view,[2] and on the following day he communicated to Sergeyev the draft of a note which, if it met with the approval of Russia, would be communicated to the Powers.

The note began thus:

Considering that from a legal point of view her situation with respect to Austria-Hungary has remained normal since the annexation of Bosnia-Herzegovina, Serbia has no intention whatever of provoking a war against the neighbouring Monarchy, and in no sense desires to modify the legal relations with that Power nor her attitude of correct neighbourliness. Nor does she any longer demand from Austria-Hungary, as a consequence of the question of Bosnia-Herzegovina, any kind of compensation, whether territorial, political, or economic.

The note then proceeded to say that if the Powers were agreed that the Bosnian question had been settled, Serbia would refrain from any future discussion. Serbia's military measures were declared to "have no connection with the Bosnian question", but to be based on "general necessities"; they would be cancelled "if Austria-Hungary is prepared on her part to restore the normal military situation on her Serbian frontier or if the Powers will give us a guarantee that Austria-Hungary will not attack us ".[3]

---

[1] Sergeyev to Izvolsky, telegram, 2 March; Siebert, p. 84. According to the British minister, Milovanovich said that Serbia "could not be expected to make formal declaration renouncing all such [territorial] claims for the future, and reserved her right to place her point of view before the conference if it met" (Whitehead to Grey, telegram, 2 March; B 641). The British government thereupon pointed out that "any reference to future claims would of course spoil the reply for purposes of communication at Vienna" (Grey to Whitehead, telegram, 3 March; B 645). Cf. Franz to Aehrenthal, telegram, 2 March; A 1085. The German ambassador in Vienna thought that Serbia was assuming the rôle of "a stubborn child who, if it cannot have everything, will take nothing at all, and now rejects even economic advantages " (Tschirschky to foreign office, telegram, 5 March; G 9418).

[2] Sergeyev to Izvolsky, telegram, No. 1, 3 March; Siebert, p. 85. Milovanovich added that "he did not give up hope that Russia, for her part, would fulfil those obligations which she had previously assumed and that she had no intention of affixing her signature to the annexation ".

[3] Sergeyev to Izvolsky, telegram, No. 2, 3 March; Siebert, p. 86: enclosure 2 in B 653. Cf. Ratibor to foreign office, telegram, 4 March; G 9415.

Izvolsky had been favourably impressed by the forecast of the Serbian reply,[1] but when the proposed text was received, he at once found objections. He thought the renunciation of all claims for compensation "very wise and correct", but the references to the Bosnian question and to the Serbian armaments "dangerous", for "they might make the calling of a conference still more difficult". In truth these passages were well calculated to make the Serbian note entirely unacceptable to Vienna and might even facilitate that Austrian military action against Serbia which the Russian minister professed to fear and for the prevention of which he had advised Serbia to modify her attitude.[2] It was therefore not surprising that he wished to see these passages eliminated. He was further of the opinion that "in the present temper of the Vienna cabinet[3] it would be useless for the Powers to address themselves to Vienna [this was his original plan],[4] and transmit reply of Serbia, and so it would be a way out of the deadlock if the latter were to do so herself directly as she would at the same time to the other Powers".[5] Grey at once agreed with this view.[6]

[1] Nicolson to Grey, telegram, 3 March; B 644.

[2] Nicolson had "noticed of late a growing opinion that Russia cannot go to war, not so much on account of her military unpreparedness, for this is not admitted, but because it would upset the finances, and above all because it might give the revolutionaries the chance for which they are looking. The latter feel that their cause is rapidly losing ground, and they hope that amid the turmoil of a war, and with a government preoccupied outside, they would be able to create difficulties in the interior, and bring back all the old troubles. It is this last consideration which is causing many people to reflect, and to moderate the high tone which was adopted not so long ago" (Nicolson to Grey, private, 10 March; B 664). Berchtold was also much impressed by the universal fear of an Austrian attack on Serbia: "there is agreement on this from the minister of foreign affairs to the members of the duma, and from the latter to the amateur politicians of the St Petersburg clubs and salons". Stolypin was doubtful of the ability of the government to resist popular indignation if Austria did attack Serbia. All responsible circles were, however, convinced of the necessity of peace for Russia and did not wish to be drawn into any adventure, and the officers of the army evinced no eagerness for war (Berchtold to Aehrenthal, 6 March; A 1132).

[3] Aehrenthal had specifically declared that he did not desire the mediation of the Powers (circular telegrams, 1, 4 March; A 1080, 1097). See below, p. 172.     [4] See above, p. 164.

[5] Izvolsky to Poklevsky, telegrams, 5 March; Siebert; pp. 87–8: Nicolson to Grey, telegram, 5 March; B 654.

[6] Grey to Nicolson, telegram, 6 March; B 656: Poklevsky to Izvolsky, telegram, 6 March; Siebert, p. 88, Kiderlen, on the basis of an outline of the

Izvolsky therefore sent to Belgrade the text of a note embodying "three direct unqualified statements" to the effect that Serbia wished to be on good neighbourly relations with Austria; that she did not ask for any compensations, territorial, economic or political; that she left her case in the hands of the Powers. To persuade the Serbian government to accept this draft, he declared the assumption justified that "the cabinet of Vienna will refrain from demanding of Serbia any explanation of her armaments";[1] that Austria was prepared to negotiate a commercial treaty with Serbia[2] and her action "will in no sense have the character of an ultimatum";[3] and that if Serbia declared that she did not wish to interfere in the question of the annexation, "this does not mean that Serbia thereby loses her right, when the proper moment arrives, of acquainting the Powers with her wishes", for "the act of annexation will not, in the last resort, receive our signature".[4]

The Serbian government, convinced on the one hand of the futility and danger of further resistance and determined on the other hand to liquidate the situation,[5] and, perhaps encouraged by somewhat vague promises of future assistance,[6] accepted the

Serbian reply (Ratibor to foreign office, telegram, 3 March; G 9415) discussed with Jules Cambon a plan according to which (1) the Powers should ask the Serbian government for written confirmation of its promises; (2) the Powers should communicate this note to Vienna; (3) Serbia should then negotiate with Austria about the concessions which the latter was prepared to make (memorandum of Kiderlen, 4 March; G 9416: Paul Cambon to Grey, 4 March; enclosure 2 in B 658). Pichon accepted the first two points of this new "Kiderlen proposal", but rejected the third. Grey declined it outright in favour of Izvolsky's suggestions (Grey to Bertie, 6 March; B 658).

[1] If Austria did make such a demand, Serbia could ask the other Powers for advice.

[2] Aehrenthal had so informed the Powers (circular telegram of Aehrenthal, 3 March; A 1097). See below, p. 172.

[3] Izvolsky to Sergeyev, telegram, 7 March; Siebert, p. 89.

[4] Izvolsky to Sergeyev, telegram, 8 March; Siebert, p. 91.

[5] Forgách to Aehrenthal, telegrams, 3, 4, 5 March, and despatch, 7 March; A 1091, 1101, 1110, 1135.

[6] A special representative in Russia, Koshutich, reported that Izvolsky "did not believe in the future of Serbia unless there was a national rebirth". In his opinion, "Serbia was condemned to a poor existence until the moment for the collapse of Austria-Hungary has arrived. The annexation had brought this moment nearer, and when it arrived, Russia would raise the Serbian question and solve it". He recognized that "a struggle with Germanism was unavoidable" (Koshutich to foreign office, 10 March; S 65). The tsar was reported to have the same feeling (Koshutich to foreign office, 6 March; Bogitshevich, *Causes of the war*, p. 112).

Russian draft, and on 10 March addressed the following note to the Powers:

Considering that from a legal point of view her situation with respect to Austria-Hungary has remained normal since the annexation of Bosnia-Herzegovina, Serbia has no intention whatever of provoking a war against the neighbouring Monarchy, and in no sense desires to modify the legal relations with that Power, while continuing to fulfil, on a basis of reciprocity, her obligations of good neighbourliness and to maintain with Austria-Hungary, as in the past, relations involving interests of a material order. Though having always put forward the view that the question of Bosnia-Herzegovina is a European question and that it appertains to the Powers signatory of the Treaty of Berlin to come to a decision with reference to the annexation and the new form of Article 25 of the Treaty of Berlin, Serbia, trusting in the wisdom and sense of justice of the Powers, leaves her cause in their hands, without reservation and without in consequence claiming from Austria-Hungary any compensation, whether territorial, political or economic.[1]

This note, which was designed by the Russian government as a conciliatory move, actually had the effect of making the crisis more acute. For in the meantime Aehrenthal had assumed the diplomatic offensive. On the very day that the agreement with Turkey was signed, he called on Izvolsky to recognize the annexation of Bosnia,[2] and on the following day he notified Grey that Serbia must accept the Austro-Turkish agreement and give guarantees of a " correct and peaceful policy ", after which Austria would enter upon direct negotiations with Belgrade on economic

[1] Gruyich to Grey, 10 March; B 662 also A 1160. The note omitted the final clause of the Russian draft, which stated that Serbia "is now ready, as heretofore, to examine with the cabinet of Vienna those questions which relate to the economic relations between the two countries".

[2] Aehrenthal to Berchtold, 26 February; A 1067. Since Izvolsky had had no personal relations with Berchtold for several months, Aehrenthal instructed the ambassador to see Stolypin, the Russian premier, and communicate the documents relating to the Buchlau interview, in order that Stolypin might understand " the real situation " and put an end to the crisis by " taking a clear position " (Aehrenthal to Berchtold, 26 February; A 1068). In view of the advice given to Serbia by Russia to abandon her claims for compensation and because he satisfied himself that Stolypin was already acquainted with the documents, Berchtold did not make the démarche (Berchtold to Aehrenthal, 6 March; A 1131). Normal relations between Berchtold and Izvolsky were resumed when the ambassador, at Izvolsky's request conveyed through the German ambassador, called on the foreign minister (Berchtold to Aehrenthal, 6 March; A 1133).

questions.[1] When informed of the Russian *démarche* in Belgrade, he notified all the Powers that he did not desire their mediation to adjust the differences between Austria and Serbia. On the contrary,

The Imperial and Royal government expected from Serbia a clear and precise declaration made direct [*sans intermédiaire*], to the effect that she renounced her claims to political compensations and that she had decided for the future to fulfil her obligations of good neighbourliness towards the Monarchy. If Serbia placed herself on this ground, we should be quite ready to negotiate directly with her on the economic questions which concerned her and to give proof in these negotiations of the greatest good will.[2]

Lest there be any doubt of what this language implied, the Hungarian premier stated in parliament that "the question is exclusively one between ourselves and Serbia and one therefore in which no third party has a right to interfere", and the semi-official *Fremdenblatt* asserted that "the Serbian question is no European question but a purely private concern of Austria-Hungary".[3]

Grey was much annoyed by this attitude. When the German ambassador attempted to explain the Austrian position, Grey declared:

This might hold good if the point was an isolated one, but it had to be considered as part of the whole difficulty of the Near East. For raising this as a whole, Austria was to blame, her action had caused us all an infinity of diplomatic trouble for nearly six months. Russian action at Belgrade had now brought a possible settlement of the whole within sight and it would be too bad if Austria spoilt it all in a point of form of *amour-propre*.[4]

He was even more emphatic to the Austrian ambassador:

If the Serbian reply was satisfactory, and if Austria announced that the other Powers were not to concern themselves about the economic concessions which were to be made to Serbia, and that the matter was to be discussed between Austria and Serbia alone, I should regard the situation not only with disappointment, but with despair.

[1] Aehrenthal to Mensdorff, telegram, 27 February; A 1072.
[2] Circular telegram of Aehrenthal, 1 March; A 1080.
[3] Cartwright to Grey, telegram, 2 March; B 636.
[4] Grey to Nicolson, telegram, 1 March; B 630. Cf. Metternich to foreign office, telegram, 1 March; G 9410.

In her note of November 14, Austria had stipulated for a preliminary agreement before a conference met, and had declared herself quite ready to enter upon an exchange of views with regard to the several points of the programme we had suggested, and Austria herself had proposed for the wording of the seventh point of this programme: "economic advantages to be obtained for Serbia and Montenegro". If Austria were now to go back on the attitude she had then taken up, I should despair of European politics....

...I hoped that Austria was not going to spoil this whole settlement by now raising an objection on a point of form which she had never raised last autumn.

When Mensdorff asked whether he "still adhered to the idea of a conference", Grey replied that "we must have some definite idea upon which to work".[1] The British foreign secretary informed the Russian and French governments of his position, and proposed that they adopt it also.[2] Izvolsky for his part did so at once.[3]

This opposition only served to stiffen Aehrenthal's back.[4] He at once declared that the economic issues between Austria and Serbia involved questions of sovereignty, "which cannot be made dependent upon the influence of third states"; only such matters as the Danube-Adriatic railway or Serbia's position as a riverain state of the Danube could be brought under international consideration.[5] "Austria could never admit" Russia's "mad claim"

[1] Grey to Cartwright, 2 March; B 643: Mensdorff to Aehrenthal, telegrams, 2 March; A 1087, 1088. Grey repeated much of this to Metternich, adding that "it was not merely a question between Austria and Serbia alone, but a question of preserving the peace of Europe" (Grey to Goschen, 3 March; B 647).

[2] Grey to Nicolson and Bertie, telegrams, 2 March; B 637, 638.

[3] Nicolson to Grey, telegram, 3 March; B 644: Pourtalès to foreign office, telegram, 2 March; G 9413.

[4] The German foreign minister, Schoen, professed to regret Aehrenthal's "unapproachable attitude with regard to other Powers" and admitted that his "obstinacy on this point put the German government in a difficult position", but he refused to promise German support at Vienna for the Serbian reply if it were satisfactory (Goschen to Grey, telegram, 4 March; B 648).

[5] Circular telegram of Aehrenthal, 3 March; A 1097. Grey received this rather coolly, insisting to Mensdorff that the problem belonged to "the whole complex of Balkan questions" which had to be settled together (Mensdorff to Aehrenthal, telegram, 4 March; A 1107: Grey to Cartwright, 4 March; B 652), and to Metternich that "Austria was going further now" than in the previous week (Grey to Goschen, 4 March; B 651). Mensdorff thought that Grey's attitude was determined in no small measure by concern for the difficult position of Izvolsky (Mensdorff to Aehrenthal, 5 March; A 1117).

that " she had a right to act as the protectress of Serbia," and this "pretension" was only "retarding the settlement of the Austro-Serbian crisis ".[1] He did, however, promise Grey that " he would make use of no sudden or violent action against Serbia ".[2]

But a diplomatic action was decided upon. Reports from St Petersburg that Russia was not prepared for war[3] and from Belgrade that Serbia was in a yielding mood[4] doubtless contributed to Aehrenthal's feeling that the moment had come to press the Serbs to the wall. He would give them to the end of March, but if by then the situation was not cleared up, he would, so he repeated to the German government, "address an ultimatum to Serbia, and that to the effect that if Serbia did not within three days make a binding declaration of peaceful intentions, Austria-Hungary would march into Serbia ".[5] As the first step in this direction, instructions were sent to Forgách, the minister in Belgrade, to inform the Serbian government that in view of the attitude maintained by Serbia the commercial treaty concluded between the Monarchy and Serbia in the preceding year would not be submitted to the Austrian and Hungarian parliaments (by implication the *modus vivendi* would not be renewed on its expiry on 31 March). The communication to be made then continued:

The Imperial and Royal government would like to hope that Serbia, yielding to the advice of the Powers, will change her attitude with respect to Bosnia and Herzegovina and will at the same time express her well-considered intention to resume relations of good neighbourliness with Austria-Hungary. The Imperial and Royal government is only waiting for a communication in this sense to open new negotiations with the Royal government concerning the

---

[1] Cartwright to Grey, telegram, 6 March; B 657.
[2] Cartwright to Grey, telegram, 4 March; B 650.
[3] Berchtold to Aehrenthal, 24 February; A 1051.
[4] Franz to Aehrenthal, telegram, 3 March; A 1091.
[5] Tschirschky to foreign office, telegram, 5 March; G 9418. Aehrenthal had already informed Bülow, in a general manner, of this plan (Aehrenthal to Bülow, private, 20 February; A 1022; G 9386). Conrad von Hötzendorf had been urging war against Serbia ever since October, but had been voted down (report of Kageneck, German military attaché, 23 February; G 9390). For Conrad's own account of his activities, see Conrad, *Aus meiner Dienstzeit*, I, 138–50, 601–55; for his negotiations with Moltke, chief of the German general staff, see above, pp. 95–7.

commercial relations and the transit between the Monarchy and the Kingdom of Serbia.

Forgách was to explain that this offer was " an act of conciliation ", that the step was not to be construed as a *mise en demeure*, and that Serbia would be given time to consider her answer; but the economic question between the two countries must be settled by direct negotiations. Furthermore, if Serbia intended to give a satisfactory reply to the Russian *démarche*, Austria would not understand a Serbian refusal to communicate it also to Vienna.[1] This *démarche*, notified to the other Powers on the following day,[2] was duly executed, and Milovanovich made the conventional reply of promising to consult his colleagues.[3] Without waiting for the Serbian answer, Aehrenthal then indicated what that answer should contain. Serbia should declare:

> In view of the fact that since the conclusion of the agreement between the Monarchy and Turkey the annexation of Bosnia and Herzegovina must be regarded as a matter which is settled on the material side and no longer open to discussion, Serbia follows the advice of the Powers and no longer maintains her earlier claims which were based on the annexation.

Forgách was to reveal to the Serbian premier the disingenuous conduct of Izvolsky since Buchlau, to argue that the Russian minister was now being guided "by regard for his personal prestige", and to convince Novakovich, the premier, that "Serbia had no reason to lend herself to this strange intrigue which ran directly counter to her own well-understood interests".[4] Thus Aehrenthal was bringing strong pressure to bear on the Serbian government while it was still considering the answer to be made to the Russian *démarche*.

[1] Aehrenthal to Forgách, telegram, 5 March; A 1109; G 9419.
[2] Circular telegram of Aehrenthal, 6 March; A 1124.
[3] Forgách to Aehrenthal, telegram, 6 March; A 1120. After several days, Milovanovich answered evasively that the question of a commercial treaty would have to be studied by the ministries of finance and commerce and asked whether the *modus vivendi* would be prolonged after 31 March; Forgách cut him short by remarking that Serbia must give an immediate and satisfactory answer "on the political part and the question of principle" (Forgách to Aehrenthal, telegrams, 9 March; A 1150, 1151).
[4] Aehrenthal to Forgách, telegram, 8 March; A 1141.

Grey continued to hold out against the direct negotiations demanded by Aehrenthal. "If Serbia", he telegraphed to Vienna, "puts her case in the hands of the Powers Austria cannot refuse to discuss it without abandoning her own position of last autumn."[1] While now favouring a preliminary accord between the Powers before a conference should meet, he declined to commit himself further until the Serbian reply had been received:

If the Serbian reply was satisfactory, we should be in a position to take stock of our "accord préalable", and to see how far we had got. With regard to the difficulty between Austria and Turkey, we had already reached an "accord préalable" which would ensure that if this difficulty was discussed at a conference there would be no risk of our being unable to come to an agreement. I hoped that a similar stage might be reached in a few days with regard to the difficulty between Turkey and Bulgaria. But the Serbian question would have to be nearer settlement before we could decide upon our future procedure.[2]

Grey was showing himself as stubborn as Aehrenthal.

Izvolsky, on the other hand, seemed disposed to yield the point at issue. While he advised Serbia to renounce all claims for compensation, economic as well as political, he recommended opening negotiations for a commercial treaty,[3] and on 9 March he informed Berchtold that he accepted the Austrian contention that the questions of a commercial treaty and railway communication "were of interest only to Austria-Hungary and could be settled only by direct negotiation between those two governments".[4] But in the meantime, Aehrenthal had put forward a demand that Russia should exert her influence in Belgrade in order that Serbia should recognize and accept the protocol between Austria and Turkey liquidating the Bosnian question.[5]

[1] Grey to Cartwright, telegram, 6 March; B 655.
[2] Grey to Cartwright, 8 March; B 659: Mensdorff to Aehrenthal, telegram, 8 March; and despatch, 9 March; A 1145, 1155.
[3] Izvolsky to Sergeyev, telegram, 7 March; Siebert, p. 89. Cf. Grey to Nicolson, 9 March; B 661.
[4] Berchtold to Aehrenthal, telegram, 9 March; A 1156.
[5] Aehrenthal to Berchtold, telegram, 8 March; A 1146. On the same day he instructed Forgách to secure this from the Serbian government (Aehrenthal to Forgách, telegram, 8 March; A 1141); see above, p. 174.

The Russian minister was greatly annoyed by this and complained that "it was difficult to believe that the Austrian government were acting in good faith, as they were always raising some new demand". He could not "see the *locus standi* of Serbia in regard to the protocol, which had not yet been accepted by the Powers, as she was not a signatory of the Berlin Treaty", and he doubted if any Serbian government would subscribe to such a demand.[1] Since Berchtold had been instructed to obtain "a clear statement of position" from Izvolsky, the latter asked to have the demand put in writing.[2] In the answer which he gave to Berchtold on 11 March, Izvolsky stated that the Serbian government had not, as Aehrenthal affirmed, inquired of him in respect of its position to the Austro-Turkish protocol, and that consequently there was no occasion for the *démarche* in Belgrade requested by Aehrenthal; he also refused to commit himself on the expected Serbian note until it had been communicated to and examined by the Powers. Berchtold thereupon, according to instructions, informed Izvolsky that Aehrenthal would be constrained to transmit to Belgrade, London and Paris certain secret documents in order "to make clear the facts" about the annexation. The Russian minister, though "upset to a high degree" by this threat, kept himself in hand and asked for a list of the specific documents, "in order to submit them to His Majesty the Emperor and the council of ministers". Berchtold refused to give this information without specific authorization, and warned Aehrenthal that "this course would produce a deep rift between the two empires".[3]

Such was the situation when the Serbian note of 10 March was presented to the Powers. In Izvolsky's opinion, the note was "satisfactory", "in spite of some details of style which have been added contrary to our advice", and he urged London, Paris and Rome to "use all their influence at Vienna and Berlin

[1] Nicolson to Grey, 10 March; B 663. He talked in the same strain to the German ambassador (Berchtold to Aehrenthal, telegram, 11 March; A 1186).

[2] Berchtold to Aehrenthal, telegram, 9 March; A 1157.

[3] Berchtold to Aehrenthal, telegram, 11 March; and despatch, 18 March; A 1185, 1269. Cf. Pourtalès to foreign office, telegram, 12 March; G 9436. Aehrenthal was apparently disconcerted by Izvolsky's demand, for he refused to authorize the communication requested (Aehrenthal to Berchtold, telegram, 12 March; A 1196).

in order to move Baron Aehrenthal to a more conciliatory attitude".[1] As for the Austro-Turkish protocol, recognition of which by Serbia was demanded by Austria, the Russian minister proposed to acknowledge receipt of the documents and to inform Vienna that Russia was now ready to negotiate with the other Powers "for the meeting of a conference which would have to examine the question of Bosnia-Herzegovina as well as the other points of the programme which had been previously accepted by all the cabinets".[2] British support was requested for both suggestions. This was immediately forthcoming, Grey declaring that he intended to tell Mensdorff that "if it [the Serbian note] did not satisfy Austria, [he] did not know what would".[3] The Italian government also supported the idea of an immediate assembling of the conference.[4]

The German reaction to the Serbian note was distinctly unfavourable. Aehrenthal's two communications to the Powers of 1 and 3 March and his note to Belgrade of 8 March[5] had received the emphatic approval of the German government,[6] and Bülow had inspired a statement in the *Norddeutsche Allgemeine Zeitung* which was intended to advertise the German position.[7] Kiderlen now promised that if the newspaper forecasts were confirmed, Germany would, "without further inquiry in Vienna" declare the Serbian note "not calculated to bring about the

[1] Izvolsky to Poklevsky, telegram, 11 March; Siebert, p. 92; enclosure in B 672.
[2] Izvolsky to Poklevsky, telegram, 11 March; Siebert, p. 91; enclosure in B 671. Cf. Nicolson to Grey, telegram, 11 March; B 666.
[3] Grey to Nicolson, 12 March; B 671, 672: Poklevsky to Izvolsky, telegram, 12 March; Siebert, p. 93. For Grey's statement to Mensdorff, see Grey to Cartwright, 12 March; B 674, and Mensdorff to Aehrenthal, telegram, 12 March; A 1193.
[4] Rodd to Grey, telegram, 13 March; B 679: Lützow to Aehrenthal, telegram, 12 March; A 1195: Monts to Bülow, 9 March; G 9509. Tittoni was, however, more interested in the alteration of Article 29 of the Treaty of Berlin, which had to do with Montenegro, than with the Serbian question. His statement to Rodd that he had told the Austrian ambassador that "unless he received a formal assurance that Article 29 would be modified in favour of Montenegro, he would not even acknowledge receipt of communication of Austro-Hungarian protocol" is not contained in Lützow's report of the conversation.
[5] See above, pp. 172, 173, 174.
[6] Szögyény to Aehrenthal, telegrams, 4, 7, 9 March; A 1102, 1136, 1152.
[7] Szögyény to Aehrenthal, telegram, 6 March; A 1122.

peaceful solution on all sides".[1] Loyalty could hardly go further.

When the Serbian note was received, it was at first described in Berlin as "a juggle with words, which might even be thought amusing if it were not part of a game in which the lives of men are at stake". The points most objected to were the reference to a "competent tribunal" and the omission of any mention of Serbian disarmament. Kiderlen asserted that "Great Britain, France and Italy would be responsible if war occurred, which seemed only too likely in view of the equivocal and irritating language" of the note. Later he talked more calmly, admitting that "after all it was possible that it [the note] might open the way to a settlement; at all events it did not absolutely shut the door against further negotiations". Finally he published a *communiqué* in the *Norddeutsche Allgemeine Zeitung* stating that "one must wait and see whether, and what, Serbia answers to the Austro-Hungarian communication" and that "a conference, if held, should have a sharply defined programme, and only deal with questions on which those participating in the conference have come to an understanding beforehand".[2] On only one point did he urge caution. Advised that Aehrenthal had threatened Izvolsky with the publication of documents,[3] Kiderlen declared that he must leave the responsibility for this to Aehrenthal, but he personally thought it wiser "not to give up this trump for as long as possible".[4]

[1] Szögyény to Aehrenthal, telegram, 10 March; A 1165.

[2] Memorandum of Schoen, 11 March; G 9422: Goschen to Grey, telegram, 12 March, and despatch, 12 March; B 668, 673: Szögyény to Aehrenthal, telegram, 11 March; A 1181. According to Goschen, Jules Cambon "pitched into" Kiderlen about the *communiqué*, saying that "it might do mischief and create the impression that Germany did not care whether war ensued or not". Kiderlen replied that that impression would be quite wrong, adding: "We certainly do not want war—as Russia would be sure to get a beating and that would mean a revolution followed by a republic. That would not suit our book at all. Especially as we are not ready for one ourselves" (Goschen to Grey, private, 13 March; B 680). Kiderlen suggested that perhaps the moment had come for Austria to come to an understanding with Turkey "for mutual far-reaching support against Serbia". Aehrenthal replied that the Turkish grand vizier had given a written promise not to allow Serbian war materials to pass through Turkish territory (Tschirschky to foreign office, telegram, 12 March; G 9426). See above, p. 122.

[3] Aehrenthal to Szögyény, telegram, 10 March; A 1164.

[4] Memorandum of Kiderlen, 12 March; G 9425.

Sure of German support, Aehrenthal had no hesitation in declaring the Serbian note unsatisfactory. To the Serbian minister in Vienna, Simich, he pointed out that the note, being addressed to the Powers, could not be considered a reply to the communication which Austria had recently addressed to the Serbian government. Though it constituted "a first step in a better direction", it was not acceptable to Austria because it tried to keep the Bosnian question "open" by putting it up to the decision of the Powers—whereas for Austria that question had been settled by the agreement with Turkey and was "a matter which could no longer be discussed".[1] Austria now offered Serbia her hand for an understanding, in spite of Serbian provocations, which no other Power would have tolerated for so long, and if Serbia were prepared to become "a peaceful and loyal neighbour", the Monarchy was ready to grant large economic concessions. Finally, Aehrenthal informed Simich that at Buchlau, Izvolsky had agreed to the annexation.[2]

These views were communicated to the Powers,[3] but Aehrenthal was evidently determined to go ahead regardless of them. Irritated by the action of the Serbian government on 9 March in calling up the last ban of the reserves and subjected to great pressure by the Austrian military party,[4] he held a ministerial council on 13 March, at which it was decided to bring the 63 battalions in Dalmatia and Bosnia to war strength and to send

[1] Aehrenthal to Forgách, telegram, 11 March; A 1176. Forgách's opinion had been more favourable (Forgách to Aehrenthal, telegram, 10 March; A 1161).

[2] Simich to foreign office, 12 March; S 66. Simich declared that the Serbian note had made a good impression in Vienna business circles; he had also heard that the Emperor Francis Joseph was in favour of concessions to Serbia.

[3] Circular telegram of Aehrenthal, 11 March; A 1180: Cartwright to Grey, telegram, 12 March; B 667: memorandum of Schoen, 12 March; G 9425.

[4] So the British ambassador was informed by his German colleague, who added something of his own to the conversation. "Germany", said Tschirschky, "had little interest in the fate of Serbia, but she had a great one in the fate of Austria-Hungary. She would stand by her ally and protect her if necessary" (Cartwright to Grey, telegram, 14 March, and despatch, 15 March; B 681, 689). For the activity of the military party, see Conrad, *Aus meiner Dienstzeit*, I, 148–56. The Archduke Francis Ferdinand was, however, opposed to war (Chumlecky, *Erzherzog Franz Ferdinands Wirken und Wollen*, pp. 97–100).

15 additional battalions at full strength into these provinces, provided a satisfactory answer had not been received from Serbia by 16 March, that is, within three days. At long last the military party had triumphed.[1] On the same day, Aehrenthal reminded the Serbian government that "more than a week has passed since our note was delivered and it was not proper to delay an answer longer"; Forgách was informed that "stronger pressure" was under consideration, and he was asked to report by Monday, 16 March, his personal opinion as to the chances of a satisfactory reply.[2]

Forgách apparently did his best to make the Serbian minister of foreign affairs understand the seriousness of the situation, and was supported by his German, French and British colleagues.[3] But the Serbian government, although it debated the question for days, could not bring itself to submit unconditionally to the Austrian demands, and Milovanovich avoided consulting Forgách about the text of the reply, although he had promised to do so.[4] On 14 March the Serbian note was handed to Forgách

---

[1] Report of Kageneck, military attaché, 13 March; Tschirschky to foreign office, telegram, 14 March; Szögyény to Bülow, private, 15 March; G 9429, 9430, 9434.

[2] Aehrenthal to Forgách, telegram, 13 March; A 1197.

[3] Forgách to foreign office, telegrams, 12, 14 March; A 1188, 1189, 1190, 1203, 1204, 1205, 1206.

[4] Izvolsky, after having expressed his approval of certain passages in the Serbian circular of 10 March (see above, p. 177), had intended to offer no further advice to Serbia. But when Berchtold, the Austrian ambassador, informed a French newspaper correspondent in St Petersburg that the Serbian circular would compel his government to send Serbia "very shortly an ultimatum" (Nicolson to Grey, telegram, 12 March; B 669), the Russian minister reconsidered the situation and decided to "advise Serbian government, in informal conversation with Austrian minister, to find formula which will satisfy Austria" (Nicolson to Grey, telegram, 14 March, and despatch, 15 March; B 682, 690: Pourtalès to foreign office, telegram, 15 March; G 9433). Grey supported this suggestion and urged Serbia not "to jeopardize the interests of peace, not to mention the commercial advantages, so essential to Serbia, which are likely to result from an early and precise understanding with Austria" (Grey to Whitehead, telegram, 15 March; B 685). This advice was, however, received too late in Belgrade. The king and Milovanovich were reported to have opposed the reply actually sent, but were overborne by Protich, the Radical minister of finance, and Stoyanovich, the Young Radical minister of education (Whitehead to Grey, telegram, 15 March; B 686: Ratibor to Bülow, 16 March; G 9443: Forgách to Aehrenthal, telegram, 15 March, and despatch, 17 March; A 1210, 1245).

and transmitted to Vienna; unfortunately it was published in the press before it had been received by Aehrenthal.

The note began by recalling the statement made in the note of 10 March: " Serbia, considering that juridical relations between herself and Austria-Hungary have remained normal, desires to continue to fulfil towards the neighbouring Monarchy on the basis of reciprocity the duties of a good neighbour and to maintain with her the relations concerning their mutual interests of a material order ", and then continued:

The Royal government is therefore of the opinion that it would be most in conformity with the material interests of the two parties and with the bonds created by the treaty signed last year, which has already been given the force of law in Serbia, if the governments of the Monarchy were to submit this treaty of commerce for the approval of the parliaments at Vienna and Budapest, although the term fixed for the ratification has expired. The acceptance of this treaty by the parliaments would at the same time furnish the most certain means of avoiding any interruption of treaty relations. Its rejection by the parliaments would serve to fix a definite point of departure for negotiations for a new treaty or on the other hand to make clear that the views of the parliaments, with their agrarian tendencies, make it advisable to abandon in general any idea of concluding a treaty with a conventional tariff between Serbia and Austria-Hungary. In case Austria-Hungary, in consequence of insufficient time, or for reasons of a parliamentary nature, should not be able by 31 March to secure ratification of the treaty which Serbia has concluded with her, the Royal government would be ready to accept, if it were proposed to them, a further provisional application of the treaty up to 31 December of this year.[1]

By common consent the Serbian reply was held unsatisfactory. Not only Forgách,[2] but also his British, French and Italian colleagues condemned it.[3] In the British foreign office it was found "insolent" and "impertinent", for it put not only Serbia,

[1] A 1214: B 683: G 9431.

[2] Forgách to Aehrenthal, telegrams, 14, 15 March; A 1207, 1210: Ratibor to foreign office, telegram, 15 March; G 9432. Novakovich, the Serbian premier, attempted to justify the note to Forgách and offered all kinds of pacific assurances; Forgách thought that "he seemed not really to be conscious of the significance of the Serbian reply" (Forgách to Aehrenthal, telegram, 15 March; A 1213: Ratibor to Bülow, 16 March; G 9443).

[3] Ratibor to Bülow, 16 March; G 9443: Forgách to Aehrenthal, telegram, 15 March; A 1212.

but also "*the Powers*", that is, Serbia's friends, in the wrong;[1] possibly the explanation was that Serbia wished to provoke pressure by the Powers to which she might gracefully yield.[2] Aehrenthal of course declared the document "entirely unsatisfactory", and informed the Serbian minister in Vienna that "the prospects of an understanding between Vienna and Belgrade had again become less favourable", while he notified Forgách that he would take his time about answering,[3] waiting, presumably, until the military measures decided upon two days before had been carried out. In Berlin the Serbian chargé was told that his government could prove its pacific dispositions only by disarmament.[4] Bülow went so far as to say that the "situation was serious, but that he still thought war might be avoided";[5] thereby creating the impression that he was "for the moment perhaps even more Austrian than the Austrians".[6]

As a way out of the situation, Grey now came forward with two suggestions. The first was to revive the question of a conference, which seemed possible now that the Austro-Turkish difficulty had been adjusted,[7] the Turco-Bulgarian controversy practically arranged,[8] and an alteration of Article 29 of the Treaty of Berlin in favour of Montenegro agreed upon in principle;[9] this idea had the warm support of Italy.[10] But it did

[1] Minutes on B 683. Cf. Metternich to foreign office, telegram, 16 March; G 9444.

[2] Metternich to foreign office, telegram, 16 March; G 9445. Cf. Whitehead to Grey, telegram, 15 March; B 686.

[3] Aehrenthal to Forgách, telegram, 13 March; A 1209.

[4] Memorandum of Schoen, 16 March; G 9442. On the following day a somewhat defiant *promemoria* was transmitted to Schoen by the chargé, according to which Serbia refused to make any declaration to Austria "which would signify the giving up of our national interest and aspirations" and left her case to the Powers (G 9447); Schoen could only repeat the advice that Serbia should disarm "without delay".

[5] Goschen to Grey, telegram, 16 March; B 691.

[6] Goschen to Grey, 16 March; B 698.

[7] See above, p. 119. When Aehrenthal complained that he had not received Grey's reply to his communication of the Austro-Turkish protocol (Cartwright to Grey, telegram, 12 March; B 670), Grey expressed his "satisfaction" to Mensdorff and offered the touchy Austrian minister his "sincere congratulation" (Grey to Cartwright, telegram, 13 March).

[8] See above, pp. 141–2.

[9] Grey to ambassadors, telegram, 16 March; Grey to Cartwright, telegram, 16 March; B 692, 695.

[10] Rodd to Grey, telegram, 13 March; B 679.

not contribute much to a solution of the Austro-Serbian question, and Aehrenthal was as determined as ever not to enter a conference until that question had been settled on his own terms. Furthermore, Grey realized that "in order to settle a conflict between two states so different in size and power, the weaker must show more good will than Serbia has up to now been inclined to do".[1] His second move, therefore, was to sketch out in his own mind and to communicate to the Austrian ambassador in London the sort of reply which he thought Serbia might make and which should satisfy Austria, a suggestion with which Mensdorff found no fault and which he transmitted to Aehrenthal.[2] Grey's draft ran as follows:

Serbia might have given [sic] assurance that she would take no measures which directly or indirectly would cause difficulties or disturbances in Austrian territory, she would while maintaining her independence and integrity observe all the obligations of friendship and good neighbourhood, she would be glad to take advantage of Austrian offer to enter into direct negotiations for a commercial treaty and if desired she might add that it was not for her to make alterations in the Treaty of Berlin, but that she would accept what was duly recognized by the Powers who were parties to the Treaty.

He added that "if Austria did not ask for anything to which Powers might take exception", he thought that "combined pressure might be forthcoming at Belgrade to get a more favourable reply". Without waiting to hear from Vienna, Grey informed the other capitals of this plan, and added:

We should ask whether such assurances would be accepted by Austria and whether if in addition to them Serbia undertook to replace her army on normal peace footing on which it was before recent troubles Austria would promise not to attack Serbia. If Austrian reply was favourable we should engage to do all we can to induce Serbia to send a note on these lines to Austria.[3]

[1] Poklevsky to Izvolsky, 17 March; Siebert, p. 96.
[2] Grey to Cartwright, telegram, 16 March; B 697: Mensdorff to Aehrenthal, telegram, 16 March; A 1237. Grey declined to follow a suggestion of Izvolsky that "some friendly advice" should be given to Berlin and Vienna "to be conciliatory and generous" (Nicolson to Grey, telegram, 14 March; B 682); Grey feared that "we should only be told that what was needed now was representations at Belgrade" (Grey to Nicolson, telegram, 16 March; B 694).
[3] Grey to ambassadors, telegram, 17 March; B 702.

In other words, if Serbia was to be made to eat humble pie, she was not to be left at the mercy of Austria.[1] Aehrenthal promptly replied that Grey's proposal was "very good as far as it went, but it omitted all reference to one essential point required by Austria, namely a beginning of disarmament"; he was prepared, however, to give assurances that Austria-Hungary "had no wish to attack or injure Serbia".[2] On the basis of these exchanges, Aehrenthal and Grey began negotiations for a formula which ultimately, though not without great difficulty, led to a successful issue. But in the meantime Germany had entered the lists with a proposal of her own.

[1] Grey made it clear to Metternich, the German ambassador in London, that "some such assurance would be a necessary condition of disarmament on Serbia's part, for the air had been thick with rumours that Austria intended to attack Serbia in any case, though I had always expressed my personal disbelief in these rumours" (Grey to Goschen, 17 March; B 707).

[2] Cartwright to Grey, telegram, 17 March; B 704, 705. Whether the assurance was entirely sincere must be open to doubt, in view of the decisions taken in Vienna a few days before, but it was accepted by Grey.

# CHAPTER XII

## The Crisis: Germany's Intervention

IN NOTIFYING Russia of the Austro-Turkish protocol of 26 February, Aehrenthal had threatened that if Russia did not advise Serbia to recognize this settlement of the Bosnian question, he would be compelled to publish certain secret documents which would reveal Izvolsky's complicity in the annexation.[1] The Russian minister tried to counter this move by a threat of his own to publish the Austro-Russian agreement of 1904,[2] but he was so alarmed by the prospect of his negotiations with Aehrenthal becoming known that he forthwith appealed to Berlin to stay the hand of the Austrian minister.[3] Meanwhile Aehrenthal, impressed perhaps by the warning of his ambassador in St Petersburg that publication of the documents would produce " a deep rift " between Austria and Russia[4] and faced with a renewed suggestion from Italy that a conference was now in order,[5] had also appealed to Berlin. He asked whether it could not be proposed to the Powers " and especially Russia " that recognition of the Austro-Turkish protocol should be effected by means of identic notes addressed by the Powers to the Austrian government;[6] this would make it easier to hold a conference, which Aehrenthal, out of consideration for Tittoni, did not reject out of hand.[7]

Hitherto Germany had kept in the background of the tortuous

---

[1] See above, p. 177.

[2] This was signed in the autumn of 1904 and provided, according to a statement of Nicholas II to William II, for " the observation of the loyal and strict neutrality in case one of the empires should be in a state of war, alone, and, without provocation on its part, with a third country, the latter wishing to endanger the existing status quo " (G, vol. XXII, No. 7345).

[3] Pourtalès to foreign office, telegram, 12 March; G 9436.

[4] Berchtold to Aehrenthal, telegram, 11 March; A 1185.

[5] Lützow to Aehrenthal, telegram, 12 March; A 1195.

[6] Tschirschky to foreign office, telegram, 12 March; G 9435 : Aehrenthal to Szögyény, 12 March; A 1191.

[7] Aehrenthal to Szögyény, 12 March; A 1198 : Szögyény to German foreign office, 15 March; G 9519.

negotiations which had been going on for months. Although resolutely supporting the position of Aehrenthal, Bülow had not attempted to control the course of events which had slowly but surely brought Europe to the verge of war; for a time much of his energy had been consumed in liquidating the problems created by the famous interview of William II in the *Daily Telegraph*, and in foreign affairs his interest had been concentrated on the negotiations which led to the Franco-German convention of 8 February 1909 relating to Morocco. Moreover the foreign minister, Schoen, was easygoing and in poor health. But by March the internal situation had become less acute, and the foreign office was being more and more dominated by Kiderlen, the German minister in Bucharest, who had been brought in to assist the ailing Schoen and who thought of himself as a second Bismarck. It was known in Berlin that Austria was preparing to use force against Serbia if the situation was not soon cleared up,[1] and, said Kiderlen, "it would be too silly if Europe fell to fighting and hundreds of thousands of men were killed for the *beaux yeux* of those Serbian pigs ".[2] Evidently, positive and vigorous action was necessary. When, therefore, on 14 March, the Russian ambassador, Count von der Osten-Sacken, made a personal appeal to Bülow, in the name of Izvolsky, to prevent Aehrenthal from publishing the compromising documents, the German chancellor expressed his willingness to help Izvolsky out of his hole, provided that Russia would force Serbia to remain quiet, and to work out a *combinazione* which would enable Russia to do this without stultifying herself and compromising Izvolsky. Bülow suggested that if the Powers were to recognize the annexation of Bosnia by an exchange of notes with Austria, "Russia would then be in a position to use firmer language in Belgrade, either alone or with the other Powers, as she deemed more suitable". If, however, Izvolsky did not care to avail himself of this plan and continued to oppose recognition of the *fait accompli*, "we should, to our regret, have to let things take their course". "*Fortiter in*

[1] See above, p. 154.
[2] E. Jaeckh, *Kiderlen-Waechter, der Staatsmann und Mensch* (Stuttgart, 1924), II, 25.

*re, suavissime in modo*" is Bülow's description of his *démarche*.[1]
He was doubtless sincere in wishing to build a golden bridge
for Russia's retreat, for in spite of, or rather because of, the
alliance with Austria, friendly relations with Russia were an
important factor in German policy. He may also have felt that
the time had come for Germany to reassert herself as an active
member of the alliance, for in notifying Aehrenthal of his
action, he expressed the view that the proposal, which had
indeed emanated from Aehrenthal, was more likely to find
acceptance in St Petersburg if it were made by Berlin than if
it came from Vienna.[2] Incidentally, the proposal would, if
accepted, obviate the necessity for a conference, which the
German government did not consider "opportune", even within
the limits suggested by Tittoni.[3] With the launching of this
German plan, the Bosnian crisis entered upon its final stage.[4]

The moment for the German action was well chosen. At a
secret sitting of the duma on 8 March, Guchkov, the leader of
the Octobrists, had declared that the army was not ready for
war and that a policy of reserve, while not popular in the country,
was the only right one;[5] while Izvolsky had asserted that Russia
would not move "even if Austria-Hungary occupied Serbia".[6]
But the statement of Berchtold, the Austrian ambassador, to a
French journalist that Austria would have to send Serbia an
ultimatum "very shortly",[7] made a decision imperative.
Accordingly a council of war was held at Tsarskoye Selo on

---

[1] Bülow, *Denkwürdigkeiten*, II, 400–1: Bülow to Pourtalès, telegram,
14 March; G 9437.
[2] Bülow to Tschirschky, 14 March; G 9438: Szögyény to Aehrenthal,
telegram, 14 March; A 1208.
[3] *Aide-mémoire* to Szögyény, 15 March; G 9511: Szögyény to Aehrenthal,
telegram, 16 March; A 1232.
[4] According to Freiherr von Schoen, *Erlebtes* (Stuttgart, 1921), p. 77:
"Prince Bülow was not indisposed to let things become acute and to accept
a trial of strength between the bloc of the Central Powers and the not yet
consolidated Triple Entente, in the firm conviction that no Power would
draw the sword and that Russia, if it came to bending or breaking, would
climb down from her presumptuous height and enjoin her vassal Serbia to
keep quiet. I had the same confidence, but thought it wise not to draw the
bow too tight." Schoen's caution was, as will be seen, overborne by Kiderlen.
[5] Hintze to William II, 13 March; G 9428.
[6] Koshutich to foreign office, telegram, 10 March; S 65.
[7] Nicolson to Grey, telegram, 12 March; B 669.

13 March. The military and naval leaders and the minister of finance were agreed that it was out of the question for Russia to go to war, but the tsar appears to have reserved his decision.[1] At the same time doubts were being manifested as to the utility of the *entente* with Great Britain, and "there is a feeling", so the British ambassador observed, "that neither the *entente* nor the French alliance has been of much benefit to Russia during present crisis, while aid which Germany has given Austria-Hungary has been cited in contrast".[2]

Such was the situation when the German proposal was presented in St Petersburg. Pourtalès represented it as an effort on the part of Germany to be helpful to Russia, and Izvolsky readily admitted the "friendly intentions". But he expressed the fear that if he accepted the proposal, a conference would no longer be necessary and that Austria would "act towards Serbia as she pleased"; his influence in Belgrade, he said, was overestimated, and he was not responsible for the latest Serbian note. He would, therefore, have to take the orders of the emperor.[3] But Izvolsky was probably resigned to accepting the proposal. For while on this same day he communicated to Berchtold, as a reply to the notification of the Austro-Turkish protocol,[4] a demand for a conference,[5] he assured the ambassador that "all rumours of Russian preparations for war were invented", and that Russia would remain quiet "even in case it came to a 'military promenade' of our [Austrian] troops to Belgrade"; also that he had advised the Serbian government to get in

---

[1] Berchtold to Aehrenthal, telegram, 16 March, and despatch, 24 March; A 1243, 1347: Pourtalès to foreign office, telegrams, 14, 17 March; G 9439, 9451 : Popovich to foreign office, telegram, 16 March; S 69.

[2] Nicolson to Grey, telegram, 17 March; B 701.

[3] Pourtalès to foreign office, telegram, 15 March, and despatch, 16 March; G 9440, 9441. Izvolsky complained to Pourtalès that it was Aehrenthal who had abandoned the policy of Austro-Russian co-operation in the Balkans and by his threats to Serbia made it impossible for Russia to revert to that policy. "Believe me," he said to the German ambassador, "the present crisis will pass, *mais l'avenir est long*". Pourtalès tried to pin him down to an acceptance, in principle, of the old policy, but Izvolsky rejoined that time would show that he was right—as indeed it did.

[4] See above, p. 171.

[5] Berchtold to Aehrenthal, telegram, 15 March; A 1222; Izvolsky to Poklevsky, telegram, 15 March; Siebert, p. 94: Pourtalès to foreign office, telegram, 17 March; G 9516.

touch with Forgách as to the terms of the Serbian reply to Austria.[1]

The tsar, when consulted on the following day, decided for peace.[2] But before giving an answer to Germany, Izvolsky deemed it wise to consult London and Paris. After explaining the proposal to them and recognizing its "conciliatory spirit", he continued:

It seems to me that this effort of Germany to bring about a relaxation of the tension must be encouraged, and her proposal might be adopted in principle, with the proviso that the form of the Austrian action must be precisely established and, furthermore, guarantees for the meeting of the conference be demanded.

He also submitted a draft of the reply which he intended to make.[3] The British and French governments were invited to express their opinions.

The British action was somewhat unfavourable. Grey noted that the proposed Russian reply was "obscure since it contains no reference to a conference". Great Britain had stood out for a conference in deference to Russian wishes; "if the Russian government now considers it possible to abandon this idea, the British government is also prepared to be satisfied with an exchange of notes". But in that case the Serbian question "would probably assume an acute development, Austria having obtained from the Powers all that she requires". In Grey's opinion therefore, "it would be desirable to obtain first a pacific settlement of the relations of Serbia to Austria and to await the results of the steps which I have proposed", that is, the negotiation of a formula acceptable to Austria and pressure on Serbia

---

[1] Berchtold to Aehrenthal, telegrams, 15 March; A 1223, 1224. Izvolsky mentioned to Berchtold reports that in the event of a conflict with Serbia, four Austrian corps would be mobilized in Galicia against Russia. Aehrenthal replied that the reports were "invented" and that he did not believe the rumours of Russian preparations (Aehrenthal to Berchtold, telegram, 17 March; A 1256). Cf. Nicolson to Grey, 20 March; B 728.

[2] Berchtold to Aehrenthal, 24 March; A 1347. Charykov, Izvolsky's assistant, informed the German ambassador that the proposal would probably be accepted (Pourtalès to foreign office, telegram, 16 March; G 9448).

[3] Izvolsky to Poklevsky and Nelidov, telegrams, 17 March; Siebert, pp. 98–100.

to adopt it.[1] The French attitude appears to have been identical.[2] When questioned by Nicolson, Izvolsky replied that "of course he desired a conference, which he considered essentially necessary", and he added to his projected reply a sentence stating that an exchange of notes did not replace the necessity of a conference.[3]

Before the Russian reply was presented to the German ambassador, a decisive ministerial council was held at Tsarskoye Selo on 20 March, at which, it is said, partial mobilization was proposed and rejected,[4] for "a definitely negative answer was given by all the competent ministers" to the question whether Russia could go to war.[5] On the same day, Izvolsky handed his reply to Pourtalès. It began by saying that the proposal of the German government was "thoroughly appreciated" and that Russia was ready to continue trying to bring Serbia to reason.

Unfortunately [the reply continued] the cabinet of Vienna is very little disposed to recognize the good will which Serbia, in spite of the difficulties she has to combat, has displayed. On the contrary, it is making more and more demands, and according to the latest news from Vienna, it is to be feared that war has already been decided upon.

Be that as it may, the Russian government, which from the very beginning of the crisis has neglected nothing to bring about a peaceful solution of the questions in dispute, hastens to accept the proposal of the cabinet of Berlin. If the latter can secure that the cabinet of Vienna will undertake an action with the other governments in the sense

[1] Grey to Nicolson, telegram, 18 March; B 714: Poklevsky to Izvolsky, telegram, 19 March; Siebert, p. 102. In the British foreign office the first reaction to Bülow's proposal was not unfavourable, but "our attitude must depend entirely on that of M. Izvolsky" (minute of Hardinge on B 700).

[2] Bertie to Grey, telegram, 20 March; B 724.

[3] Nicolson to Grey, telegram, 20 March; B 722. Izvolsky explained to Nicolson that he had "purposely" made his reply "a little obscure", "as he did not wish to state fully his views until he was in possession of what Austria-Hungary would propose...if he had met the German communication by a *fin de non-recevoir*, Russia would have incurred the reproach of frustrating a friendly endeavour to preserve peace. He had, therefore, felt bound to show a disposition to accept in principle the German proposals" (Nicolson to Grey, 20 March; B 729).

[4] Hintze to William II, 3 April; G 9505.

[5] Taube, *La politique russe d'avant-guerre*, p. 228. The decision "was influenced partly, perhaps decisively, by telegrams from Colonel Martchenko, the Russian military attaché at Vienna, in which the danger of German military co-operation with Austria-Hungary against Russia was clearly explained" (Steed, *Through thirty years*, I, 299).

indicated by the German government, that is, if the cabinet of Vienna should ask the Powers for a formal sanction of the alteration of Article 25 of the Treaty of Berlin through an exchange of notes, the Russian government will consider it its duty to be receptive to this action in the sincere wish to find in it the elements of a solution which would be equally satisfying to all the Powers signatory of the Treaty of Berlin.

Meanwhile the cabinet of St Petersburg, in accordance with the explanations of Count Pourtalès, believes that it should be expressly established that in the opinion of the cabinet of Berlin, the *modus procedendi* suggested by it does not exclude the necessity of the meeting of a European conference.[1]

The Russian minister also informed the ambassador that he would be willing to use his influence at Belgrade to secure acceptance of the formula being negotiated between Grey and Aehrenthal.[2]

In the interval between the German *démarche* and the Russian reply, the attitude of Berlin had begun to stiffen. On 16 March the *Post* published an article, written by Kiderlen at Bülow's suggestion and reproduced in the *Norddeutsche Allgemeine Zeitung*, defending German policy from the charge brought by the *Berliner Tageblatt*, the *Frankfurter Zeitung*, and even the conservative *Kreuzzeitung* of being too subservient to Austria: in the event of conflict, it would not be "Austrian, but our own interests which would determine our place at the side of Austria-Hungary".[3] When the French and Italian ambassadors spoke to Schoen about Tittoni's proposal for a conference, the German minister professed to find it acceptable in principle, but "again reiterated his opinion that he would prefer an exchange of opinions and notes to a conference".[4] The emperor, speaking

[1] Pourtalès to foreign office, telegram, 20 March; G 9458.

[2] Pourtalès to foreign office, telegram, 20 March; G 9459. Cf. Berchtold to Aehrenthal, 24 March; A 1346. To both Pourtalès and Nicolson, Izvolsky expressed the fear that Aehrenthal did not desire a peaceful solution, for he was constantly raising his demands on Serbia; at the moment the Austrian minister had rejected Grey's draft for a Serbian note (see below, p. 211) and was insisting on a sharper text (Pourtalès to foreign office, telegram, 21 March; G 9463: Nicolson to Grey, 21 March; B 733).

[3] Szögyény to Aehrenthal, 15 March; A 1234.

[4] Memorandum of Schoen, 16 March; G 9515: Goschen to Grey, 16 March; B 698.

to the Austrian ambassador at an official dinner, waxed eloquent
on the theme of German support of Austria, which might be
summed up in the phrase *Tua res agitur*;[1] when he learned that
Izvolsky had assured Berchtold that Russia would not abandon
her neutrality in the event of an Austro-Serbian conflict, he
exclaimed, "There! Something definite at last! Now forward
and plunge in!"[2] Perhaps in consequence of a report that
mobilization of the Kiev military district was under consideration,[3] a council was held, under the presidency of the emperor,
"at which military measures which might eventually have to
be taken were discussed".[4] From Vienna the news was that
Aehrenthal much preferred Bülow's plan to the conference advocated by Tittoni;[5] from London that Grey was not particularly
keen for a conference and would agree to an exchange of notes
if Russia yielded.[6] Finally, there was much indignation in Berlin
over the provocative language of Nelidov, the Russian ambassador
in Paris, who had said that if Austria attacked Serbia, Montenegro
would instigate a revolt in Herzegovina and that ultimately all
the Powers, including England, would be drawn into war.[7]

[1] Szögyény to Aehrenthal, 16 March; A 1233. Before this was known in
Vienna the Archduke Francis Ferdinand expressed to a member of the
German embassy his heartfelt gratitude for the "incomparable loyalty" of
the German Emperor. He denied that he was pressing for war: "there is really
little or nothing for us to get out of Serbia"; but Austria would insist on
guarantees from Russia that "Serbia will keep really and permanently quiet"
(memorandum of Brockdorff-Rantzau, 17 March; G 9453). Bülow replied
that Germany had entire confidence in the "proved wisdom" of Francis
Joseph and the "prudent counsels" of his ministers (Bülow to Tschirschky,
telegram, 18 March; G 9454).
[2] Marginal note on G 9451.
[3] Pourtalès to foreign office, telegram, 14 March; G 9439. The report was
transmitted to the chief of staff and the war minister. According to Izvolsky,
all that had happened was the return to Kiev of some troops which had been
sent to the Caucasus during the troubles in that region (Nicolson to Grey,
20 March; B 728).
[4] Goschen to Grey, telegram, 18 March; B 709.
[5] Tschirschky to foreign office, telegram, 17 March; G 9517: Aehrenthal to
Szögyény, telegram, 18 March; A 1259. Aehrenthal had decided not to reply
to Tittoni's suggestion until the result of the German action in St Petersburg
was known (Aehrenthal to Lützow, telegram, 16 March; A 1240).
[6] Metternich to foreign office, telegram, 20 March; Tschirschky to foreign
office, telegram; G 9520, 9519: Mensdorff to Aehrenthal, 19 March; A 1282.
Metternich's view was correct; see above, p. 190.
[7] Radolin to foreign office, telegram, 15 March; Bülow to Radolin, telegram,
17 March; G 9449 and note *.

Such was the situation when the Russian reply to the German *démarche* was received in Berlin. In the eyes of William II, it was a "refusal", and "an insolent answer".[1] A German counter-reply was despatched on the following day, 21 March. Since it was the most important document of the long Bosnian crisis and has given rise to endless discussion, its full text is quoted:

I [Bülow] request your Excellency [Pourtalès] to tell M. Izvolsky that we learn with satisfaction that he recognizes the friendly spirit of our proposal and appears willing to fall in with it.

You will then inform M. Izvolsky that we are ready to propose to the Austro-Hungarian government that it should ask the Powers, on the basis of the Austro-Turkish agreement already communicated to them, to consent to the elimination of Article 25 of the Treaty of Berlin. But before we make such a proposal to Austria-Hungary, we must know definitely that Russia will answer the Austrian note in the affirmative and declare, without any reservation, her formal agreement to the abolition of Article 25. Your Excellency will therefore say to M. Izvolsky in a specific manner that we expect a precise answer— yes or no; we shall have to consider any evasive, conditional [*verklau-sulierte*] or unclear answer as a *refusal*. We would then draw back and let matters take their course; the responsibility for all subsequent events would then fall exclusively on M. Izvolsky, after we have made a final sincere effort to help M. Izvolsky clarify the situation in a manner acceptable to him.

If you should find M. Izvolsky receptive, you can allow it to be seen that we will support him on a proposal emanating from him for adjusting formally the question of the recognition of Bulgaria.

You will not yourself advert to the complaints raised by M. Izvolsky against the Austrian policy towards Serbia. If this is done by the minister, I request you to remind him that even on the Russian side the Serbian reply has been recognized as unsatisfactory and that he himself has repudiated responsibility for it. In that connection recall to him the unsuitable language of the Serbian government [in its *promemoria* of 17 March].[2]

In any case say to M. Izvolsky that in face of the increasingly provocative attitude of the Serbs matters press for a decision and that we therefore expect an immediate *clear* answer to our question.

The question of a conference has nothing to do with our *démarche*; the decision whether it is necessary or useful will have to be reserved,

[1] Marginal note on G 9458.
[2] See above, p. 183.

now as before, to an exchange of views among the Powers. We should have to regard dragging it into the specific question now under discussion as an attempt at obstruction and consequently as a refusal of our proposal.[1]

What was the motive of this communication? Was it an ultimatum, either in intention or in fact? Years later the Rumanian politician Take Jonescu asserted that Kiderlen, who drafted the note, boasted to him:

> I knew that the Russians were not ready for war, that they could not go to war in any case, and I wanted to make what capital I could out of this knowledge.... Never would Schoen and Co. have ventured to do what I did on my own responsibility.[2]

Schoen himself, also writing after the war, admitted that the language was "very forceful".[3] Unfortunately the contemporary testimony is scanty. Kiderlen himself recorded in his diary on 20 March:

> I have finally succeeded in having clear and plain language used to Izvolsky. The chancellor to-day signed my note to Pourtalès in St Petersburg for Izvolsky.[4]

To the Austrian ambassador he declared that the purpose of the *démarche* was "to press M. Izvolsky to the wall and expedite a clear and precise answer".[5] Apart from these two utterances, we are forced to form a judgment on the bases of Kiderlen's character and the text of the note. Kiderlen was undoubtedly fond of strong words and a believer in vigorous action; he was not afraid to rattle the sabre and was, if need be, even ready to draw it.[6] In March 1909 he was evidently prepared to face the

---

[1] Bülow to Pourtalès, telegram, 21 March; G 9460.

[2] Take Jonescu, *Souvenirs* (Paris, 1918), p. 49; English translation, *Some personal impressions* (New York, 1920), p. 62. James Morgan Read, *Das Problem der deutschen Vermittlung beim Ausgang der Bosnischen Krise* (Berlin, 1933), p. 53, doubts the authenticity of the language.

[3] Schoen, *Erlebtes*, p. 79.

[4] Jaeckh, *Kiderlen-Waechter*, II, 26.

[5] Szögyény to Aehrenthal, telegram, 21 March; A 1299. Holstein, who had retired from the foreign office in 1906 but maintained intimate relations with Kiderlen, congratulated him on his "'nerve' in imposing this humiliation on Izvolsky", all the more so "because I [Kiderlen] had 'nobody' behind me" (Jaeckh, II, 29).

[6] This is well demonstrated by his conduct in the Moroccan crisis of 1911.

inevitable consequences if his action failed to achieve the result anticipated. The essential point of the note was the statement that if Russia declined the German proposal, "we would then draw back and let matters take their course". In the circumstances of the moment, this could only mean that Germany would make no effort to restrain Austria and that the latter would probably invade Serbia. Pressure on Russia could hardly go further, short of a definite ultimatum. In so far as no time limit was fixed, the note was not an ultimatum, but it did have the tone of an ultimatum, and, in the opinion of the present writer, was so intended; it was in keeping with Kiderlen's nature for him to reason that only such a tone would cause Russia to yield, and he himself never sought to explain away his action. Perhaps the best commentary was made by Bülow. In public the chancellor defended his course as having saved the peace of Europe, but in June 1909, just before his retirement, he said to William II: "Don't repeat the Bosnian action",[1] as if he realized that the course had not been a happy one after all.[2] Whether Bülow,

---

[1] Bülow, *Denkwürdigkeiten*, II, 513.

[2] The verdict of historians is far from unanimous. Most German writers defend the German policy, but at least three of them view it critically. J. Haller, *Die Aera Bülow* (Stuttgart, 1922), p. 7, calls the *démarche* "a veiled threat"; E. Brandenburg, *Von Bismarck zum Weltkriege* (Berlin, 1924), p. 284, asks, "Was it necessary for Germany to intervene in this fashion and take upon herself the odium of having humiliated Russia?"; A. Frankenfeld, *Oesterreichs Spiel mit dem Kriege* (Dresden, 1928), p. 94, says that Germany demanded a "diplomatic capitulation" and that the real purpose of the action was to shatter the Triple Entente. J. Ancel, in H. Hauser (ed.), *Histoire diplomatique de l'Europe (1871–1915)* (Paris, 1929), II, 95, describes the German note as an "ultimatum"; P. Renouvin, *La crise européenne et la grande guerre, 1904–1918* (Paris, 1934), p. 87, says that "the *démarche* had the tone of an ultimatum"; R. Recouly, *De Bismarck à Poincaré* (Paris, 1932), p. 270, is content to speak of "a vigorous *démarche* by Germany". G. P. Gooch, *History of modern Europe, 1878–1919* (London, 1923), p. 420, did not commit himself: "On March 23 [*sic*]...Prince Bülow applied what he asserted to be gentle pressure, but what was regarded throughout the world as something closely resembling an ultimatum"; in his *Recent revelations of European diplomacy* (London, 1927), p. 30, Gooch wrote: "Neither in the so-called 'ultimatum' to Russia of March 1909, which he drafted for Bülow, nor in the *Panther's* spring, did Kiderlen seek for war; but his blows on the diplomatic table were little calculated to create confidence in the pacific aims of the German Empire." According to G. Lowes Dickinson, *The European anarchy, 1904–1914* (New York, 1926), p. 178, the note "does not seem to have been conceived as an 'ultimatum', and it was sent only after a friendly consultation of the chancellor with the Russian ambassador"; R. B. Mowat, *The concert*

who had resented Aehrenthal's cavalier tactics at the beginning
of the crisis, and Kiderlen, who never liked the Austrians,
wished to deprive Aehrenthal of a great personal triumph over
Izvolsky, as has been suggested by a shrewd contemporary
observer,[1] cannot be determined from the available documents.

Pourtalès presented the German note to Izvolsky on 22 March.
The Russian minister replied that he would have to consult the
council of ministers and take the order of the emperor, "since
the attacks directed against his policy forced him, in the present
critical situation, not to take the slightest step on his own
responsibility" (on which William II commented "coward!").
He added that "it would be a simple matter" if Russia had to
do only with Germany, and he would at once give "the desired
clear answer", but he could not trust Aehrenthal.[2] In spite of
the "courteous" tone employed by Pourtalès,[3] Izvolsky was
thrown into such a funk by the German summons, which he
was asked by the ambassador to keep confidential, i.e. to conceal
from Nicolson,[4] and which he regarded as having "the character
of a diplomatic ultimatum",[5] that he at once requested a

*of Europe* (London, 1930), p. 271, says that the note "was in effect an
ultimatum". Fay, *The origins of the World War*, II, 391, writes: "It was not
an ultimatum. It was an attempt on Germany's part to bridge the gulf
between Russia and Austria and prevent outbreak of war between Serbia
and Austria."

[1] Steed, *Through thirty years*, I, 300–1.

[2] Pourtalès to foreign office, telegram, 22 March; G 9465.

[3] So Izvolsky seems to have described it to the French ambassador (Bertie
to Grey, telegram, 24 March; B 759). Tcharykow, *Glimpses of high politics*,
p. 270, speaks of the "ultimatum" as "couched, I must admit, in the most
amiable form".

[4] Pourtalès to Bülow, 1 April; G 9502.

[5] So he subsequently told Nicolson (Nicolson to Grey, 23 March; B 753).
It is important to note that Berchtold received the same impression of Izvolsky's
attitude from what Pourtalès himself said (Berchtold to Aehrenthal, 4 April;
A 1467). Months later, however, Izvolsky gave a very different version to the
British ambassador in Vienna, whom he met in Venice. "He complained to
me", reported Sir Fairfax Cartwright, "of the distorted accounts [of the
so-called German ultimatum delivered in St Petersburg during the height
of the Serbian crisis] which had appeared in the European press. He asserted
that nothing approaching to an ultimatum had been delivered to him; in fact,
Germany had acted in a friendly spirit and had merely declared that if war
broke out between Austria and Russia it would be very difficult for her not
to stand by her ally [actually, no such statement appears in the German
communications—B. E. S.]. She had no desire to see war break out between
Russia and Austria, and still less to see war having to break out between herself

ministerial council. He explained to the ministers that if Russia refused the German proposal, "it was clear that Austria, in accordance with the statement of the German ambassador, would attack Serbia and the whole responsibility for the conflict would be thrown upon Russia"; he may also have expressed the fear that an attack on Serbia might also "develop into an attack by Germany and Austria on Russia".[1] The council agreed to the acceptance of the German proposal, and the decision was referred to the tsar for approval.

Before learning of the German *démarche*, Nicholas II had telegraphed to William II concerning the first German proposal. He said that Bülow's plan seemed "to indicate Germany's wish to find a peaceful way out of the present difficulties" and that Izvolsky had been instructed "to show every disposition to meet him half way". The tsar hoped that "with your powerful help and through your influence in Vienna we may be able to settle the matter in a just way", for "we are doing and shall do our best to quiet Serbia". But he feared that Aehrenthal and his advisers "want war" with Serbia, which "will put an end to every possibility of a good understanding in the future between Austria and Russia".

I now once more appeal to you [Nicholas concluded] in the strong hope that you may still withhold him from further fatal errors. Any final estrangement between Russia and Austria is sure to evolve also on our relations with Germany. And I need not repeat how deeply such a result would grieve me. I am as strongly convinced as you that Russia and Germany must be as closely united as possible and

and her friendly neighbour Russia. In fact, according to Izvolsky's account, Pourtalès came to Izvolsky like a cooing dove bearing a message of peace. To such communication Izvolsky found himself compelled to reply in a most civil manner" (Cartwright to Hardinge, private, 20 September 1909; B 870). This was exactly the German version! (see below, p. 246). On which occasion Izvolsky told the truth, it is impossible to say.

[1] He used this argument subsequently to Nicolson (Nicolson to Grey, private, 24 March; B 764). Since the German proposal had emanated from Izvolsky's request that Bülow dissuade Aehrenthal from publishing documents which would compromise Izvolsky (see above, p. 187), the theory was circulated in Vienna that "the Russian minister collapsed not before the threat of war but before the threat of the publication of his own letters. According to this story Izvolsky invented the story of the terrible ultimatum to justify his conduct to the emperor and the council of ministers" (Cartwright to Tyrrell, private, 7 April; B 829).

form a strong hold for the maintenance of peace and monarchical institutions.[1]

The tsar did not wait to receive an answer to this appeal and at once gave his consent to the proposal of his foreign minister.[2]

Accordingly, Izvolsky sent for Pourtalès late on the evening of 23 March and communicated to him the formal reply of the Russian government:

> The German government has informed the Imperial government that it is prepared to propose to Austria-Hungary that it should ask the Powers, on the basis of the Austro-Turkish agreement communicated to them, to give their formal consent to the abolition of Article 25 of the Treaty of Berlin. The Russian government does not hesitate to declare that if the cabinet of Vienna makes such a request to the Powers, Russia will not fail to give her unconditional assent. By giving this new proof of our desire to settle the present difficulties, we hope that the cabinet of Berlin will bring its whole influence to bear on the cabinet of Vienna in order to induce it to accept the English proposal and to arrive at an understanding between Austria-Hungary and Serbia.[2]

Thus did Russia yield to the imperative demand of Germany, that is, in form. In truth, "the Russian minister capitulated in March 1909 not to a German ultimatum", one of Izvolsky's advisers has remarked, "but to the practical [matérielle] impossibility—this must be admitted and recognized openly—of making war on Austria".[3]

Izvolsky at once telegraphed to London and Paris what he had done, saying that "we have no other choice than to accept the German proposal", and calling "especial attention to the great sacrifice which we are making in the interest of peace". Since Berlin and Vienna evidently wished to avoid a conference, he had not mentioned it, but "we by no means intend to give it up, and we are of the opinion that the exchange of notes proposed at Berlin does not exclude such a possibility".[4] The last remark

[1] Nicholas II to William II, telegram, 22 March; G 9465.
[2] Pourtalès to foreign office, telegram, 23 March; G 9468. Text in Siebert, p. 104.
[3] Taube, La politique russe d'avant-guerre, p. 228.
[4] Izvolsky to Nelidov and Poklevsky, telegram, 23 March; Siebert, p. 104. The British ambassador in Vienna disputed Izvolsky's contention that he had to accept the German proposal in order to prevent an Austrian attack on

must have been designed to salve the wounded feelings of Grey,[1] for it was not likely that either Berlin or Vienna would consent to a conference once the notes had been exchanged.

After the Russian council of ministers had made its decision but before the Russian answer was communicated to the German ambassador, Izvolsky sent for Nicolson to tell him what had happened. He described the German proposal as " a peremptory ' mise en demeure' ", as "a diplomatic ultimatum"; if Russia refused or evaded it, " Germany would ' lâcher [l'] Autriche sur la Serbie' ". Therefore Russia would agree to the proposal, for the Central Powers were pushing her to the wall:

The military preparations in Galicia were on a scale which was ominous, the immediate readiness of Germany for war was undoubted, and Russia was alone. France, even diplomatically, had supported Russia " très mollement ": and she could not be depended upon; while, though England had been loyal throughout in her support, it was limited to diplomatic support. Russia was practically for active action isolated, and she was unable to face alone, in her present condition, the powerful combination of the Central Powers.

Nicolson, for once, was " puzzled as to what to say ", but finally charged Izvolsky with " abandoning his former standpoint " and endangering the *Entente*. Could he not in the first place consult with the French and British governments? Izvolsky replied that there was " no time ": " any delay would be misconstrued and might precipitate a catastrophe ".[2] On the following day

Serbia. On Sunday, 21 March, Cartwright informed the Russian chargé that he believed Aehrenthal would be satisfied if the Powers could give him private assurances that when a conference met they would raise no objection to the recognition of the Austro-Turkish protocol. "The Russian chargé d'affaires telegraphed this information home immediately I had told it to him; therefore on that night Izvolsky was in possession of information that Austria-Hungary did not press for an immediate and unreserved declaration that the Powers would raise no further objections to the abrogation of Article 25. Why should he then on the following day have informed Nicolson and the French ambassador that apparently without resistance he had given more to Germany than he really knew Austria-Hungary was demanding?" (Cartwright to Tyrrell, private, 7 April; B 829).

[1] See above, p. 190.

[2] Nicolson to Grey, 23 March; B 753. According to Nicolson, *Lord Carnock*, p. 302, " Nicolson, as a matter of fact, was somewhat relieved that M. Izvolsky had not thought fit to consult England and France before deciding upon the acceptance of the ultimatum. A request for advice would have been difficult to evade ". After Nicolson, Izvolsky saw Admiral Touchard, the French

he told Nicolson that "they had positive information that all was in readiness for an invasion of Russia by Austrian forces and for an attack by Austria on Serbia in the event of Russia refusing to accept the German demand". To this the ambassador retorted that on the previous day what Izvolsky had professed to fear was "a combined attack by Germany and Austria on Russia, and that Russia was alone and could not resist the combination, as she was doubtful of France", and he, Nicolson, could not see the connection between the German demand and an Austrian attack on Serbia, especially as Aehrenthal was declaring that he had no intention of attacking Serbia unless directly provoked. Izvolsky then explained:

Of course the whole plan had been arranged between Germany and Austria. If Austria attacked Russia the Franco-Russian alliance did not come into force; no *casus fœderis* arose.[1] Such an event would occur only if Germany attacked either France or Russia. Similarly, Germany was not bound to assist Austria if the latter attacked Russia. She was only bound to come to the aid of Austria if Russia initiated the offensive, but evidently of late there had been some amplification of the engagement,[2] as there was not a shadow of doubt that if Austria were getting the worst of the conflict Germany would then step in.

In spite of Nicolson's objection, he insisted that "the Austro-German combination was stronger than the triple *entente*"; in any case, "Russia did not want a war", which "would throw back all the progress effected, and would probably revive all the troubles from which Russia was just emerging".[3] Nicolson was profoundly discouraged that "a great nation" should "tamely accept a peremptory summons".

When we have passed through the present "Sturm und Drang" period [he wrote to his chief], I should not be greatly surprised if we were to find both France and Russia gravitating rapidly towards the Central Powers, as neither of the former, distrustful of each other,

ambassador; Nicolson understood that "there were some remarks exchanged as to the want of support which France had given and would have been likely to give".

[1] The pertinent clause of the Franco-Russian alliance read: "If Russia is attacked by Germany, or by Austria supported by Germany, France shall employ all her available forces to fight Germany."

[2] This was correct. See above, pp. 95–7.

[3] Nicolson to Grey, 24 March; B 761.

feels that she can stand alone against the power of the central combination.

Our entente, I much fear, will languish, and possibly die. If it were possible to extend and strengthen it by bringing it nearer to the nature of an alliance, it would then be possible to deter Russia from moving towards Berlin.... We should not forget that in a very few years Russia will have regained her strength, and will again be a most important factor.[1]

In Berlin, of course, there was great satisfaction with the result of the German action.[2] The foreign office prepared a telegram for the emperor to send to the tsar in reply to the latter's message of 22 March;[3] the language reveals the confidence that Russian resistance was definitely broken. After expressing his pleasure that the German proposal had been accepted, William said:

I regret that matters have changed in Serbia since I wrote to you on the 9th of January.[4] For the Serbian government has, contrary to the good counsels of your government, assumed a more and more provoking attitude. I am convinced that even to-day the government of the Emperor Francis Joseph wishes to avoid taking military measures against Serbia, but I am afraid that Austria will finally be forced to do so by the menacing attitude of Serbia.

No great power can allow itself to be menaced by revolutionary plots next to its frontier, as Serbia continues to indulge in vis-à-vis Austria. I am accordingly unable to put any pressure on the Vienna government.

After a reference to German assistance at the time of the Japanese war and during the revolutionary troubles, the emperor continued:

I trust that matters in Serbia will not interfere with our friendship nor trouble your relations with the Emperor Francis Joseph even if Austria should be forced against her will to take military measures. Then your wish will come true which I share with all my heart that God may help us to bring the present crisis to a rapid and, as regards us, peaceful settlement.[5]

[1] Nicolson to Grey, private, 24 March; B 764.
[2] Szögyény to Aehrenthal, telegram, 24 March; A 1336: Bulazell to Izvolsky, telegram, 24 March; Siebert, p. 105.
[3] See above, p. 198.          [4] See above, pp. 92–3.
[5] William II to Nicholas II, telegram, 27 March; G 9485. Rumour of the imperial telegram evidently got abroad in St Petersburg, for Izvolsky told

Even before this telegram was despatched, Bülow had decided to use the advantage gained. He informed Aehrenthal that Germany would now make analogous *démarches* in the other capitals and requested the Austrian minister to desist from his negotiations with Grey over the note to be addressed by Serbia to Austria[1] until the other Powers had accepted the German proposal.[2] Bülow evidently intended to carry things with a high hand, for, without waiting to obtain Aehrenthal's approval of this course, he despatched identic notes on the same day to London, Paris and Rome informing those cabinets of the Russian acceptance of the German proposal and inviting their adherence. "We regard the decision of M. Izvolsky", he said, "as an important step in the peaceful solution of the crisis and believe that the procedure proposed by us will give special emphasis to the *démarche* which, on English initiative, is being planned for Belgrade".[3] Since Pichon, the French foreign minister, had expressed himself as "very pleased" with the result of the German action in St Petersburg, which had removed the danger of war,[4] the German chancellor may well have anticipated no difficulties from his proposal. But he was due for a rude awakening.

By this time the negotiations between Grey and Aehrenthal concerning the note which Serbia should address to Austria had reached a somewhat difficult pass.[5] The British minister was endeavouring to secure a declaration "which would be in substance satisfactory to Austria, irreproachable in form, and free from all irritating language", but he did not propose to "join in advising anything which was humiliating",[6] and he did not intend to recognize the annexation of Bosnia until the

Nicolson that "there was no truth in the report that the Emperor William had written to the Emperor of Russia on the subject of the abrogation of Article 25. No pressure of that kind had been exercised" (Nicolson to Grey, telegram, 31 March; B 814).

[1] See above, pp. 184–5.
[2] Bülow to Tschirschky, telegram, 24 March; G 9468: memorandum of German embassy in Vienna, 25 March; A 1337.
[3] Bülow to Metternich, Radolin and Monts, telegrams, 24 March; G 9469.
[4] Radolin to foreign office, telegram, 24 March; G 9471.
[5] The negotiations are described in the next chapter.
[6] Grey to Goschen, 23 March; B 755.

Austro-Serbian controversy had been adjusted. At the moment Grey and Aehrenthal were far from agreeing on the terms of the note. Moreover, news of the German action at St Petersburg had reached London.[1] The British foreign office was therefore not in a yielding mood, and learning that the German ambassador was going to make the *démarche* which had already been carried out in St Petersburg,[2] "we were ready for him, and purposely made our reply somewhat stiff, as we resented German interference in this matter altogether".[3] When Metternich called to communicate the German proposal, he was given a statement in writing, as follows:

The assurance of a readiness to accept Baron d'Aehrenthal's declaration respecting the annexation at a future conference affects only one of the various questions which have been raised by the action of Austria last autumn. At the present moment His Majesty's government are deeply interested in the preservation of the peace of Europe and therefore in a settlement of the Serbian crisis in particular. The assurance for which the German government ask while involving an alteration of the Treaty of Berlin leaves the Serbian question unsettled and makes no provision for the solution of other questions relating to the Treaty of Berlin in which England and the other European Powers are equally interested. His Majesty's government are not disposed to give the assurance required until the Serbian question has been settled in a pacific manner on lines satisfactory to them and the other Powers and until a solution has been assured of other questions arising from the annexation of Bosnia by Austria especially the alteration of Article 29. When this result has been obtained His Majesty's government will be ready to agree to any peaceful settlement based on mutual good-will amongst the Powers.

Metternich remarked that "this was a very grave decision which imperilled peace". Grey then replied:

This could only mean that Austria intended to attack Serbia or to dictate terms to her if we did not do what Austria asked. The British government would never consent to act under pressure of this kind. If we gave an unconditional promise without any assurance

[1] Nicolson to Grey, telegrams, 23 March; Bertie to Grey, telegram, 24 March; B 748, 749, 759.
[2] The counsellor of the embassy, Kühlmann, in making the appointment for Metternich, had let the secret out (memorandum of Montgomery, 24 March; B, p. 735).
[3] Hardinge to Nicolson, private, 30 March; B, p. 764.

that Austria was going to deal with moderation as regards Serbia and Montenegro we should simply be making her more free than she was before to treat them as she liked. However little British interests might be directly involved we could not make ourselves a party to proceedings of this kind. To give unconditional assent as asked gave no security that peace would follow.[1]

Bülow at once realized that he had overshot the mark and telegraphed to Metternich explaining that his proposal had been intended to "make it easier for the Serbs" to come to terms with Austria and that there had been no thought of pressure on England; but if the proposal were rejected, "Germany must decline responsibility for all subsequent events".[2] Grey received the explanations with reserve. For the moment, he "had nothing more to say":

[1] Grey to Goschen, telegram and despatch, 25 March; B 768, 770: Metternich to foreign office, telegram, 25 March; G 9474. The British answer "had the admirable effect of stiffening France, who was rather 'wobbly' in her attitude" (Hardinge to Nicolson, private, 30 March, B, p. 764; for the details, see Bertie to Grey, telegram, 27 March; B 783. The French reply to the German demand ran thus: "The French government does not hesitate to declare that if Austria requests it to give an unconditional consent to the modification of Article 25 of the Treaty of Berlin, as Russia has done, it will give an answer in the affirmative. But since the maintenance of peace is the highest aim of French policy, it urgently requests Baron Aehrenthal not to make this inquiry in Paris until an agreement has been reached in the negotiations now under way in Vienna concerning the note to be addressed to Austria by Serbia" (Radolin to foreign office, telegram, 25 March; G 9476: Izvolsky to Bulazell, telegram, 26 March; Siebert, p. 106). Izvolsky promptly disclaimed responsibility for the British and French answers (Pourtalès to foreign office, telegram, 26 March; G 9481) and requested Berlin to urge Austria not to impose "too hard conditions" for Serbia (memorandum of Schoen, 27 March; G 9483: Izvolsky to Bulazell, telegram, 26 March: Siebert, p. 107). Tittoni refused to accept the German proposal unless he were assured in advance by a note, the text of which he submitted, that Austria would consent to the abrogation of Article 29 of the Treaty of Berlin concerning Montenegro (Lützow to Aehrenthal, telegrams, 25 March; A 1355, 1356, 1357); Aehrenthal at once agreed to this (Aehrenthal to Lützow, telegram, 26 March; A 1374).

[2] Bülow to Metternich, telegram, 26 March; G 9575. Bülow remarked that the first French answer had been more conciliatory and that the French reservation had been added subsequently, as if he suspected British representations to France. For the German irritation, see Bulazell to Izvolsky, telegram, 26 March, Siebert, p. 107: Szögyény to Aehrenthal, telegram, 26 March; A 1362. The emperor expressed his disgust thus: "Well, this is what we get for all our politeness towards Paris. They are an unreliable gang wholly in the tow of England" (note on G 9482). Kiderlen noted on this day that "the crisis is now at its high point" (Jaeckh, II, 29).

We were, I hoped, on the point of an agreement with Baron Aehrenthal as to the terms of a Serbian note. If the Powers could induce Serbia to send this note modification, and Austria gave a conciliatory reply, the whole question might be settled together.

Only if Serbia refused to follow the advice of the Powers, in which event he "could not accept any responsibility for what might happen after that", would he reconsider the position.[1] In other words, England expected Germany to use her influence in Vienna to secure from Aehrenthal a conciliatory attitude towards the Serbian note. This Bülow had no intention of doing,[2] but he appears to have been piqued by the failure of the Entente Powers to invite Germany to join in the representations at Belgrade,[3] and he therefore decided, at the last moment,[4] to participate in the *démarche* if Aehrenthal so desired.[5] Thus, in contrast to the success achieved in St Petersburg, German policy obtained little satisfaction from its efforts in London and Paris, for Grey was able to maintain his position that he would not

[1] Grey to Goschen, 27 March; B 787: Metternich to foreign office, telegram, 27 March; G 9486. Grey told Mensdorff, the Austrian ambassador, that "parliament and public opinion would never forgive the government if it gave its approval in advance and then afterwards war or an ultimatum resulted"; but he gave a verbal assurance that if a peaceful solution were reached, England would recognize the annexation (Mensdorff to Aehrenthal, telegram, 27 March; A 1382). It will be noted that both Bülow and Grey declined responsibility for what might happen if their respective proposals were declined or failed. But the import was not the same in each case. Bülow conveyed the threat that Germany would not restrain Austria from war against Serbia. What Grey meant was that if Serbia, whose interests he had been endeavouring to protect, proved stubborn or recalcitrant, he would leave her to her fate ("he would no longer interest himself in the question", as he put it to Mensdorff).

[2] Bülow to Tschirschky, telegram, 29 March; G 9490.

[3] Szögyény to Aehrenthal, telegram, 29 March; A 1407: Goschen to Grey, telegram, 30 March; B 807. Kiderlen blamed England for this, and perhaps rightly, for the opinion in London was that "the German government had identified themselves so conspicuously with the Austrian attitude in this question that it seemed out of place to invite them to offer friendly advice to Serbia to submit to that of the Powers" (minute of Hardinge on B 807).

[4] Bülow was opposed to German participation, lest it appear the result of British intimidation (Bülow to William II, 27 March; G 9484), but yielded to the emperor's suggestion that Germany should join in the action if Austria desired it.

[5] Memorandum of Kiderlen, 29 March; G 9492: Szögyény to Aehrenthal, 29 March; A 1406. For the action of the German minister in Belgrade, see the next chapter, pp. 226–7.

consent to the abrogation of Article 25 until a peaceful solution of the Austro-Serbian question was assured. One can hardly avoid speculating as to what might have happened if Izvolsky, instead of returning a precipitate answer to the German demand, had consulted the British and French governments, as Nicolson begged him to do. Certainly Grey's comment was pertinent: "M. Izvolsky did not give either us or France the chance of saying whether we should help him to make better terms."[1] Perhaps the end would not have been different, for Germany and Austria-Hungary were determined to have their way with Serbia, but Russia might have been spared a humiliation of having, "for apparently no valid cause, to submit to the dictation of a foreign Power",[2] a humiliation which she burned to revenge and which profoundly affected her policy in the years to come.

[1] Minute on B 801.
[2] Nicolson to Grey, 29 March; B 801.

# CHAPTER XIII

## The Serbian Note of 31 March 1909

WHILE THE GERMAN intervention was running its course, the negotiations begun by Sir Edward Grey with Baron Aehrenthal concerning the note which Serbia was to present to Austria-Hungary[1] gradually came to a head. The British proposal was that if Austria would agree to accept assurances from Serbia that she would conduct herself as a good neighbour and reduce her army to a peace-footing, the Powers were to do their utmost to induce Serbia to address a note in that sense to Austria.[2] As soon as Russia and France had assented to this proposal,[3] Grey transmitted it to Vienna and Belgrade,[4] and expressed to Berlin the hope that the German government would support it.[5] The question of peace or war now depended on the Austro-Hungarian government.

Undoubtedly, Aehrenthal's attitude had become more resolute.

[1] See above, p. 183. Cf. also Egon Gottschalk, "Die diplomatische Geschichte der Serbischen Note vom 31. März 1909", *Berliner Monatshefte*, x (1932), 787–803.

[2] See above, p. 184.

[3] Nicolson to Grey, telegram, 18 March; B 712. Italy also agreed to the plan (Rodd to Grey, telegram, 20 March; B 723).

[4] Grey to Cartwright, telegram, 19 March; B 719. Cartwright was instructed that "if there is least reason to suppose that this method of procedure will not be satisfactory to Baron d'Aehrenthal you should inform us at once what method would be preferable". Mensdorff, the Austrian ambassador, was of the opinion that the British foreign office had grown quite disgusted with Izvolsky, who seemed to have "lost his nerves"; nevertheless, the Russian minister had to be supported "through thick and thin" because British policy rested on the maintenance of the *entente* with Russia. "In this inclination towards Russia regard for important Asiatic questions—Persia, India—plays a great rôle. But in addition there is alarm, which is growing in quite childish fashion, over the too-powerful Germany; this provides a reason for seeking the support of the tsarist empire, which in conjunction with France may be in a position to exert pressure on the German legions that are represented to the peaceful Englishman by his newspapers as landing in British ports on the North Sea" (Mensdorff to Aehrenthal, 19 March; A 1282).

[5] Grey to Goschen, telegram, 19 March; B 718. Bülow expressed his approval of the British proposal to the Austrian ambassador in Berlin and declared that he was convinced of "the honourable intentions" of the British government (Szögyény to Aehrenthal, telegram, 20 March; A 1288).

After the decision had been taken on 13 March to reinforce the troops in Bosnia and Dalmatia,[1] he informed the chief of the general staff that in the course of the next two weeks he would use reserved language: "The Serbs have made things easy for us."[2] In other words, if Serbia had not yielded by the end of the month, military operations would begin, and on 19 March instructions were sent to the Austrian ministers in Belgrade and Cetinje to arrange with their German colleagues for placing the legations under the protection of Germany in the event of a rupture.[3] Aehrenthal also explained to Tschirschky his future plans in respect of Serbia, in case the British mediation should fail.

He had already let it be known in Berlin and St Petersburg by means of holograph letters from his imperial master to the rulers of Germany and Russia[4] that Austria would not infringe the independence and integrity of Serbia. He had given up the idea of a partition of Serbia between Austria, Rumania and Bulgaria,[5] because this would produce throughout Europe a high degree of excitement, the consequences of which were difficult to foresee. On the other hand, the incorporation of all of Serbia in the Monarchy would be a mistake from the point of view of Austro-Hungarian internal politics. Consequently, there would be nothing left but to impose a war indemnity on Serbia of 500 millions and to hold Belgrade as a pledge. Care must be taken that the payment of this indemnity should be made in the smallest possible yearly instalments in order to keep Serbia under Austrian pressure for as long as possible. Naturally, the question of the dynasty in Serbia would then become acute. "It is altogether a matter of indifference to me who rules in Serbia, for I hope that in the future the king of Croatia [i.e. the Austrian emperor] will replace the ruler of Belgrade." Eventually, Serbia may well have a republican constitution.[6]

[1] See above, p. 180.
[2] Conrad, *Aus meiner Dienstzeit*, I, 156.
[3] Aehrenthal to Forgách and Kuhn, telegrams, 19 March; A 1271. Instructions for the conduct of the ministers had already been sent on 3 March. On this same day, Wickham Steed, the Vienna correspondent of the *Times*, was informed that the Archduke Francis Ferdinand had told his Jesuit confessor that "there will be no war" (Steed, *Through thirty years*, I, 298). This provides additional evidence that the archduke was opposed to war (see above, p. 180), but it does not prove that he would have been able to stay the hands of Aehrenthal and Conrad if Serbia had not finally capitulated.
[4] Letters of 18 January and 28 January 1909; see above, pp. 97, 89.
[5] The plan of August 1908; see above, pp. 11–12.
[6] Tschirschky to Bülow, 19 March; G 9457.

Possibly this shift in policy was not unconnected with the most recent news from St Petersburg, for Izvolsky had informed Berchtold that Russia would not object to a military occupation of Serbia.[1] But while the means of the Austrian policy might be changed, the end remained the same: the subjection of Serbia to Austrian control, and Aehrenthal was committed to military intervention if necessary. Whether he preferred a peaceful, diplomatic solution, at least for the time being, is uncertain.[2] In the circumstances of the moment, it would probably have been safe to reject Grey's overture. However, he did not do so, but proceeded to draft a note which Serbia might address to the Austrian government, at the same time giving assurances that Austria would not resort to war against Serbia until he and Grey had agreed on the text of the note and until the British government had had time to urge Serbia to accept it.[3]

Aehrenthal's draft was thus phrased:

Serbia recognizes that her rights have not been affected by the *fait accompli* brought about in Bosnia-Herzegovina. She declares that having learned of the arrangement come to at Constantinople between Austria-Hungary and the Ottoman Empire by which the new state of affairs has been materially settled, she abandons the attitude of protest and opposition which she had maintained towards the annexation since last autumn, and in addition she undertakes to change the direction [*cours*] of her present policy towards Austria-Hungary in order to live henceforth on terms of good neighbourliness with the latter.

In conformity with her pacific declarations, Serbia will reduce her army to its strength of the spring of 1908 in respect of its organization, distribution [*dislocation*] and effectives. She will disarm and dismiss the volunteers and the bands and will prevent the formation of new irregular units along the frontiers of Austria-Hungary and Turkey.

[1] Berchtold to Aehrenthal, telegram, 15 March; A 1224. See above, p. 188.
[2] The opinion of the British ambassador was that the Emperor Francis Joseph was definitely for peace and that it was therefore in Aehrenthal's personal interest to solve the crisis peacefully (Cartwright to Grey, 29 March; B 802). The German ambassador, on the other hand, declared it to be "no secret" that "originally and also recently" Aehrenthal had regarded war as "unavoidable and, for internal as well as for external political reasons, desirable" (Tschirschky to Bülow, 2 April; G 9528).
[3] Aehrenthal to Mensdorff, telegram, 19 March; A 1278: Cartwright to Grey, telegram, 19 March; B 720: Tschirschky to foreign office, telegram, 19 March; G 9455.

Far from claiming the right to impose obstacles to the normal development of the Serbian army, Austria-Hungary contents herself with asking for the withdrawal of the exceptional measures which involve a threat directed towards herself.[1]

Grey did not find this draft to his liking:

It is too much to expect Serbia to say definitely that she has not been prejudiced by the annexation or to use language which might be construed as an apology for her attitude; and other Powers, who are parties to the Treaty of Berlin, can hardly be expected to advise Serbia to pronounce an opinion upon the annexation of Bosnia before they have done so themselves.

He begged Aehrenthal not to insist that Serbia "should say anything about the past" and to accept his draft, with the addition of paragraphs 2 and 3 if desired: "my draft meets with the approval of other Powers, and it would be a great pity to spoil the prospects of unanimity."[2] When Cartwright presented these objections to Aehrenthal, the Austrian minister definitely refused to accept Grey's original draft and declared that paragraph 1 of his own draft "contained the minimum demands of Austria-Hungary". It was "absolutely necessary" that "Serbia should give assurances without any loss of time, that 'dès à présent' she desisted from all pretensions as to the two provinces"; if the Serbian professions were sincere, "he did not see what objection there could be on their part to renounce definitely and at once all official aspirations to Bosnia".[3] Cartwright

---

[1] Aehrenthal to Cartwright, 19 March; A 1280: Cartwright to Grey, telegram, 19 March; B 721. For Aehrenthal's justification of his demands, see Cartwright to Grey, telegram, 19 March; B 720. The third paragraph was, of course, not part of the note to be signed by Serbia.

[2] Grey to Cartwright, telegram, 20 March; B 725. Grey said much the same things to Mensdorff several days later (Mensdorff to Aehrenthal, telegram, 22 March; A 1315). Asquith warned the ambassador that if it came to war between Austria and Serbia, public opinion in Europe would turn against Austria as it had against Great Britain during the Boer war (Mensdorff to Aehrenthal, telegram, 22 March; A 1314).

[3] Cartwright to Grey, telegram, 21 March; B 732. The ambassador explained Aehrenthal's intransigeance thus: "Austrian minister of foreign affairs showed considerable anxiety as to a sudden change of ministry at Belgrade which might bring about a repudiation by the new Serbian government of engagements entered into by their predecessors. This fear makes it all the more necessary for him to obtain without loss of time a clear declaration from Serbia that she officially abandons for good her pretensions to Bosnia" (Cartwright to Grey, telegram, 22 March; B 735). For events in Serbia, see below pp. 225–6.

suggested that the difficulty might be got around by including in the note the following statement: "and that she [Serbia] will consequently comply with such decision as the Powers may take in respect of Article 25 of the Treaty of Berlin".[1] This proposal Aehrenthal agreed to submit to the emperor.[2]

On the following day the Austrian minister submitted to the ambassador proposals which he hoped the British government would accept as "reasonable":

If the Powers will give him written assurance that they will raise no objection to Austro-Turkish proposal whenever it goes before conference he will be satisfied with a formula containing a declaration from the Serbian government that she [*sic*] will accept alteration in Article 25 of Treaty of Berlin which may be made by the Powers in conference. This declaration may be made to the Powers but must be made also directly to Austria-Hungary.[3]

He also communicated a declaration which would be signed by the Powers and a revised draft of the note to be addressed by Serbia to Austria.[4] The latter read as follows, Aehrenthal's changes from his original draft being printed in italics:

Serbia recognizes that her rights have not been affected by the *fait accompli* brought about in Bosnia-Herzegovina *and that she will*

[1] Cartwright's draft, 21 March; A 1302.

[2] Aehrenthal to Cartwright, private, 22 March; A 1313.

[3] Cartwright to Grey, telegram, 22 March; B 736.

[4] A 1313, annexes A and B; B 737. Izvolsky subsequently complained that Cartwright had suggested the proposal to Aehrenthal (Nicolson to Grey, telegram, 31 March; B 813). In reply to an inquiry from Grey, Cartwright said: "On Sunday the 21st of March, after a long discussion which I had with Baron von Aehrenthal, I found that it was highly improbable that the mediation scheme would come to anything unless Austria-Hungary was reassured with regard to the recognition by the Powers of the Austro-Turkish protocol. As it seemed improbable that the Powers would feel inclined to give such official assurances as Austria-Hungary required, I asked Baron von Aehrenthal whether he would be satisfied if I could persuade you to approve of the idea that each Power individually should privately give Austria-Hungary assurances that they would raise no objection to the abrogation of Article 25 of the Berlin Treaty when the conference should meet, it being naturally taken for granted that by that date the Serbian crisis would be over. Baron von Aehrenthal replied that he could not immediately give me a definite answer as to this suggestion, but after thinking it over for a little time he said that on the whole he felt inclined to accept it as a possible solution of a difficulty. He promised to let me know his views on this matter without loss of time. On the following day I received a private letter from him containing the texts of the two formulae which I telegraphed to you" (Cartwright to Grey, private, 1 April; B 820).

*consequently comply with such decision as the Powers shall take in respect of Article 25 of the Treaty of Berlin. Yielding to the counsels of the Great Powers, Serbia undertakes from this time* to abandon the attitude of protest and opposition which she has maintained towards the annexation since last autumn, and in addition undertakes to change the direction of her present policy towards Austria-Hungary in order to live henceforth on terms of good neighbourliness with the latter.

The second paragraph of the note followed the original draft, to which Grey had raised no objection.[1]

Meanwhile Grey, who continued to maintain that "Baron d'Aehrenthal's draft [i.e. his first draft] expects something like an apology which is directly humiliating to Serbia and a recognition by Serbia of Austro-Turkish protocol in advance of the Powers which is indirectly humiliating to them, especially to Russia", had prepared a new text which, he contended, secured everything that Aehrenthal demanded, "but without humiliation to other Powers or to Serbia". If Aehrenthal accepted it, he believed that "the Serbian difficulty may be disposed of in a few days and the main questions settled by exchange of notes or conference as Powers may prefer in a very short time".

If Austria cannot accept this [he continued] the responsibility for disappointing all these hopes must be with her. We shall have done all we can, our part will be finished and if peace is sacrificed we shall have no course but to justify parliament here the part we have played by explaining what we have done to secure peace and how it came to fail.[2]

Strong language, though not so sharp as that being used by Germany at St Petersburg on this same day,[3] and with it Grey had shot his last diplomatic bolt.

[1] See above, p. 210.
[2] Grey to Cartwright, telegram, 22 March; B 739. The telegram was despatched at 10.45 p.m.; Cartwright's telegram containing the revised draft by Aehrenthal was received at 6.30 p.m. But evidently the British proposal had been formulated before Aehrenthal's new draft was received (cf. Mensdorff to Aehrenthal, telegram, 22 March; A 1315). Whether Aehrenthal's draft was considered before the British proposal was sent off to Vienna, cannot be determined (see editorial note on B 747).
[3] See above, p. 194. Metternich reported Grey as saying that if his proposal failed, "he would draw back and let things take their course" (Metternich to foreign office, telegram, 22 March; G 9466). For the meaning of this language, see above, p. 206.

The British proposal for a Serbian note was thus phrased:

Since Serbia possesses no legal rights to the annexed provinces of Bosnia and Herzegovina, the Serbian government, on the invitation of the Powers, declares that it recognizes and formally accepts every modification effected in the Treaty of Berlin, whether by a *fait accompli*, as a result of a material agreement [*accord matériel*] come to between Austria-Hungary and Turkey, or in any other manner, which shall obtain the approval of the Powers signatory of the Treaty of Berlin.

The Serbian government gives formal assurances to the Austro-Hungarian government that it will not take unfriendly measures with respect to the latter which, either directly or indirectly, may create difficulties or disorders in Austria-Hungary and in Bosnia-Herzegovina, and that, in fully safeguarding the independence and integrity of the Kingdom of Serbia, it will, from this time and in the future, observe all the obligations of friendship and good neighbourliness which should govern the relations between two friendly and neighbouring [*limitrophes*] states.

Relying on the formal assurances of the Austro-Hungarian government that it cherishes no plan of aggression against Serbia and claims no right to infringe [*ne prétendre ni porter atteinte à*] the independence, integrity and free development of the latter or to impose obstacles to the normal development of the Serbian army, the Serbian government, carrying out the request of the Powers, undertakes from this time to reduce the Serbian army to its normal strength in time of peace—that is, a year ago—and to withdraw the exceptional measures which it has recently taken. In addition, the Serbian government will disarm the irregular bands and will prevent the formation of similar new units along the frontiers of Austria-Hungary and Turkey.

Being certain that these friendly assurances will be met on the part of the Austro-Hungarian government in a spirit of reciprocity, the Serbian government will hasten to take advantage of the offer made to it by the latter to begin direct negotiations for the conclusion of a commercial treaty and it is ready from this time to enter upon *pourparlers* to this end.

As a diplomatic document, this text was less precise and rather more involved than what Aehrenthal had proposed, and he promptly rejected it.[1] His own text contained "the minimum

---

[1] Cartwright to Grey, telegram, 23 March; B 747: Aehrenthal to Mensdorff, telegram, 23 March; A 1324. Aehrenthal objected to paragraph 2 because it said nothing about a change in Serbian policy and to paragraph 3 because Austria had never shown any inclination to threaten the independence of Serbia.

assurances" which Austria must have. "These assurances Austria will be glad to obtain through the mediation of the Powers. If this mediation fails she must with regret obtain them in other ways." He therefore once more begged Grey to "consider carefully" the Austrian draft before rejecting it.[1] But the British minister maintained his position because the Austrian draft "entailed either humiliation or war" and threatened to publish a Bluebook.[2] A deadlock had been reached.

A way out was provided, perhaps without design, by Izvolsky. To the surprise and annoyance of the British foreign office,[3] the Russian foreign minister did not at all like Grey's proposed note "as it seemed to him to go even further than that suggested by Baron d'Aehrenthal" who, he imagined, "would gladly accept it if it were proposed to him".[4] He accordingly preferred Aehrenthal's version, provided certain modifications were made which he communicated to Grey.[5] By this time it was known in London that Izvolsky had yielded to the German demand for recognition of the annexation.[6] In the circumstances the British government, deeming it absurd to be more Russian than the Russians, could hardly do otherwise than discard its own draft and adopt that of Aehrenthal, provided the modifications desired by Russia could be obtained. On this basis Grey telegraphed to Vienna a revised version of the Austrian text:

Serbia recognizes that her rights have not been affected by the *fait accompli* brought about in Bosnia-Herzegovina and that she will consequently comply with such decision as the Powers shall take in

[1] Grey to Cartwright, telegram, 23 March; B 745. Aehrenthal told Cartwright privately that the advice of the Powers at Belgrade would be without result "unless it is accompanied by a categorical declaration by them to the effect that if Serbia refuses to conform to this advice the Powers will then abandon her to her fate" (Cartwright to Grey, private telegram, 23 March; B 743). Grey replied that this would not be necessary if his draft were adopted (Grey to Cartwright, private telegram, 23 March; B 744).
[2] Grey to Cartwright, telegram and despatch, 23 March; B 750, 756: Mensdorff to Aehrenthal, telegrams, 23 March; A 1325, 1326, 1327, 1328.
[3] Hardinge to Nicolson, private, 30 March; B, p. 765.
[4] Nicolson to Grey, 23 March; B 754.
[5] Poklevsky to Grey, 24 March; Grey to Nicolson, telegram, 24 March; B 757, 762.
[6] See above, p. 204.

respect of Article 25 of the Treaty of Berlin. Yielding to the counsels of the Great Powers, Serbia undertakes from this time to *refrain from an* attitude of protest and opposition *in the question of Bosnia-Herzegovina* and in addition undertakes to change the direction *of her policy* towards Austria-Hungary in order to live henceforth on terms of good neighbourliness with the latter.

*Relying on the assurances of the Austro-Hungarian government*, Serbia will reduce her army to its strength in the spring of 1908 in respect of its organization, distribution and effectives. She will disarm and dismiss the volunteers and the bands and will prevent the formation of new irregular units *on her territory*.[1]

Thus Grey at last adopted substantially the Austrian draft. But he warned Mensdorff that he would not advise Serbia to accept this note if it had to be imposed on her by war.[2]

Meanwhile, of course, Aehrenthal had learned of the Russian surrender, and was soon informed that Izvolsky would accept any formula which could be agreed upon with Grey.[3] He heard that Grey's original formula had been communicated to the Serbian government before his own approval had been secured.[4] He was being badgered by the German government for negotiating at all with Grey and for continuing to toy with the idea of a conference for registering the decisions reached.[5] He had already decided that the negotiations with Grey must be concluded in time to permit the presentation of the note in Belgrade

[1] Grey to Cartwright, telegram, 24 March; B 758: A 1353.
[2] Mensdorff to Aehrenthal, telegram, 24 March; A 1341. Metternich expressed to Grey the opinion that "Serbia would accept anything which the Powers advised" (Grey to Goschen, 23 March; B 755); Cartwright reported the Serbian minister in Vienna as volunteering the statement that "the Serbian government would accept almost any formula proposed" (Cartwright to Grey, telegram, 23 March; B 745). Grey also remarked to Mensdorff that "he was frequently in the mood to declare (he will not do it or at least not yet) that the whole Berlin Treaty was null and void" (Mensdorff to Aehrenthal, telegram, 24 March; A 1342).
[3] Berchtold to Aehrenthal telegram, 25 March; A 1358: Pourtalès to foreign office, telegram, 25 March; G 9473. The British government was not informed of this until several days later (Nicolson to Grey, telegram, 28 March; B 790).
[4] Forgách to Aehrenthal, telegram, 24 March; A 1330. Cf. Whitehead to Grey, telegram, 21 March; B 731.
[5] Bülow to Tschirschky, telegram, 24 March; G 9468: communicated by Tschirschky, 24 March; A 1337. Cf. Szögyény to Aehrenthal, telegrams, 24, 25 March; A 1336, 1351.

on 27 March,[1] but he now determined to break off the negotiations and resume his liberty of action.[2]

Such was the situation when on 25 March Aehrenthal received from Cartwright the modifications proposed in his second draft. Since Grey had abandoned his own proposal and substantially accepted the Austrian, Aehrenthal decided to continue the negotiations after all. But of the five changes desired, he objected to all but the last, and Cartwright had to argue with him for a long time before he would agree to submit the matter to the emperor. As regards paragraph 3 of the first Austrian draft,[3] which Grey had insisted "should form a declaration on the part of the Austrian government",[4] Aehrenthal declared his readiness to give it "in a more formal manner", but objected to its being communicated to Serbia. Finally he promised that "he would take no step while the present negotiations lasted". He did not, however, intimate that he had set a time-limit in his own mind.[5]

On the following day he communicated to Cartwright what proved to be the final text:

Serbia recognizes that her rights have not been affected by the *fait accompli* brought about in Bosnia-Herzegovina and that she will consequently comply with such decision as the Powers shall take in respect of Article 25 of the Treaty of Berlin. Yielding to the counsels of the Great Powers, Serbia undertakes from this time to *abandon the* attitude of protest and opposition *which she has maintained towards the annexation since last autumn*, and in addition undertakes to change the direction *of her present policy* towards Austria-Hungary in order to live henceforth on terms of good neighbourliness with the latter.

*In conformity with these declarations and relying on the pacific intentions of Austria-Hungary*, Serbia will reduce her army to its strength in the spring of 1908 in respect of its organization, distribution and effectives. She will disarm and dismiss the volunteers and

[1] Aehrenthal to Szögyény and Berchtold, telegram, 24 March; A 1333.

[2] Draft of a telegram to London, not sent, 25 March; A 1352. To Berlin, Aehrenthal explained that he would consent to a conference only if its programme were strictly limited (Aehrenthal to Szögyény, telegram, 24 March; A 1334).

[3] See above, p. 211.

[4] Grey to Cartwright, telegram, 24 March; B 758. Aehrenthal had already informed Grey that this was dependent upon an agreement being reached on the terms of the note (Aehrenthal to Mensdorff, telegram, 24 March; A 1339).

[5] Cartwright to Grey, telegram, 25 March; B 766.

the bands and will prevent the formation of new irregular units on her territory.[1]

He impressed on the ambassador "the urgent necessity" of an immediate agreement and said that "he would wait until Sunday" (28 March) for Grey's reply. "If this reply should unfortunately prove unsatisfactory, he would be compelled to assume that the mediation of the Powers had failed, and would be reduced to send in Austrian reply to last Serbian note."[2] Mensdorff was being instructed to see Grey on the next day[3] and repeat formally the assurances desired concerning the declaration of the Austrian government, but this could not be done officially "as it was inconsistent with the dignity of a Great Power to declare solemnly that she had no intention of interfering with natural development of the army of a neighbouring country". If Grey accepted Aehrenthal's text, the Serbian crisis could be settled "before the end of next week".[4]

At this point the situation became complicated by the attempt of Germany to secure from the British government a promise to recognize the annexation analogous to that extorted from Russia.[5] Grey had refused, it will be recalled, to give the desired undertaking until he had assured himself, by his negotiations then in progress with Aehrenthal, that the note to be handed in by Serbia could be accepted by that state. Between the original German *démarche* (25 March) and the subsequent explanations (27 March), Grey telegraphed to Cartwright:

We are to give what I now gather from the German embassy to be an immediate and unconditional assent to abolition of Article 25 of Treaty of Berlin, the Powers will then be given an opportunity (though even this is not certain) of inducing Serbia under pressure if need be to write a note in terms dictated by Austria. Should they feel unable to do this Austria will presumably issue an ultimatum to Serbia, and the assent of the Powers to the abolition of Article 25 will

[1] Cartwright to Grey, telegram, 26 March; B 773: A 1367.
[2] This would be done on 29 March (Aehrenthal to Mensdorff, telegram, 26 March; A 1364).
[3] Aehrenthal to Mensdorff, telegram, 26 March; A 1365.
[4] Cartwright to Grey, telegram, 26 March; B 776. Aehrenthal, when informing Tschirschky of these proposals, expressed the hope that the attitude of England or Serbia would cause the negotiations to fail (Tschirschky to foreign office, telegram, 26 March; G 9478).    [5] See above, pp. 203–7.

in no way have ameliorated the situation. His Majesty's government have no wish to assert special interests of their own in the matter, which go beyond the facts of the case, but they cannot accede to the request which has been made without some assurance that they are not being placed in the position or made parties to the procedure described and that their assent will contribute to a peaceful and not a forcible solution of present difficulties.[1]

As the news of the British attitude rolled into Vienna from Berlin and London,[2] Aehrenthal was furious. Cartwright expressed to Grey the opinion that "the German government inspired Baron von Aehrenthal to believe that your desire was to avoid giving a clear reply to the question put to you, so that you should be able to continue to worry Austria-Hungary over the matter of the annexation of Bosnia-Herzegovina...and that the final recognition of the Austro-Turkish protocol was to be still further delayed".[3] At any rate Aehrenthal sent for Cartwright and once more informed him that unless he received by the following evening (Sunday, 28 March) the assurance that Great Britain would give a favourable reply without reservations to the Austrian request for recognition of the abrogation of Article 25, he would break off his negotiations with Grey, consider the mediation of the Powers to have failed, and address a note directly to the Serbian government. Cartwright persuaded the indignant minister to be satisfied with verbal assurances which would be conveyed from Grey through Cartwright and sent a "very urgent" telegram to Grey requesting the necessary authority.[4] Aehrenthal himself despatched instructions to Mensdorff in the same sense.[5] The Austrian demand was practically an ultimatum.

Fortunately the issue was not put to the test. On the day before Grey had decided to accept Aehrenthal's final draft if he insisted on it.

It appears to His Majesty's government [Grey telegraphed to St Petersburg, Paris and Rome] that, in view of the general tenour of

[1] Grey to Cartwright, telegram, 26 March; B 774.
[2] Szögyény to Aehrenthal, telegrams, 26 March; Mensdorff to Aehrenthal, telegrams, 26 March; A 1361, 1362, 1368, 1369, 1370, 1371.
[3] Cartwright to Grey, 29 March; B 802. Cf. Szögyény to Aehrenthal, telegram, 26 March; A 1362.
[4] Cartwright to Grey, telegram, 27 March; B 785.
[5] Aehrenthal to Mensdorff, telegram, 27 March; A 1379.

the note, it is hardly worth while to risk the cause of general peace by splitting hairs upon the interpretation to be placed upon certain words which in any case cannot make the note palatable to the Serbian government although no doubt they will accept it under the collective pressure of the Powers whatever its ultimate form may be.

We shall have done our utmost to secure a more satisfactory wording, and it seems to us that it would be more politic to accept whatever text may be ultimately agreed upon between His Majesty's ambassador at Vienna and Baron d'Aehrenthal and thus cut the ground from under the feet of those who wish to force an ultimatum to be followed by an attack upon Serbia. Such a course would even seem to be preferable in the interests of Serbia herself, to say nothing of Europe as a whole.[1]

Grey thus admitted his diplomatic defeat, but no other course was open since the Powers of the Triple Entente were not prepared to go to war and surrender was the only means to prevent an Austrian invasion of Serbia. On the next day, after Aehrenthal's final text had been received,[2] Grey telegraphed his acceptance to Vienna, on the understanding that "if Serbia presents this note to Austria she will receive a conciliatory reply and that the Powers in advising her to send the note will not be exposing her to a rebuff".[3] He communicated the note to St Petersburg, Paris, Rome and Belgrade, asked the Russian, French and Italian governments to join with Great Britain in urging its acceptance by the Serbian government,[4] and, in spite of Aehrenthal's objection, instructed the British minister in Belgrade to inform the Serbian government of Aehrenthal's assurance that Austria would not attempt to impede the normal development of the Serbian army. The Serbian government was also to be told that "if the Serbian government are so unwise as to refuse the advice of the Powers, we shall not be able to do anything more for them, and they will have to abide by the consequences of their refusal".[5] These telegrams were sent about 3 p.m. Thus, when Cartwright's telegram containing

[1] Grey to Nicolson, Bertie and Rodd, telegrams, 26 March; B 771. The Italian and French governments at once accepted Grey's views (Rodd to Grey, telegram, 27 March; Bertie to Grey, telegram, 27 March; B 779, 783).

[2] See above, p. 217.

[3] Grey to Cartwright, telegram, 27 March; B 781. Cf. Mensdorff to Aehrenthal, telegram, 27 March; A 1380.

[4] Grey to Nicolson, Bertie and Rodd, telegram, 27 March; B 782.

[5] Grey to Whitehead, telegram, 27 March; B 780.

Aehrenthal's near-ultimatum arrived at 7.50 p.m., the main issue had been settled, and late the same evening Grey replied that "after Serbia has written the note in the terms agreed and Austria has accepted it as satisfactory we shall be prepared to assent without reserves to the abrogation of Article 25, if Baron d'Aehrenthal asks for it". The ambassador was therefore authorized to give the verbal assurances desired by the Austrian minister,[1] which he did on the following day, that is, before the time-limit had expired.[2]

Aehrenthal at once expressed his "great satisfaction", promised that he would not ask for the abrogation of Article 25 until the mediation at Belgrade had succeeded or failed, repeated the assurances that "Austria has no hostile intentions against Serbia and would not attack her if she disarmed", and conveyed similar assurances to the French and Italian ambassadors in Vienna. Later in the day, he informed Cartwright that the Emperor Francis Joseph "was much relieved at the prospect of a peaceful settlement of the present crisis, and was very grateful to you [Grey] for having contributed to bring this about".[3]

[1] Grey to Cartwright, telegram, 27 March, 11.20 p.m.; B 786: Mensdorff to Aehrenthal, telegram, 27 March; A 1382. Grey also said that if Serbia refused to send the agreed note, Great Britain would assent to the abrogation if the other Powers did so, and that in any case, her assent was conditional upon the alteration of Article 29 to the satisfaction of Italy (see below, p. 230). Mensdorff did not receive Aehrenthal's urgent telegram until the small hours of the night; since there seemed to be some discrepancy between the minister's demands and what Grey had told him during the afternoon, he wrote to the latter at 2 a.m. on 28 March requesting an interview, concluding with the hope that "this is the final stage of the negotiations and that a complete settlement will soon be arrived at and foreign secretaries and ambassadors not obliged to sit up till this time of night" (Mensdorff to Grey, 28 March; B 789, a). Grey, who was planning to go away for the week-end, replied that he had said his "last word" and could not go further without consulting the cabinet (memorandum of Grey; B 789, b); he referred the ambassador to Hardinge. The latter succeeded in allaying Mensdorff's fears by reading to him Grey's telegram to Cartwright quoted above (Mensdorff to Aehrenthal, telegram, 28 March; A 1397).

[2] Freiherr von Musulin, Das Haus am Ballplatz (Munich, 1924), p. 168, gives a vivid picture of the state of mind at the Ballplatz on 28 March, "a day of highest tension and excitement for us all", before the British reply was received about 6 p.m.

[3] Cartwright to Grey, telegrams, 28 March; B 793, 794: Aehrenthal to Mensdorff, telegrams, 28 March; A 1393, 1394: Tschirschky to foreign office, telegram, 28 March; G 9488. Aehrenthal also said that he had arranged with Italy for the alteration of Article 29 (Cartwright to Grey, telegram, 28 March; B 795).

Having secured what he had set out to obtain, the Austrian minister was willing enough to show his gratitude to Grey, whether he sincerely felt it or not. Thus ended the long struggle between the two ministers which had begun in October 1908. Though, on the whole, Aehrenthal got the better of the Englishman, yet the latter had forced him to stay the hand of the Austrian military party and thus allow time for a pacific solution. Unlike Izvolsky, Grey did not lose his nerve and must be credited with a greater sense of realities than his Russian colleague. He refused to be bluffed (though it may perhaps be said that Aehrenthal called his own bluff), and he saved England's face by not giving an unconditional assent to the abrogation of Article 25. In short, Grey deserves much credit for the successful ending of the long crisis without recourse to war.

The British proposal to adopt Aehrenthal's draft was at once accepted by France, Italy, and Russia,[1] and instructions were sent to their ministers in Belgrade to advise the acceptance of the proposed note by the Serbian government without delay.[2] German participation in the *démarche* was, however, not invited, presumably in order to exhibit British irritation with the recent German actions. The German government professed to resent the omission,[3] but an invitation would have sounded strange

[1] Bertie to Grey, telegram, 28 March; Rodd to Grey, 28 March; Nicolson to Grey, telegram, 28 March; B 792, 797, 790. Izvolsky complained, however, that "there is no longer any mention of a promise on the part of Austria not to attack Serbia if the latter follows the advice of the Powers", and thought it essential for the Powers to communicate to the Serbian government the assurances which Aehrenthal had given them.

[2] Grey to Whitehead, telegram, 29 March; B 798. Grey seems to have feared that Serbia might attempt to modify the note, for he asked that the Serbian answer should be shown to the British ambassador in Vienna before being presented to Aehrenthal.

[3] Szögyény to Aehrenthal, telegram, 29 March; A 1407; Goschen to Grey, telegram, 30 March; B 807. Hardinge proposed to say, in case of inquiry by the German government: "The German government had identified themselves so conspicuously with the Austrian attitude in this question that it seemed out of place to invite them to offer friendly advice to Serbia to submit to that of the Powers" (minute on B 807); no questions were, however, asked by Berlin. As a matter of fact, it had been the original German intention not to take part in the representations at Belgrade (Bülow to William II, 27 March; G 9484), on the ground that they were not likely to produce any results; but the emperor urged participation, if Aehrenthal desired it, in order to avoid the reproach of pushing Austria into war (marginal note on G 9484). Kiderlen thereupon asked what Aehrenthal's wishes were (memorandum of

enough in view of the speech which was delivered on the same day by Bülow, the German chancellor, in the reichstag.

The speech, one of the most famous in the prince's career, ranged over the whole field of international relations. In dealing with the Bosnian question he defended German policy from the charges both of having taken an uncertain attitude towards Austria and of running undue risks in support of its ally. Germany had placed herself squarely on the side of Austria because it was in her own interest to do so, because " a diplomatic defeat of our ally must necessarily react on our own position in Europe ".

I have read somewhere [he continued] a scornful word about our vassalage to Austria-Hungary. The word is silly. In this matter there is no struggle for precedence, as between the two queens of the Nibelungenlied; but in our relations with Austria-Hungary we will not short-circuit [ausschalten] the Nibelungen loyalty which on both sides we wish to observe.

Declaring that Austrian policy had been throughout justified, Bülow defined the German attitude thus:

We have taken and shall take no step which can leave the slightest doubt of our determination not to abandon any vital Austro-Hungarian interest. And just as little are we disposed to see conditions imposed on Austria-Hungary which are incompatible with the dignity of the Habsburg Monarchy.

He condemned the warlike attitude of Serbia and laid the responsibility for the consequences on those who encouraged her; but the aspirations of Serbia were not worth a war, "let alone a world conflagration", and the recent change in Russian policy strengthened his confidence that " Europe's need of peace will be strong enough to avoid such a world conflagration ".[1] In face of this ringing utterance, it was hardly necessary for the German minister in Belgrade to participate in the representations to the Serbian government.

The action of the Entente Powers and Italy was taken just in the nick of time. Although in his negotiations with Cartwright

Kiderlen, 29 March; G 9492: Szögyény to Aehrenthal, telegram, 29 March; A 1407); the Austrian minister refused to express an opinion (Aehrenthal to Szögyény, telegram, 30 March; A 1417).

[1] *Fürst Bülows Reden*, ed. O. Hoetzsch (Berlin, 1909), III, 184–90.

and Grey Aehrenthal had repeatedly declared that he desired a
peaceful settlement with Serbia, either he was not sincere or he
did not expect a pacific issue. For he took steps to prepare
public opinion for a rupture. During the autumn documents
had been received from the legation in Belgrade purporting to
be minutes of the Serbian irredentist society *Slovenski Yug* or
reports of the Serbian foreign office on Serbian propaganda
against the Dual Monarchy;[1] according to this evidence numerous
members of the Serbo-Croat coalition at Zagreb had been in
treasonable relations with Belgrade. This material was communicated by the Ballplatz to an eminent historian, Dr Heinrich
Friedjung, who proceeded to formulate a stirring indictment
against Serbia. After being held in reserve for some weeks,[2]
his article was released for publication in the *Neue Freie Presse*
on 25 March, when Aehrenthal's negotiations with Grey were
not yet concluded. It accused Serbia and the Yugoslav political
leaders of Croatia of working for the disruption of the Habsburg
Monarchy, and its conclusions were thus stated:

Should it be ordained that the Austrian arms shall thoroughly
purge Belgrade of the nest of conspirators and help the healthy elements
of the Serbian people to triumph, this would be a civilizing deed of
great value—not merely an advantage for the Austro-Hungarian
Monarchy, but also the liberation of a whole people from a company
of conspirators divided among themselves and sowing evil on every
hand, while they plunder the Serbian state by the purchase of
armaments and the preparations for war....Deep, however, as is the
rottenness of the Serbian state, it is not the office of a great power to
act as controller of morals on its frontiers. But it is its duty to assure
the safety of its own frontiers.[3]

[1] Three are printed in A 98, 598.
[2] Steed, *Through thirty years*, I, 310.
[3] Quoted in R. W. Seton-Watson, *The Southern Slav question* (London,
1911), pp. 203–4. The article led to a libel suit against its author by one of the
accused Serbo-Croat deputies. In the course of the trial it was proved that
the documents on which Friedjung, in entire good faith but with little critical
acumen, had rested his case were forged in Belgrade and, seemingly, with
the complicity of the Austrian legation (Seton-Watson, pp. 209–328). There
was a lengthy correspondence on the matter between the Ballplatz and Forgách;
the latter denied the charges against himself and his subordinates and insisted
that the documents were genuine. The dragoman of the legation, who was
accused of forging the documents, was examined by the officials of the
Ballplatz and exonerated (A 1769, 1972, 2312, 2323, 2424, 2432).

The article was all the more significant because it was already known in Vienna that Izvolsky had yielded on the main issue and had decided to recognize the annexation.[1]

Aehrenthal, it is true, professed to be satisfied with the prospect of a peaceful settlement. "A war with Serbia", he told the German ambassador, "would certainly have cost from 600 to 800 million crowns." The incorporation of Serbia in the Monarchy or its partition between Austria, Bulgaria and Rumania was not practical or, at the moment, even in the interest of the Monarchy:

> In our century such a policy of force was difficult to justify and would have provided a dangerous amount of inflammable matter for the future. Things in the Southern Slav lands must, he thought, be allowed to ripen slowly, and in view of the difficulties of the dualistic system and the still unconsolidated situation of the annexed provinces, it would be necessary to proceed carefully and step by step.[2]

Nevertheless, on the following day, 29 March, a ministerial council was held at which the so-called "yellow" mobilization against Serbia and Montenegro was decided upon. "Baron Aehrenthal now counted on war", rejoiced Conrad von Hötzendorff, the chief of the general staff.[3] Only complete submission on the part of Serbia would avoid an appeal to arms.

The cool reception by the Powers of its note on 14 March[4]

---

[1] Steed, II, 310, says: "Late in the evening of March 24th, Baron von Aehrenthal heard from Prince Bülow that Russia would recognize the annexation of Bosnia-Herzegovina. Feeling that Friedjung's article might now be dangerous, the foreign office instructed the *Neue Freie Presse* to withhold it; but the printing presses were already in motion and a large number of copies of the newspaper had been distributed." As a matter of fact, a telegram from Berlin (A 1335) announcing the glad news was received at 3.10 p.m. on 24 March, and a fuller statement (A 1336) arrived at 7 p.m. It would seem that there was ample time to stop the publication of the article.

[2] Tschirschky to Bülow, 28 March; G 9493.

[3] Conrad, *Aus meiner Dienstzeit*, I, 162. Conrad had for a week been pressing the Emperor Francis Joseph and Aehrenthal for such a decision. He complained that Germany seemed to prefer a peaceful solution (G 9490, note *).

[4] See above, pp. 182–3. Serbian attempts to justify the note met with distinct rebuffs, not only in Berlin (comment of Schoen on Serbian memorandum, 17 March; G 9447), but also in London (Grey to Whitehead, 24 March; B 765: Gruyich to foreign office, telegram, 18 March; S 71) and St Petersburg (Koshutich to foreign office, telegram, 18 March; S 73). Milovanovich subsequently explained to the British ambassador in Vienna that

had brought the Serbian government to realize the seriousness of the situation.[1] Feeling themselves abandoned by both Great Britain and Russia, the Serbs let it be seen that they would yield to the pressure of the Powers, that they even desired it.[2] From Paris came warnings that the Austrian military party was straining at the leash.[3] The government wisely refused to extend its military preparations, that is, to order mobilization,[4] and replaced the Crown Prince George, who was one of the most violent advocates of resistance, by his brother Alexander.[5] Forgách thought that the Serbs hoped to secure easier terms by submitting to the Powers and urged that Serbia must yield to Austria, but finally admitted that the precise terms of the note mattered little.[6]

Thus, after six months of tension, Serbia was brought to heel. By 29 March the ministers of Great Britain, France, Italy and Russia had received instructions to present the Aehrenthal-Grey note to the Serbian government and to urge its immediate acceptance. As Russia, however, desired Germany to participate in the representations and the German minister had received no instructions,[7] the *démarche* was postponed until the following day. When on the morning of 30 March Prince Ratibor was

the Serbian memorandum had been intended to serve two purposes, "in order to satisfy public opinion in his country, it had presented to the world in a concrete form the national aspirations, secondly, in his own mind it served as a means of bringing about the combined pressure of the Powers at Belgrade to moderate Serbian pretensions, and so enable public opinion to accept a peaceful and not too humiliating a solution of the dispute with Austria. Without the memorandum the pressure of the Powers would not have been brought to bear upon Serbia and she would have been left to herself to meet an ultimatum from Austria" (Cartwright to Grey, 17 August 1909; B, vol. IX, Part I, No. 39).

[1] Forgách to Aehrenthal, telegram, 17 March; A 1244.

[2] Forgách to Aehrenthal, 20, 22, 25 March; A 1287, 1307, 1348. Chomyakov, the president of the Russian duma, and Milyukov, the leader of the Cadets, both insisted that Russia could not fight and that Serbia must submit, contenting herself with hopes for the future (Koshutich to foreign office, telegrams, 19, 23 March; S 76, 82).

[3] Vesnich to foreign office, 24, 26 March; S 84, 88.

[4] Forgách to Aehrenthal, telegrams, 24 March; A 1331, 1332.

[5] Forgách to Aehrenthal, telegrams, 26, 28 March; A 1359, 1387: Whitehead to Grey, telegram, 26 March; B 772.

[6] Forgách to Aehrenthal, 19, 22, 26 March; A 1274, 1308, 1360.

[7] Forgách to Aehrenthal, telegram, 29 March; A 1404.

still without instructions,[1] Forgách appealed to his colleague to participate, and he agreed to do so.[2] The note was accordingly presented at 11 a.m. The British, French, Italian and Russian ministers conveyed in writing the assurances of Aehrenthal that he "had always expressed the desire to exercise no pressure on the Serbian government if it yielded to the counsels of the Powers, and that he had never had the intention of placing obstacles to the free development, security and integrity of Serbia".[3] Signor Baroli, the Italian minister, added in sharp tones that Italy would not again take part in such a *démarche*: if Serbia rejected the note, she would be left to her fate. That same evening the ministers were informed that the note had been accepted and would be communicated to the Austro-Hungarian government on the following day.[4] And it was communicated, the text corresponding exactly to that agreed upon.[5]

Aehrenthal declared that "the Monarchy had now achieved a complete success and that every ground for military intervention had disappeared",[6] and despatched a circular telegram to the capitals, Balkan as well as European, stating that the controversy with Serbia had been closed and friendly relations restored.[7]

[1] In reply to a request for further instructions, the British minister was told that "any further delay is very undesirable", and he was to proceed if necessary without his German colleague (Grey to Whitehead, telegram, 30 March; B 804).

[2] Aehrenthal expressed his satisfaction with Ratibor's action (Aehrenthal to Szögyény, telegram, 30 March; A 1417). Kiderlen, however, was annoyed. "The note contained no guarantee for Serbia's future conduct, and he could not shut his eyes to the possibility that through some act on the part of Serbia Austria would in spite of all be forced to take military action. He would therefore have preferred that Germany should have incurred no responsibility with regard to the note" (Goschen to Grey, telegram, 31 March; B 810).

[3] Aehrenthal protested against this declaration, on the ground that he had never intended his assurances to be communicated to the Serbian government (Aehrenthal to Mensdorff, telegram, 2 April; A 1442). Grey replied that he had understood that they were to be communicated, and the matter was of no consequence (Mensdorff to Aehrenthal, telegram, 3 April; A 1453).

[4] Forgách to Aehrenthal, telegrams, 30 March; A 1414, 1415, 1416: Whitehead to Grey, telegrams, 30 March; B 805, 808: Ratibor to Bülow, 31 March; G 9497.

[5] Aehrenthal to Forgách, telegram, 31 March; A 1424: Cartwright to Grey, telegram, 31 March; B 809.

[6] Conrad, *Aus meiner Dienstzeit*, I, 163. "I was of another opinion," adds the disappointed chief of staff.

[7] Telegram of 31 March; A 1428.

He also instructed Forgách to begin negotiations with Serbia for a commercial treaty.[1] Well might he be content, for he had successfully defied the Entente Powers and humiliated Serbia.[2] But his representative in Belgrade took a gloomy view of the situation. Belgrade was quiet, reported Forgách, but the hatred of Austria and the " Russian hypnosis " would prevent any " real reversal " of Serbian policy. The desire for revenge would be he order of the day. Austria might establish "very good political relations" with Serbia by supporting her aspirations at the expense of Turkey or by creating, eventually, a customs union; but the first would be a mistaken policy, and the second was impossible because of the internal political conditions and the agrarian tendencies of the Monarchy. Only time could show whether Serbia had learned her lesson from the crisis through which she had passed.[3] How little Serbia had learned her lesson, from the Austrian point of view, can be estimated from the fact that she showed herself receptive to Russian suggestions of a Balkan alliance and promptly opened negotiations with Bulgaria to that end—but that story lies beyond the scope of this study.

Having brought about the submission of Serbia in agreement with Great Britain, the Austrian foreign minister expected to receive at once the latter's consent to the abrogation of Article 25 of the Treaty of Berlin, and he telegraphed to London asking

[1] Aehrenthal to Forgách, telegram, 31 March; A 1424. A serious difficulty in the way of a satisfactory commercial treaty was the agrarian opposition in both Austria and Hungary to the admission of Serbian products (Aehrenthal to Forgách, 15 April; A 1518: Cartwright to Grey, 16 April; B 840). It was not until 1910 that a treaty was finally signed and ratified.

[2] He thanked Bülow effusively for the German support, but said that he would instruct the Austrian press not to speak too much of the humiliation of Russia (Aehrenthal to Szögyény, telegram, 31 March; A 1426). Cf. Tschirschky to Bülow, 2 April, G 9528.

[3] Forgách to Aehrenthal, 3 April; A 1447. Conrad, I, 181–3, prints what purports to be an instruction of the Serbian foreign minister Milovanovich, dated 17 April 1909, to the Serbian minister in Vienna concerning "the continuation of the Great Serbian propaganda in Austria-Hungary", and this is quoted as genuine in Fay, *The origins of the World War*, I, 400–1. The document appears, however, to have been one of the forgeries published by the Vienna *Reichspost* in connection with the Friedjung trial (Seton-Watson, *The Southern Slav question*, pp. 233, 401–6). This or a similar document was reported upon to Berlin by the German ambassador in Vienna (Tschirschky to Bülow, 22 April; G 9529).

for it.[1] He was, however, to wait more than two weeks for it: Grey had made his consent dependent not only on a peaceful solution of the Austro-Serbian difficulty, but also on a satisfactory settlement of the questions affecting Montenegro under Article 29 of the Treaty.[2] And this proved more difficult than had been anticipated.

---

[1] Aehrenthal to Mensdorff, telegram, 1 April; A 1434. A formal demand was addressed to all the Powers on the following day (circular telegram of Aehrenthal, 2 April; A 1443).

[2] See above, p. 221.

# CHAPTER XIV

## *Montenegro and Article* 29

O N the very day when the Serbian note was presented in
Vienna, Metternich, the German ambassador in London,
asked Grey whether Great Britain would now consent
to the abrogation of Article 25, provided Austria found the
Serbian note satisfactory, or whether the British consent would
depend on the modification of Article 29 respecting Montenegro.
The British foreign secretary replied that the matter of Article 29
"should be settled between Austria and Italy, either before or
simultaneously with the promise to recognize the abolition of
Article 25", and that he "had really left the matter in the hands
of Italy".[1] Since he did not know exactly what Italy desired,
he telegraphed to Rome to ask "exactly what the conditions are
upon which he [Tittoni, the Italian foreign minister] is insisting
and whether he has ascertained that they are satisfactory to
Montenegro".[2] Izvolsky, on the other hand, resented the
initiative of Austria and Italy, which would imply that the
Powers recognized "a kind of protectorate of those two Powers
over Montenegro and the entire Adriatic Sea",[3] and produced
a scheme of his own.[4] Since Austria and Italy, as will be seen,
were not in fact fully agreed, the possibility of complications
had to be faced.

[1] Grey to Goschen, 31 March; B 816: Metternich to Bülow, 31 March;
G 9499. An answer in the same sense was returned to Mensdorff when he
presented the formal request of Aehrenthal for the British consent (Mensdorff
to Aehrenthal, telegrams, 5 April; A 1474, 1475). Metternich also wished to
know if Grey still favoured a conference; to which Grey replied that "we
ourselves had taken so active a part recently that I was disposed to defer to
the wishes of the other Powers as to the method of settlement". Metternich's
question may have been inspired by reports from Constantinople that England
was urging Turkey to insist upon a conference for the purpose of ratifying
the Austro-Turkish protocol and the pending agreement with Bulgaria
(Marschall to foreign office, telegrams, 29, 30 March; G 9523, 9524, 9525);
see above, p. 142. There is no record in B of any such British suggestions.

[2] Grey to Rodd, telegram, 31 March; B 812.

[3] Izvolsky to Benckendorff, telegram, transmitted to Grey, 3 April; B 824.

[4] The Russian circular is reproduced in A 1460.

Article 29 of the Treaty of Berlin laid serious restrictions on the sovereignty of Montenegro within her own territory. Paragraph 4 prohibited any fortifications on the Boyana River except within six kilometres of Scutari. Paragraph 5 denied to the little state warships or a war flag. By paragraph 6 the port of Antivari and all Montenegrin waters were closed to men-of-war of all nations. According to paragraph 7 no fortifications could be erected between Lake Scutari and the Montenegrin littoral. Paragraph 8 entrusted the policing of Antivari and the Montenegrin coast to Austria-Hungary, and by paragraph 9 Montenegro had to adopt the maritime legislation in force in Dalmatia, in return for which Austria extended her consular protection to the Montenegrin merchant marine. Under paragraph 10 Montenegro was bound to negotiate with Austria concerning the construction of a road and a railway across her new territory; while paragraph 11 stipulated for "complete freedom of communication" on these highways. Not unnaturally Montenegro was restless under these restrictions.

Probably Aehrenthal hoped to see them preserved. At any rate he ignored the question when making his plans for the annexation of Bosnia.[1] But when he conducted his negotiations with Izvolsky at Buchlau, the Russian foreign minister had asked for modifications in Article 29 and Aehrenthal had to promise to take them under consideration.[2] He was also doubtless well aware that Italy was sensitive on this matter, although it had not been discussed at the interview with Tittoni early in September.[3] Furthermore, it was an important feature of the Austrian policy towards Serbia to play discreetly on the rivalry between that country and Montenegro and, within limits, cater to the whims and ambitions of Prince Nicholas. Whatever the precise motives of Aehrenthal may have been, the Austrian minister in Cetinje, Baron Kuhn, was authorized, when he informed the prince of the annexation of Bosnia, to say that if Nicholas took a "correct and sympathetic attitude" towards the

---

[1] There is no reference to Montenegro or Article 29 in his memorandum of 9 August (see above, pp. 10–12) or in the discussions in the ministerial councils of 19 August and 10 September (see above, pp. 12–13, 18).
[2] See above, p. 21.          [3] See above, pp. 14–15.

annexation, Austria was prepared to grant him certain subventions for the building of roads and to enter into negotiation for the modification of Article 29.[1]  To deprive Serbia of Montenegrin sympathy in the approaching crisis was worth while as an end in itself; but in addition such a policy was essential for dealing with Italy.  For Tittoni, having failed to induce Aehrenthal to postpone his Bosnian action, declared that he could recognize the annexation only if Austria renounced her privileges under Article 29. Since Aehrenthal had already decided to do this, he could yield to Tittoni with easy grace and thus assure himself of Italian support in his dealings with the other Powers.[2]

So far as Italy was concerned, Aehrenthal's calculations were not unjustified by the results.  It is true that Tittoni supported the proposal of the British and Russian governments for a conference and urged that it be held in Rome;[3] but he admitted privately that he was not sympathetic to the proposal.[4]  He also agreed with Aehrenthal that Serbia should not receive any territorial compensation,[5] claimed to have persuaded that state to reduce its claims,[6] and urged moderation on the government in Belgrade.[7]  Although Victor Emmanuel III delayed more than two months before answering, in colourless and non-committal fashion, the letter of Francis Joseph announcing the annexation,[8] the Italian government kept aloof from the lively controversies between Aehrenthal on the one hand and Izvolsky and Grey on the other which filled the next few months[9] and

[1] Aehrenthal to Kuhn, 3 October; A 112.
[2] See above, p. 44.  Renewed assurances concerning Article 29 were conveyed to Tittoni in November (Aehrenthal to Lützow, telegram, 24 November; A 637).
[3] Lützow to Aehrenthal, telegrams, 15, 21 October; A 293, 360.
[4] Lützow to Aehrenthal, telegram, 7 October; A 179.
[5] Grey to Egerton, 19 October; B 395: Lützow to Aehrenthal, telegram, 8 November; A 533.
[6] Monts to Bülow, 23 November; G 9122.  Secretly, however, Tittoni gave Serbia considerable encouragement, promising Italian diplomatic support for her pretensions as long as Russia desired it (see above, p. 70); but this was not known to Aehrenthal.
[7] Forgách to Aehrenthal, telegram, 1 November; A 478.
[8] Victor Emmanuel to Francis Joseph, 12 December; A 732.
[9] Tittoni professed to favour an Austro-Russian-Italian *entente* (see above p. 44) and continued to support the idea (Monts to Aehrenthal, telegram, 14 December; A 744), but apparently did nothing to promote it.

took no part in the complicated negotiations involving Turkey and Bulgaria. But Tittoni's policy of co-operation with Austria was not popular with his countrymen,[1] and his position was so compromised, in spite of the vote of confidence passed by parliament in December, that his resignation began to be rumoured.[2] It was probably this situation which led the minister, when in February the Serbian question began to grow acute,[3] to revive the idea of a conference.[4] But he presently watered this down, for the programme suggested was limited to the approval of the Austro-Turkish protocol, the Turco-Bulgarian agreement, and the modifications which might be made in Article 29.[5] This pleased Aehrenthal so much that, although he preferred an exchange of notes to a conference, he agreed to negotiate on the modifications to be made in Article 29, on condition that there was "a complete change in the attitude of Prince Nicholas towards the Monarchy".[6] Presumably this was what Tittoni had been waiting for:[7] asserting that he would resign rather than recognize the abrogation of Article 25, as proposed by Germany,[8] before the modification of Article 29 had been settled, he submitted the draft of a note which Austria should address to the Italian government.[9] According to this plan, Austria would agree to the suppression of paragraphs 5, 7, 8, 9, 10, 11 of the

[1] There was little to show for this co-operation, for Aehrenthal rejected a suggestion of his ambassador (Lützow to Aehrenthal, telegram, 11 January; A 877) that the time had come to take up the question of an Italian university (see above, p. 60) in Austria. Since a conference seemed no longer to be under consideration, there was no necessity for buying Italian support (Aehrenthal to Lützow, 13 January; A 886).

[2] Lützow to Aehrenthal, 16 February, 2 March; A 1000, 1089. See above, pp. 98–9. The premier persuaded Tittoni not to resign (G. Giolitti, *Memoirs of my life* (London, 1923), p. 207).

[3] See above, pp. 144 ff.

[4] Lützow to Aehrenthal, telegram, 24 February; A 1050.

[5] Lützow to Aehrenthal, telegram, 12 March; A 1195.

[6] Aehrenthal to Lützow, telegram, 18 March; A 1267.

[7] He pretended to prefer a conference to an exchange of notes, saying that he had tried to overcome Grey's objections to a conference with limited programme (Lützow to Aehrenthal, telegram, 20 March; A 1295), but did not urge his view. He was evidently courting favour with Aehrenthal when he said that "for the rest, the attitude of the British government throughout the crisis was not clear to him, and now and then almost completely unintelligible" (Lützow to Aehrenthal, telegram, 23 March; A 1329).

[8] See above, p. 194.

[9] Lützow to Aehrenthal, telegram, 25 March; A 1357.

article in question, while paragraph 6 was to be changed so as to read: "The port of Antivari shall retain the character of a commercial port: no works can be erected there which will transform it into a military port."[1]

During these months, the relations between Austria and Montenegro had been anything but satisfactory. Instead of responding cordially to Aehrenthal's overture of 7 October,[2] Prince Nicholas protested against the situation of his country, declared that he would no longer be bound by Article 29,[3] presented a note of protest to the Austrian minister,[4] and asked for a rectification of frontier with Herzegovina.[5] Not content with this, the prince issued a fiery proclamation to his people[6] and allowed a demonstration against the Austrian legation.[7] He also despatched a note of protest to the Powers.[8] Finally a partial mobilization was ordered, though it was explained as being only for defensive purposes.[9]

Aehrenthal did not at first take these outbursts seriously and, knowing the greed of the prince, offered him 500,000 crowns, as well as the modification of Article 29, in return for a correct attitude.[10] But when Nicholas continued defiant, a sharp communication was sent to Cetinje. Austria would consent to modification of Article 29 and would accord large economic advantages; the prince would be appointed to the honorary command of an Austrian regiment and invited to visit Francis Joseph, provided Montenegro abandoned her hostile attitude. But she had to make the choice "between the advantages of our friendship and the weight of our hostility, which she has never

---

[1] Lützow to Aehrenthal, 26 March; A 1375.

[2] See above, p. 231.

[3] Kuhn to Aehrenthal, telegrams, 7 October: A 171, 172.

[4] Kuhn to Aehrenthal, telegram and despatch, 8 October; A 185, 190. Aehrenthal refused to accept the note and ordered its return (Aehrenthal to Kuhn, telegram, 14 October; A 274).

[5] Kuhn to Aehrenthal, telegram, 8 October; A 186. A week later the plea was renewed with the argument that a territorial concession would cause Montenegro "to separate from Serbia and become our ally" (Kuhn to Aehrenthal, telegram, 15 October; A 283).

[6] Kuhn to Aehrenthal, telegram, 8 October; A 187.

[7] Kuhn to Aehrenthal, telegram, 9 October; A 209.

[8] Kuhn to Aehrenthal, 12 October; A 252.

[9] Kuhn to Aehrenthal, telegram, 15 October; A 282.

[10] Aehrenthal to Kuhn, telegram, 10 October; A 223.

before felt", and "a clear answer" was demanded.[1]  Such an answer neither the prince nor his premier would give.[2] So to protect itself against a recalcitrant Montenegro, the Austrian government decided to arouse the latent hostility of the Albanians,[3] and Baron Macchio, the minister in Athens, was recalled to Vienna to direct the action.[4]  Since the Catholic Albanians were reported ready to move against Montenegro,[5] instructions were sent to the consul in Scutari to prepare the ground by getting in touch with certain individuals; munitions, food supplies and even money were to be the inducements.[6]  But it was not expected that anything effective could be accomplished before the spring.

For this reason, as well as because Aehrenthal was fully occupied with much more important matters, no effort was made to clarify the situation for months.  Nicholas continued to hold out for a territorial concession;[7] in particular, he wanted Spizza, an Austrian town which dominated the port of Antivari.[8]  As a matter of course, Aehrenthal rejected any and all such demands and warned the prince against trying to "exert pressure by his military preparations and other intrigues".[9]  This, however, did not deter the Montenegrin government from sending a circular to the Powers urging its claims before the conference (which was still expected to meet).[10]  As late as Christmas Day, Nicholas informed the ministers of Great Britain, France, Russia

[1] Aehrenthal to Kuhn, telegram, 17 October; A 308.
[2] Kuhn to Aehrenthal, telegrams, 18, 19 October; A 322, 331. The prince continued to justify his military preparations and at the same time tried to minimize their import (Kuhn to Aehrenthal, telegrams, 21 October; A 352, 353).
[3] Aehrenthal to Kral, at Scutari, and Rappoport, at Salonica, telegrams, 21 October; A 361.
[4] For Macchio's views, see his letter to Aehrenthal, 22 October; A 368. Aehrenthal's reply, 25 October; A 401.
[5] Kral to Aehrenthal, telegram, 23 October; A 376.
[6] Macchio to Kral, 27 October; Macchio to Aehrenthal, 29 October; A 443, 449.
[7] Kuhn to Aehrenthal, telegram, 25 October; A 395.
[8] Kuhn to Aehrenthal, 11, 13 November; A 548, 562.
[9] Aehrenthal to Kuhn, 21 November; A 619.
[10] Kuhn to Aehrenthal, telegram, 25 November, and despatch, 27 November; A 640, 658. Aehrenthal refused to receive the note (Aehrenthal to Kuhn, telegram, 26 November; A 651). On the question of possible territorial concessions to Montenegro, see a memorandum by Lord Fitzmaurice, 21 October; B 400.

and Italy that he would fight for Spizza if necessary![1] The prince also sent General Yanko Vukotich to Constantinople with the hope of concluding an alliance with the Porte,[2] and a special envoy to St Petersburg to enlist Russian support;[3] while the skupshtina addressed telegrams to the duma and the Italian parliament asking for help.[4]

The Austrian government appears to have paid no attention to these provocations. But when on 22 January Prince Nicholas summoned the foreign representatives in Cetinje, except the Austrian minister, and asked them to telegraph to their governments a fiery protest against the Austrian military preparations,[5] Aehrenthal evidently thought the time had come to act. So the consul in Scutari was instructed to pay out money to the principal agent in Albania and to make arrangements for the landing of arms in the event of war.[6]

When, however, Izvolsky decided to abandon Serbia[7] and communicated to Cetinje a copy of the note addressed to Belgrade,[8] Montenegro's position was hopeless. Aehrenthal accordingly attempted a new overture, for which a recent summons of the Austrian minister to the konak[9] provided the entering wedge. The offer was made in general terms, but Aehrenthal promised to show "the greatest possible spirit of accommodation", provided the offer was accepted promptly; if he feared the opposition of his people, the prince could declare that he had to follow the advice of the Powers.[10] Although Nicholas tried to argue that "it was too late" to turn back, he did promise to observe a correct attitude pending the decision of the conference and asked Aehrenthal

[1] Kuhn to Aehrenthal, telegram, 25 December; A 795. The Powers apparently ignored this outburst, except that the British minister in Cetinje was instructed to "discourage the threatening language" of the prince (Kuhn to Aehrenthal, telegrams, 6, 7 January; A 849, 858).

[2] Lowther to Grey, telegram, 16 November; B 449: Pallavicini to Aehrenthal, telegram, 19 November; A 609.

[3] Kuhn to Aehrenthal, 9 December; A 707.

[4] Kuhn to Aehrenthal, telegram, 15 December; A 748.

[5] Kuhn to Aehrenthal, telegram, 22 January; A 914.

[6] Aehrenthal to Kral, telegrams, 30 January, 18 February; A 944, 1011.

[7] See above, p. 163.

[8] Kuhn to Aehrenthal, telegram, 5 March; A 1114. The Italian minister supported the Russian advice.

[9] Kuhn to Aehrenthal, telegram, 5 March; A 1115.

[10] Aehrenthal to Kuhn, telegram, 7 March; A 1137.

to prepare a bridge for his retreat.[1] If the wily prince still hoped for even a small territorial compensation, he was disappointed, for Aehrenthal would do nothing more than repeat his previous assurances.[2] Nicholas probably realized that the game was up, for he promised to cancel the mobilization of six additional battalions.[3] But instead of submitting to Austria, he finally placed his cause in the hands of Sir Edward Grey.[4] Grey, however, had decided to leave the matter to Italy.[5]

The Italian government had, in fact, already bestirred itself.[6] Its proposals were promptly accepted in principle by Aehrenthal, but when the text[7] of the proposed note was received, he asked for an addition to the effect that Austria would agree to the modifications of Article 29 only "when Montenegro has resumed, vis-à-vis the Monarchy, a correct attitude and relations of good neighbourliness".[8] Indeed without waiting for Tittoni's acceptance,[9] Aehrenthal asked him to induce Prince Nicholas to address the necessary note to the Austrian minister in Cetinje.[10] Presumably the Austrian minister thought that everything was settled except the formalities.[11] Actually, a nasty contretemps resulted.

---

[1] Kuhn to Aehrenthal, telegram, 10 March; A 1166. On the same day Nicholas replied to the Russian note by promising to submit to the decision of the Powers (Kuhn to Aehrenthal, 10 March; A 1167).

[2] Aehrenthal to Kuhn, telegram, 3 March; A 1200. A little later Tittoni, who had received a letter from the prince, urged Aehrenthal to make a concession which would be the equivalent of Spizza (Lützow to Aehrenthal, telegram, 20 March; A 1295), but Aehrenthal refused (Aehrenthal to Lützow, telegram, 21 March; A 1303).

[3] Kuhn to Aehrenthal, telegram, 22 March; A 1310.

[4] Kuhn to Aehrenthal, telegram, 28 March; A 1391.

[5] See above, p. 230.          [6] See above, p. 233.          [7] A 1375.

[8] Aehrenthal to Lützow, telegram, 28 March; A 1400.

[9] Tittoni's acceptance (Lützow to Aehrenthal, telegram, 29 March; A 1413) was not received until the following morning. Since Tittoni had declared that he was now prepared to recognize the abrogation of Article 25 "sans réserves" in view of Aehrenthal's acceptance of his plan for modifying Article 29 and that a conference was no longer necessary in view of the forthcoming démarche in Belgrade (see above, p. 222) (Lützow to Aehrenthal, telegram, 29 March; A 1401), Aehrenthal doubtless felt sure of Tittoni's position.

[10] Aehrenthal to Lützow, telegram, 29 March; A 1412.

[11] The consul in Scutari was instructed to stop his work among the Albanians for the purpose of arousing them against Montenegro (Aehrenthal to Kral, telegram, 1 April; A 1439).

Tittoni agreed to do as was desired, but his method of procedure caused great annoyance in Vienna. For he telegraphed to Cetinje requesting the Montenegrin government to address to the Italian minister a note which would then be transmitted to Austria-Hungary by Italy. The note was thus phrased:

The government of the prince is ready to conform to such decision as may be taken by the Great Powers in respect of Article 25 of the Treaty of Berlin; it will maintain henceforth relations of friendship and good neighbourliness with the Imperial and Royal government of Austria-Hungary.

Aehrenthal protested that he could not accept Italian mediation for the transmission of the Montenegrin note, which must be communicated "directly", and he demanded that the second clause of the note be modified to read:

it [the government of the prince] undertakes from the present to abandon the attitude of protest and opposition which it has observed with respect to the annexation of Bosnia and Herzegovina since last autumn and in addition it undertakes to maintain henceforth relations of friendship and good neighbourliness with the Imperial and Royal government of Austria-Hungary.[1]

To this Tittoni replied that he had not understood that Aehrenthal insisted on a direct communication of the Montenegrin declaration and that he could see no "real difference" if the declaration were handed first to the Italian minister; nevertheless, he would advise Montenegro to make the declaration direct to Austria.[2] On the other hand, he refused to change the text of the declaration.[3]

At this point the situation threatened to be complicated by the intervention of Russia, who proposed the elimination of

---

[1] Lützow to Aehrenthal, telegram, 1 April; Aehrenthal to Lützow, telegrams, 2 April; A 1438, 1444, 1445.

[2] Lützow to Aehrenthal, telegram, 3 April; A 1456.

[3] Lützow to Aehrenthal, telegram, 3 April; A 1457. Aehrenthal tried to blame Lützow for the misunderstanding, but the ambassador defended himself vigorously (Aehrenthal to Lützow, telegram, 4 April; Lützow to Aehrenthal, telegram, 6 April; A 1464, 1482). The irritated minister then reproached Tittoni, but the latter refused to be impressed (Aehrenthal to Lützow, telegrams, 7, 8 April; Lützow, to Aehrenthal, telegram, 10 April; A 1491, 1496, 1505).

paragraphs 5-11 of Article 29.[1] This differed from the Austro-Italian plan by including paragraph 6 in the elimination—which would permit the fortification of Antivari, and it was promptly criticized by the French and British governments.[2] As Grey had, in fact, already accepted the Italian proposals, he informed Izvolsky that he "considered it worse than useless to press for alterations of the article in excess of what had already been proposed".[3] The Russian minister received this news with great bitterness. "Why," he wished to know, "without saying a word to him, had His Majesty's government instructed the British representative at Cetinje to warmly support the Italian proposal?" The British action was "un coup mortel à ma position", and he would have to resign. He professed to believe that Grey was thus showing his annoyance because Russia had accepted the German demand of 23 March without reference to London; in any case it was "regrettable that questions affecting Montenegro should be settled without Russia having been consulted".[4] Izvolsky's outburst made a "very deep" impression in London.[5] Nicolson was therefore instructed to point out that

had it not been for the action of His Majesty's government, working in co-operation with that of Italy, the modification of Article 29 as a condition of the abrogation of Article 25 would not have been made, and if such a conditional promise to assent to the abrogation of Article 25 had not been given by His Majesty's government, Serbia would by now probably be in the occupation of the Austrian armies.

The British government "had no intention of deviating a hair's breadth from their policy of supporting Russia in the Near East".[6] Izvolsky readily accepted these arguments and assurances, and intimated that he would not resign unless Stolypin were forced out of office by a reactionary intrigue.[7]

[1] Russian circular, 2 April; A 1460.
[2] Grey to Benckendorff, 3 April; Bertie to Grey, telegram, 5 April; B 825, 826.    [3] Grey to Nicolson, telegram, 5 April; B, p. 822.
[4] Nicolson to Grey, 6 April; B 828. The ambassador also sent a telegraphic summary of the conversation (B, p. 822).
[5] Benckendorff to Izvolsky, telegram, 8 April; Siebert, p. 115. Benckendorff implored Izvolsky not to resign.    [6] B, p. 822.
[7] Nicolson to Grey, 8 April; B 830. The possibility of Stolypin being forced out caused grave concern in London, for it was feared that Russian policy would then be reoriented in favour of Germany, unless Great Britain

During this Anglo-Russian interlude, the Montenegrin
government, being pressed by both Italy and Great Britain,[1]
had issued two notes, one to the Italian minister, a second to the
Austrian minister with a copy of the first note and a declaration
addressed to the Austrian government. The note to the Italian
minister embodied the substance of the desired declaration and
volunteered the statement that Antivari should remain a commercial port, "ce qui mettra son libre développement à l'abri
des inconvénients auxquels sont souvent exposés les ports
militaires". In the note to the Austrian minister the hope was
expressed that "rien n'entrave plus le développement et le
raffermissement de bons rapports entre la Monarchie et la
Principauté".[2] At the same time Prince Nicholas sent for the
Austrian minister to inform him that the Montenegrin army
would be withdrawn from the frontier and to ask that Aehrenthal
would show a conciliatory attitude in the matter of a commercial
treaty.[3] Although the Montenegrin declaration did not conform
entirely to the Austrian prescription,[4] Aehrenthal decided to

were willing to conclude an alliance with Russia and France. Hardinge was
against such an alliance because "although from time to time there may be a
reactionary wave in Russia the Russia of the future will be liberal and not
reactionary, and it would be a mistake to prejudice future Anglo-Russian
relations by an alliance between England and a reactionary government in
Russia which would not be regarded with sympathy in either country while
the position of the necessity for a strong combination of Powers a few years
hence to resist an attempt to create the permanent hegemony of Germany
in Europe overshadows the general political situation" (memorandum of
Hardinge, April 1909; B, appendix iii). Hardinge was therefore "much
comforted" when the tsar conferred the White Eagle on Stolypin and
Benckendorff (Hardinge to Nicolson, private, 12 April; B, p. 781).

[1] While urging Montenegro to accept the Italian proposal and note, Grey
gave Vienna to understand that he would not exert pressure if Prince Nicholas
found them unacceptable. On the other hand, he repeated his assurances
that if Italy were satisfied with the proposed modification of Article 29,
Great Britain would give her consent to the abrogation of Article 25, regardless
of Montenegro (Mensdorff to Aehrenthal, telegrams, 5, 6 April; A 1474,
1475, 1480).

[2] Kuhn to Aehrenthal, telegram, 6 April; A 1478. Prince Nicholas tried
to the last to secure the inclusion of a statement declaring that the recognition
of Antivari as a commercial port was an act of his sovereignty (Kuhn to
Aehrenthal, telegram, 7 April; A 1486).

[3] Kuhn to Aehrenthal, telegram, 7 April; A 1487.

[4] See above, p. 238. The British government learned somewhat belatedly
(6 April) of Aehrenthal's demand that the Montenegrin note be assimilated
to the Serbian reply of 31 March, and informed the Italian government that

accept it, for until he did he could not expect either Italy or Great Britain to consent to the abrogation of Article 25. He therefore telegraphed to Cetinje that he considered "relations of good neighbourliness" restored between Austria and Montenegro, and that he would consent to the alterations of Article 29 agreed to between Tittoni and himself.[1] The long controversy being over, there remained only the formalities of the exchange of the necessary notes.

Aehrenthal promptly informed Tittoni of his settlement with Montenegro and invited the Italian government to recognize the abrogation of Article 25, according to their bargain.[2] Accordingly, the Italian ambassador in Vienna on 11 April handed in the necessary note.[3] On the same day the Italian ambassador in London notified Grey that his government regarded the solution of the Montenegrin question recently arrived at as "completely satisfactory".[4] His own condition being fulfilled,[5] Grey informed Mensdorff that he was "now ready to proceed to the suppression of Article 25 of the Treaty of Berlin",[6] and a few days later[7] instructed Cartwright to address a note to Aehrenthal;[8] which Cartwright did on 17 April.[9] Two days later the French ambassador followed suit.[10] Germany, it goes without saying, had not waited for any such preliminaries and had given her consent as early as 7 April.[11]

"although His Majesty's government will do nothing to discourage the Montenegrin government from accepting the amended text, they cannot instruct their representative at Cetinje to interfere further" (B, p. 821).

[1] Aehrenthal to Kuhn, telegram, 7 April; A 1485. Cf. Aehrenthal to Francis Joseph, 7 April; A 1493.

[2] Aehrenthal to Lützow, telegram, 7 April; A 1491.

[3] Avarna to Aehrenthal, 11 April; A 1508. Aehrenthal immediately instructed the ambassador in Rome to deliver the note agreed upon (see above, p. 237), and this was done on the following day (Lützow to Aehrenthal, telegram, 12 April; A 1513).

[4] Bosdari to Grey, 11 April; B 832.          [5] See above, p. 230.

[6] Grey to Mensdorff, 12 April; Mensdorff to Aehrenthal, telegram, 12 April; A 1511, 1510.

[7] Aehrenthal showed some impatience over the delay, which was explained in London as being due to uncertainty as to the best procedure (Aehrenthal to Mensdorff, telegrams, 15, 16 April; Mensdorff to Aehrenthal, telegrams, 15, 16 April; A 1523, 1524, 1525, 1530, 1531).

[8] Grey to Cartwright, telegram, 16 April; B 839.

[9] Cartwright to Aehrenthal, 17 April; A 1536.

[10] Crozier to Aehrenthal, 19 April; A 1543.

[11] Tschirschky to Aehrenthal, 7 April; A 1484.

With Russia the course was not quite so smooth. When informed by Berchtold of the Montenegrin settlement, Izvolsky asked if the ambassador was instructed to make a *démarche* in respect of Article 29; which Berchtold denied.[1] To this Aehrenthal replied that he would communicate the Austro-Italian proposals concerning Article 29 when he had received Russia's consent to the abrogation of Article 25.[2] The Russian minister evidently took offence, for he retorted that "Russia had never failed in her engagements" and that there was no "correlation" between Articles 25 and 29.[3] Thereupon Aehrenthal suggested that the Russian note consenting to the abrogation of Article 25 and the Austrian note communicating the proposals for Article 29 might be exchanged on the same day.[4] In the end, Izvolsky on 16 April handed to Berchtold a note consenting to the abrogation of Article 25;[5] two days later Berchtold handed over a note in which the Russian government was asked to consent to the modifications of Article 29 agreed to between Austria-Hungary and Italy;[6] and on 19 April the Russian ambassador in Vienna transmitted a second note recognizing the abrogation of Article 25.[7]

On the same day Aehrenthal formally asked the consent of the British, French, German and Turkish governments to the modification of Article 29,[8] including the proposal to substitute for paragraph 6 another wording according to which Antivari should "retain the character of a commercial port".[9] The British, French and Russian governments readily agreed to the

[1] Berchtold to Aehrenthal, telegram, 9 April; A 1503.
[2] Aehrenthal to Berchtold, telegram, 12 April; A 1512.
[3] Berchtold to Aehrenthal, telegram, 14 April; A 1517.
[4] Aehrenthal to Berchtold, telegram, 15 April; A 1527. At the suggestion of Berlin (Tschirschky to Aehrenthal, private, 9 April; A 1498), Aehrenthal instructed Berchtold to arrange with Pourtalès that the Austrian and German communications concerning Article 29 should be made on the same day (Aehrenthal to Szögyény and Berchtold, telegrams, 17 April; A 1535).
[5] Berchtold to Aehrenthal, telegram, 16 April; A 1534.
[6] Berchtold to Aehrenthal, telegram, 18 April; A 1537. Text in A 1514.
[7] Urussov to Aehrenthal, 19 April; A 1545. A few days later the ambassador notified Aehrenthal that the Russian government now considered the secret Austro-Russian declaration of 1/13 July 1878 (see above, p. 3) as abrogated (Urussov to Aehrenthal, 25 April; A 1565).
[8] Circular telegram, 19 April; A 1542.
[9] See above, p. 234.

suppression of paragraphs 5, 7, 8, 9, 10, 11, but expressed the opinion that in the matter of paragraph 6 the declaration made by the Montenegrin government to the Austrian minister in Cetinje appeared "adequate" [*suffisante*] and that any change in the wording of the paragraph would have to take the form of a treaty between the Powers signatory of the Treaty of Berlin.[1] Aehrenthal and Tittoni argued that the proposed new text could be made effective by an exchange of notes between the Powers,[2] but their views evidently did not prevail.[3] So, after a reasonable delay, the Austrian government informed the other Powers that it would be "satisfied with the formal declarations of the Montenegrin government, of which the Powers had taken act".[4] It would appear as if the Entente Powers seized the opportunity a second time to deny to the ambitious Austrian foreign minister the complete triumph which he so ardently desired.

Only one point now remained unsettled. The Porte was willing to consent to the modification of Article 29, but it desired in addition the suppression of paragraph 4.[5] The British government took only "a secondary interest" in the matter[6] and apparently left the decision to others. A desultory correspondence thus ensued between Vienna and Constantinople. Austria agreed to the suppression of the second sentence of paragraph 4 which prohibited the construction of fortifications on the Boyana;[7] when the Porte insisted on the suppression of the first paragraph which guaranteed freedom of navigation on the river for Montenegro, Aehrenthal refused to proceed with the negotiations,[8] and there the matter was left.

---

[1] Grey to Mensdorff, 27 April; B 855, A 1573: Urussov to Aehrenthal, 29 April: Nemes to Aehrenthal, 9 May; A 1581, 1595.

[2] Aehrenthal to Lützow, telegram, 29 April; Lützow to Aehrenthal, telegram, 2 May; A 1579, 1582.

[3] The available documents are silent on this matter.

[4] Circular telegram of 23 May; A 1606.

[5] Turkish memorandum of 13 April; B 834: Aehrenthal to Pallavicini, telegram, 14 April; A 1515.

[6] B, p. 823.

[7] Pallavicini to Rifaat Pasha, 22 June; A 1655, Beilage.

[8] Rifaat to Pallavicini, 27 June; A 1665, Beilage.

# CHAPTER XV

## *The Aftermath*

ALTHOUGH the crisis happily passed without recourse to war, the wranglings of six foreign ministers for a period of six months represented almost the nadir of diplomacy. The two principals in the controversy both miscalculated badly. Aehrenthal had expected to impose the annexation of Bosnia-Herzegovina on Turkey without compensation (apart from the evacuation of the Sandjak), to deal a mortal blow to Serbian ambitions, and to harness Bulgaria to the chariot of Austrian policy. Actually he had to pay a substantial sum in cash to Turkey; he was forced to wait for nearly six months before he could extort from Serbia a reluctant submission to the *fait accompli* which left the Serbs sullen and more determined than ever to realize their ambitions at the expense of Austria-Hungary; and he saw Bulgaria pass over to the Russian camp. Izvolsky fared no better. In order to secure the opening of the Straits, he was prepared to sacrifice Serbia to Austria. Yet he found the French and British governments hostile to his plans; while Russian opinion, strangely indifferent to the Straits, was stirred to the depths by the Serbian cause and, by forcing Izvolsky to come forward as its champion, placed him in a difficult, not to say impossible, position in respect of Aehrenthal. In the end, he had to abandon Serbia and submit to humiliation at the hands of Germany. Even the winning over of Bulgaria cost considerable money. Between them, Aehrenthal and Izvolsky destroyed the Austro-Russian *entente* which for some years had preserved a kind of balance in the Balkans; brought their countries face to face in what proved to be a mortal duel; and envenomed their future policies by a bitter personal antagonism.

The German Emperor resented Aehrenthal's action, but allowed himself to be won over by Bülow; the latter let himself support a policy about which he had not been consulted. At the end of the crisis Bülow took a step which, while it paved the way for a peaceful solution, was interpreted in Russia as a humiliation and in Great Britain and France as a warning. Tittoni was in perhaps an impossible situation: he did not dare oppose—such was the weakness of Italy—a policy of which he disapproved. But his shuffling between the two groups was disgusting and prejudiced him in the eyes of his countrymen. Grey thought to bring Aehrenthal to terms by appealing to the public opinion and public law of Europe. When he failed, he was driven to support Serbian claims with which he was not in sympathy, only in the end to abandon them. It was to his credit, however, that his level-headedness at the end of the crisis probably contributed in no small measure to the maintenance of peace. Pichon, who had his own problem in Morocco, wisely kept out of the imbroglio except when the question of peace or war arose, but he thereby earned the ill-will of Izvolsky. In extenuation of the conduct of all the ministers of the Powers not directly interested, it may be said that they were caught in the chains of the alliances or *ententes* to which their governments were committed, and they saw no avenue of escape.

The Central Powers undoubtedly won a notable diplomatic victory, and the two emperors exchanged congratulatory letters;[1] a little later William II and his consort visited Francis Joseph in Vienna and were warmly received. Yet the victory was a Pyrrhic one, the consequences of which were not long in manifesting themselves. The Russian surrender to Germany became generally known in Russia on 27 March and a storm of indignation at once broke out. It was directed in the first instance against Izvolsky, and voices were heard demanding a *rapprochement* with Germany and Austria;[2] in court circles the view was freely expressed that Great Britain and France had left Russia in the lurch.[3] But soon the general wrath was directed against Germany.[4] According to the German view, this was

[1] Francis Joseph to William II, 22 April; William II to Francis Joseph, 7 May; A 1555, 1598, G 9508.
[2] Nicolson to Grey, 29 March, 8 April; B 801, 831: Berchtold to Aehrenthal, 4 April; A 1470: Popovich to foreign office, telegram, 30 March; S 93.
[3] Hintze to William II, 1, 3 April; G 9504, 9505.
[4] Pourtalès to Bülow, 1 April; G 9501: Berchtold to Aehrenthal, 1 April; A 1468.

brought about by Izvolsky, who let it be known that Germany had presented an ultimatum before which Russia had had to retreat.[1] The Russian press indulged in such unrestrained criticism of Germany that on 1 April the *Norddeutsche Allgemeine Zeitung* published a denial of any pressure or threat, asserting that the Russian foreign minister had himself recognized the "friendly character and purely peaceful purpose" of the German proposal. Meanwhile Pourtalès had complained to Izvolsky, and the latter promised to publish a *démenti*. This duly appeared in the *Rossiya* on 4 April; it stated that there had been no intimidation by Germany and that Russia had agreed to the German proposal solely to obviate an armed conflict between Austria and Serbia.[2] But because the article was slow in appearing, it was attributed to German pressure, and the story of the German ultimatum was more widely believed than ever. Such is the German version of the origin of the "legend" that Germany had issued an ultimatum to Russia; in the absence of Russian evidence, its correctness cannot be determined.

Some weeks later, perhaps because Izvolsky was away on a holiday, Bülow proposed that certain documents be published

---

[1] Pourtalès to Bülow, 6 May; G 9532. Nicolson, the British ambassador, was accused by the diplomatists of the Central Powers of spreading the version that the German action had been of a threatening character, the equivalent of an ultimatum (Berchtold to Aehrenthal, telegram, 3 April; A 1458: Pourtalès to Bülow, private; G 9503). Nicolson's reports contain no record of any such action on his part, but it is of course quite possible that he repeated what Izvolsky had told him. Izvolsky himself asked Nicolson whether the latter "had stated that answer he had given German ambassador had been decided upon without consulting England and France". "I told him", said Nicolson, "a member of his own ministry had asked me point-blank whether I had known of the German demand before or after the meeting of the council of ministers. I had replied that I had heard of it afterwards. It was true that there was a lady present at the time, but I could not deny a fact which, moreover, was in most of the foreign press. He then said he had heard I had mentioned to a foreign diplomat that he had been threatened with publication of an alleged Buchlau protocol. I told him this was not a fact. He added that same insinuation as to the threat had appeared in a telegram to *Daily Telegraph* from Vienna and in another telegram from Berlin. I replied that it was clear that I could have nothing to do with what appeared from the above two capitals" (Nicolson to Grey, telegram, 31 March; B 813). It is interesting to note that the French foreign office heard that when Izvolsky attempted to resist the German pressure Pourtalès had exclaimed, "Alors c'est la guerre" (Nemes to Aehrenthal, 3 April; A 1455).
[2] Popovich to foreign office, telegram, 4 April; S 96.

which would reveal the German action of March in its true light.[1] Charykov, who was acting minister in Izvolsky's absence, agreed, but pointed out that Vienna would have to be taken into consideration and suggested that certain passages should be eliminated.[2] Bülow empowered Pourtalès to settle this question of "editing" with Charykov,[3] but when the ambassador broached the matter, the acting minister showed much less enthusiasm, saying that Stolypin objected to the omission of any passages and that Vienna might be irritated when it learned the Russian view as to the abrogation of Article 25.[4] Bülow and Pourtalès therefore decided to do nothing more until Izvolsky returned and to saddle him with the responsibility for not publishing the documents.[5] Izvolsky himself brought up the question as soon as he saw Pourtalès, and made it clear that he was opposed to publication. Though sourly admitting that Germany had enabled Russia "to get out of a dangerous situation with all honour", he insisted that it was the German action which had permitted Aehrenthal to triumph.[6] So after a decent interval, Pourtalès, to Izvolsky's great relief, informed the minister that in view of his objections, the German government dropped its proposal for the publication of the documents.[7] Sixteen years were to elapse before the documents saw the light in the *Grosse Politik* (1925).[8]

It did not need this polemic to convince the Austrian and

[1] Bülow to Pourtalès, 13 May; G 9534. The documents suggested for publication were G 9435, 9440, 9448, 9460 (the note of 21 March), 9461, 9464, 9468.

[2] Pourtalès to Bülow, telegram, 16 May, and despatch, 17 May; G 9535, 9537. Charykov said that he had always been of the opinion that Germany had rendered Russia a "very valuable service", for her "negative formula" had permitted Russia to consent to the abrogation of Article 25 without recognizing the annexation of Bosnia.

[3] Bülow to Pourtalès, telegram, 18 May; G 9536.

[4] Pourtalès to Bülow, 28 May; G 9541.

[5] Bülow to Pourtalès, telegram, 29 May; Pourtalès to foreign office, telegram, 30 May; G 9542, 9543.

[6] Pourtalès to Bülow, 3 June; G 9547.

[7] Pourtalès to Bülow, 11 June; G 9548.

[8] It seems unlikely that the truth will ever be known about Izvolsky's actions and reactions. The Russian diplomatic documents of the period will doubtless be published in due course by the Soviet government, but these documents will hardly contain information about Izvolsky's manœuvres.

German governments that their relations with Russia were bound for some time to be delicate. What they seem to have hoped for was the ultimate withdrawal of Izvolsky and a shift of policy in the direction of Berlin and Vienna. As if to emphasize their desire to let the past be forgotten, both Francis Joseph and William II wrote to the tsar, the former in brief terms expressing his satisfaction that the Balkan crisis had been solved peacefully,[1] the latter effusively and in strong denunciation of the press.[2] Nicholas replied in commonplaces to his Austrian "brother",[3] but with more warmth to his German cousin,[4] suggesting indeed a meeting in Finnish waters. The meeting took place on 17 and 18 June and went off well enough, the monarchs avoiding political discussions, while Schoen, in rebutting Izvolsky's recriminations against Aehrenthal, declared his conviction that Austria cherished no designs on Salonica.[5] But the reports of Pourtalès left no doubt of the deep suspicion of Germany and the deep animosity towards Austria-Hungary which prevailed in broad sections of Russian opinion and the press.[6] As Aehrenthal's attitude was, not unnaturally, one of reserve,[7] the only course was to let time do its work, if it could.

The prospects, however, were not cheerful. In July 1909 a Pan-Slavist conference was held in St Petersburg, and a secret circular sent by the executive committee to the Slav organizations in the Balkans indicated what might be expected from Russian policy. It bade the Balkan peoples wait patiently while Russia reorganized her army and internal administration, for all classes of Russian society wished to see Russia "take up energetically her mission as protectress of the Slav world". Serbia and

[1] Francis Joseph to William II, 24 April; A 1564.
[2] William II to Nicholas II, 8 May; G 9533.
[3] Nicholas II to Francis Joseph, 4 May; A 1584.
[4] Nicholas II to William II, 20 May; G 9533, note *.
[5] Schoen to foreign office, telegram, 18 June, and memorandum, 18 June; G 9551, 9552. Careful preparations were made on the German side to treat the tsar with the utmost circumspection and to avoid contentious questions (G 9544, 9546, 9549).
[6] Pourtalès to Bülow, 22 April, 3 June, 11 June, 18 September; G 9530, 9547, 9548, 9569.
[7] Aehrenthal to Szögyény, private, 16 April; Aehrenthal to Berchtold, 16 April; A 1529, 1533.

Montenegro must make ready to seize the Sandjak and the provinces of Bosnia-Herzegovina. Bulgaria must prepare to recover the frontiers of San Stefano and advance to the gates of Constantinople, for the days of the Young Turk regime were numbered. "Then the moment will come when Russia, in union with the other Slav peoples, will come into action in order to realize the Slav ideal and to prevent Austria and Germany from exploiting Turkey to their advantage." Meanwhile, all Slavs were to work together, particularly by excluding German commerce and industry from their lands. Russia would provide them with the money for their military preparations or secure it from France and England. "Certainly in two or three years at the most the time will come when the Slav world, under the leadership of Russia, must strike the great blow."[1] This document embodied at least to some extent the official policy of the Russian government, for the Bosnian crisis had hardly come to an end when Izvolsky set about trying to effect an alliance between the Balkan states,[2] and in October 1909 he concluded at Racconigi an agreement with Tittoni which sought to secure Russo-Italian co-operation in Near Eastern affairs. From this time Russian influence in the Balkans continued to grow, until it culminated in the creation of the Balkan alliance in the spring of 1912.

At the meeting of William II and Nicholas II in June, Izvolsky told Schoen that "the Triple Entente was an invention of the press".[3] This is not the impression left by the contemporary Russian and British documents; the two governments indeed endeavoured to strengthen the intimacy and cordiality of their relations. Benckendorff, aware that English opinion had been made nervous by the Russian surrender to Germany, assured Grey that

everything which I know about the German action [of 21 March] made me firmly believe that the latter represented a method which Russia was not likely to forget, and that if there had been any indirect

---

[1] A confidant of the German embassy in Vienna provided a summary of the document (Brockdorff-Rantzau to Bethmann Hollweg, 25 July; G 9563).

[2] Siebert, p. 137 ff.

[3] Memorandum of Schoen, 18 June; G 9552.

intention of sowing discord between Russia on the one hand and France and England on the other, this purpose would certainly not be achieved.[1]

This language was "warmly approved" by Izvolsky and repeated by the ambassador to Grey, who declared that he was "very glad" to hear it, for it "entirely accorded" with his own sentiments.[2] The British foreign secretary for his part refused to be discouraged by the pessimism of Nicolson, who had feared that "our entente will languish and possibly die" and advocated "some kind of an alliance" with Russia.[3] Though he discountenanced any idea of alliance, at least until the Russian government became "less reactionary", he said: "Meanwhile, let us keep an *entente* with Russia in the sense of keeping in touch so that our diplomatic action may be in accord and in mutual support." And he urged Russia not to be discouraged:

> She has Bulgaria on her side, she has our good will, the Slav feeling is deeply apprehensive of Teuton advance and affronted by Teuton pressure, and it is at Russia's disposal; all these are improvements in her position if only she is cool enough to see them, wise enough to use them, and will reform her internal government.[4]

These words to Nicolson were no doubt intended for Izvolsky's ear.

Nicolson, who was only too conscious of the resentment felt towards Izvolsky in all circles of the Russian public and feared his downfall, decided to give the unpopular minister "a lift up" and requested an audience of the tsar.[5] The ambassador declared that his government "desired to co-operate in the

---

[1] Benckendorff to Izvolsky, telegram, 6 April; Siebert, p. 109.
[2] Grey to Nicolson, 14 April; B 837.
[3] Nicolson to Grey, private, 24 March; B 764.
[4] Grey to Nicolson, private, 2 April; B 823. Grey remarked that Bulgaria was "worth many Serbias". Nicolson was requested by Grey to avoid using the term "triple entente" in his official telegrams and despatches. "The expression is one which is no doubt convenient, but if it appeared in a parliamentary Bluebook it would be assumed to have some special official meaning and might provoke inconvenient comment or inquiry." The ambassador was so discouraged that he hoped for "a change of government". "I am afraid", he wrote on 3 May, "that we are not likely with the present people to have a well defined firm foreign policy" (Nicolson, *Lord Carnock*, pp. 307-8).
[5] Nicolson to Grey, private, 19 April; B 842.

closest manner with the Russian government not only in the Middle East but also in the affairs of South-Eastern Europe ", that this was "one of the principal bases" of British foreign policy; this evoked from Nicholas the statement that "it is my firm intention to maintain the *entente* existing between the two countries". Nicolson then proceeded to say that

> my government fully appreciated the difficulty in which the Russian government had been placed by what was in fact a peremptory summons on the part of the German government, and that it was perfectly understood that there was no alternative in the existing circumstances but to give an affirmative reply to the German demand ...they [the British government] did not for one moment believe that in taking the course which she did, Russia had any desire to separate herself from her two partners.

As for Izvolsky, Nicolson added, he "had been suddenly thrust into a very perplexing position,...and all allowances should be made for a man who had had such a severe strain put upon him ". Nicolson also praised Stolypin "as far as I thought it was prudent to do so", and got the impression that the tsar "seemed to entertain his old friendly feelings towards the prime minister.". The ambassador likewise remarked on the dangers of an Austro-German hegemony in Europe: "were such a dictatorship established it might have very serious consequences, and...it was more than ever necessary that the Triple Entente should be maintained and consolidated "; with which the tsar "entirely agreed ".[1] How effective these representations may have been is not evident, but the fact was that neither Stolypin nor Izvolsky was replaced, in spite of rumours and intrigues.[2]

During the summer a delegation from the duma visited England and was warmly received; Stolypin assured Nicolson that the "effect which the visit has caused among the Russian

---

[1] Nicolson to Grey, telegram and despatch, 14 April; B 835, 836.

[2] Nicolson continued to be worried, but believed that the tsar was "a man of his word", who would continue to resent the German action. Once more the ambassador warned that "we must not count on the anti-German feeling being permanent" but added that "if our relations could be established on a more solid basis [that is, by an alliance] I should have no fear at all". Because he knew "the great difficulties against this being effected", he viewed with "real anxiety any change in the ministry for foreign affairs" (Nicolson to Hardinge, 21 April; B, vol. IX, Part I, No. 6).

public had been most satisfactory".[1] A little later, in August, the tsar came to Cowes and inspected the British fleet, which had been assembled for review. During the visit numerous political conversations were held between the British and Russian statesmen, Grey having a private interview with the tsar, and a complete understanding was reached on various questions. As regards the general European situation, Nicolson recorded,

> M. Izvolsky mentioned that he was being constantly reminded by Germany that Russia was sailing on a wrong tack, and that intimations were made that he should come to an arrangement with Austria. Moreover he had been approached by Italy to come to some arrangement with her. As regards Austria, past experience did not encourage him to renew an engagement with her, and moreover public opinion in Russia would be opposed to any such understanding. As to Italy he did not know on what basis an arrangement could be made.[2]

The Anglo-Russian *entente* was, so far as one can judge, strengthened rather than weakened by the repercussions of the Balkan crisis, and Bülow's boast that "by means of our strength as a Continental Power, we tore the web which encompassed us"[3] was, as the editors of the German documents observe, "reichlich optimistisch".[4]

Bülow also admitted, in 1913, what others believed in 1909: "The German sword had been thrown into the scale of European decision." Because of that fact, other swords were sharpened. The British naval scare of 1909, precipitated by rumours of secret and accelerated German shipbuilding and terminated by a doubling of the British programme, was doubtless influenced by the diplomatic action of Germany in the Balkan crisis. Equally important from the German point of view was the decision of Russia to undertake the reorganization of her army on a grand scale, and this was actually begun before the end of 1909. These British and Russian measures lay in the logic of

---

[1] Nicolson to Grey, 12 September; B, IX, i, 53.

[2] Memorandum of Nicolson, 3 August; B, VI, i, 29. Izvolsky subsequently found the basis for an arrangement with Italy at Racconigi (October 1909).

[3] Prince von Bülow, *Imperial Germany* (New York, 1913), p. 65.

[4] G 9501, note *. For a dispassionate German estimate of the real failure, as distinct from the apparent success, of Austro-German policy, see F. Stieve, *Die Tragödie der Bundesgenossen* (Munich, 1930), pp. 53–66.

the situation, for, as the Russian ambassador in Paris expressed it, when the news leaked out of the secret ministerial council at which the Russian ministers declared that Russia could not wage war,[1]

Such a public exposure of our weakness has made a most painful impression on our friends and must encourage our opponents to present the most impossible demands to Russia in the firm conviction that we shall yield. The cabinets of Paris and London have therefore drawn the conclusion that Russia, France and England must pay more attention than ever to action in common and at the same time must take the military measures necessary to convince their opponents that they have to deal with a political combination which knows how to insure respect for itself and will carry through its demands.[2]

On that note this study may fittingly close.

[1] See above, p. 189.
[2] Nelidov to Izvolsky, 1 April; Siebert, p. 114.

# APPENDIX

## *M. Nintchitch's Book*

When this book was already in page proof, M. Momtchilo Nintchitch, former minister of foreign affairs of Yugoslavia, published a two-volume work entitled *La crise bosniaque* (Paris: Alfred Costes, 1937). M. Nintchitch devotes considerable space to the history of the Bosnian question before 1908; at the end, he analyses the results of the crisis at great length. His narrative of the actual crisis (October 1908–April 1909) does not differ sensibly from that offered in this book. Although a good Yugoslav, he has written an objective study and has not hesitated to criticize the action of Milovanovich, the Serbian foreign minister of 1908–9 and his own predecessor in office, or to ring the changes on Izvolsky. On the other hand, as a diplomatist he admires the nerveless calm with which Aehrenthal carried through his policy in respect of Serbia and seemingly emerged victorious from his conflict with Izvolsky. But M. Nintchitch agrees with the present writer that Aehrenthal won a Pyrrhic victory. Attention may be called to M. Nintchitch's careful reasoning in favour of the view that at Buchlau Aehrenthal did not play fair with Izvolsky as to the time when the annexation of Bosnia would be carried out (I, 228–51). He also argues that the German action in March 1909 was not friendly to Russia, nor even loyal, for actually the German government did not attempt to stop an Austrian action against Serbia (II, 129–50). M. Nintchitch notes that early in 1909 Aehrenthal abandoned his plans for the partition of Serbia and the incorporation of part of the little state in the Habsburg dominions; this change he ascribes to the sharp letter written by Nicholas II to Francis Joseph on 30 December 1908 (II, 49–51). Aehrenthal then decided to seek a peaceful solution with Serbia and was able finally to achieve it, in spite of the pressure of the Austrian military party. Occasionally M. Nintchitch quotes from unpublished Serbian documents. Thus he gives the substance of a telegram from Pashich, then on special mission in St Petersburg, of 2 December 1908, according to which the Serbian statesman advised his government to try to calm the excited Serbian populace and to avoid provoking an armed conflict with Austria (I, 383). The story of the Serbo-Montenegrin alliance is told in detail (II, 83–7). On 15 March 1909, the Serbian chargé in Berlin telegraphed that in the German capital war between Austria and Serbia was expected shortly, "perhaps in two or three days", and that localization of the conflict was counted upon (II, 135); this no doubt helped the Serbian government to decide to abandon its opposition and come to terms with Austria. M. Nintchitch's references show that he has used all available sources of information, including several that had escaped the notice of the present writer. It is unfortunate that so excellent a book should not be provided with any kind of index.

# INDEX

Unless otherwise indicated, titles and dignities are given as of the period October 1908–April 1909. [ ] indicate that the person is referred to in the text by title rather than by name.

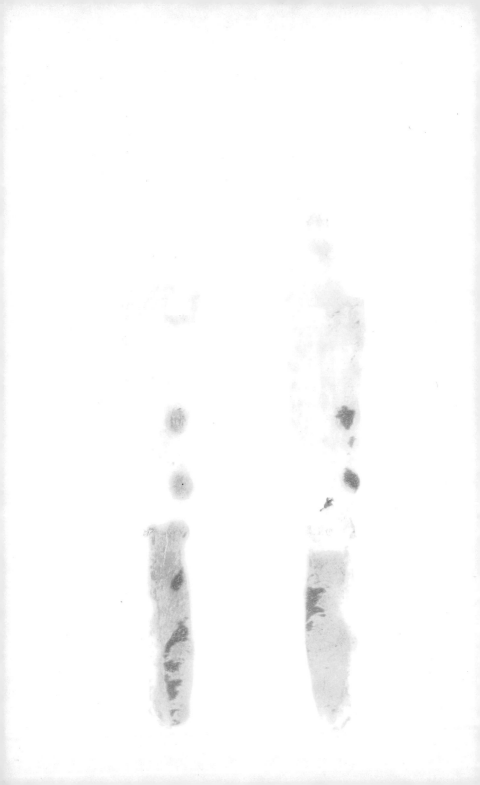